As portrayed in *Nemesis,* the tragedy of both wars—and the main lesson it holds for today's involvements—is that once Truman and Johnson approved initial modest commitments of forces, they were sucked in deeper and deeper until they were forced to abandon their objectives to avert the danger of a third world war. Filled with anecdote and personality, written with clarity and passion, *Nemesis* is both an important document for today and a fascinating look at our recent history.

ROBERT J. DONOVAN, a former newspaperman who covered the Truman and Johnson administrations as Washington bureau chief, first for the *New York Herald Tribune* and then for the *Los Angeles Times,* is the author of a recent two-volume work on the Truman presidency.

NEMESIS

By Robert J. Donovan

NEMESIS

Truman and Johnson in the Coils of War in Asia

Robert J. Donovan

7-692

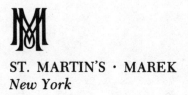

ST. MARTIN'S · MAREK
New York

Donovan, Robert J.
    Nemesis : Truman and Johnson in the coils of war in Asia.
    1. Korean War, 1950-1953—United States. 2. Truman,
Harry S., 1884-1972. 3. Vietnamese Conflict, 1961-1975—
United States. 4. Johnson, Lyndon B. (Lyndon Baines),
1908-1973. I. Title.
DS919.D66   1984   951.9'042   84-15967
ISBN 0-312-56370-1

First Edition

10 9 8 7 6 5 4 3 2 1

To the Little Five,
Who will some day be a very big five:

Abigail
Katie
Kenneth Jon
Kristin
Matthew

Contents

A photo section follows page 122.

Preface

In a span of fifteen years, two presidents, Harry S Truman, in 1950, and Lyndon Baines Johnson, in 1965, committed the United States to large but limited wars on the Asian mainland, a theater for ground warfare that had long seemed treacherous to American strategists. In all ramifications, the impact of the Korean and Vietnam wars was enormous, quite apart from the loss of 111,185 American lives and the expenditure of billions of dollars.

Truman and Johnson acted in the face of severe dilemmas and heavy pressures, often very much the same in both cases. Once battle commenced in Korea and Vietnam, the course of history in the second half of the twentieth century was altered. Deep changes were wrought in American values, American viewpoints toward the government in Washington, American manners, particularly among youth, American dress, American song, American literature, American education, American television, the American economy, and the American outlook upon the world. During the Vietnam War, American society was convulsed. What passed for the American establishment was assaulted, almost discredited by dissent. Division among classes deepened. At times it seemed as if the political system itself would be torn apart. A number of changes in the system did materialize: for example, the lowering of the voting age to eighteen.

The administrations of two of the most formidable of modern American presidents, both Democrats, were ripped to pieces. As a result of each of the two wars the Democratic party was thrown out of power. The insidious nature of both wars had a destructive effect on Truman and Johnson, personally as well as politically.

I saw it happen at close range as a reporter covering the White

House in both administrations. I was at Wake Island with Truman for his conference with General of the Army Douglas A. MacArthur in 1950. I was in the House of Representatives press gallery when MacArthur, relieved of his command in the Far East by Truman, made his melodramatic farewell address to a joint session of Congress in 1951. I covered Johnson's wartime meeting with the South Vietnamese leaders in Honolulu in 1966. Later that same year, I covered Johnson at the war conference in Manila and was with him at Camranh Bay, in South Vietnam, when he urged the troops to nail the coonskin to the wall.

Reflecting on these events, I was struck by the fact that no book examining together the conduct of the two wars had ever been written. That was surprising, because they were, after all, wars closely related in origin, cut from the same cloth of the policy of containment of communism in Asia. The experiences of Truman and Johnson were intertwined. Truman's views on the Communist challenge in Korea, which he personally discussed with Johnson, influenced Johnson's interpretation of events in Vietnam. The anguish that Truman suffered when China entered the Korean War against United Nations forces later affected Johnson's policies in Vietnam. Nowhere that I was aware of had a picture been drawn to encompass Truman's and Johnson's methods in conducting those bitter wars, as well as their remarkably similar reactions to Communist challenge and their responses to the traumas and disasters that beset both of them. Two extraordinary presidents trapped in comparable crises growing out of the Second World War, they commanded the power to blow Korea and Vietnam off the map. For fear of Soviet nuclear retaliation, they had to endure instead the torments of limited wars that cost them the support of the American people. In the process, Truman's Fair Deal and many of Johnson's Great Society programs suffered the usual wartime fate of being either sidetracked or starved of funds.

Having witnessed the dramas of Korea and Vietnam unfold under Truman and Johnson, I became convinced that they would yield new meaning and excitement if they could be woven into a single narrative. It was only after I settled down to the task that I fully realized how appropriate it was, historically, that one book try to capture the two related agonies and the lessons they may have left.

By coincidence, the book was written while United States marines were still being killed ashore in the midst of fierce civil strife in

Lebanon and large American military maneuvers were taking place in Honduras, as the Reagan administration slipped ever deeper into intervention in civil conflict in Nicaragua and El Salvador. The juxtaposition of events then and now was not only arresting, but a very disturbing reminder that Korea and Vietnam were not calamities of a kind that can be safely relegated to the past.

NEMESIS

Eighty-one-year-old former President Harry S Truman and President
Lyndon B. Johnson chat in Truman's hometown of Independence,
Missouri, on July 30, 1965. Johnson flew to Independence to sign the
Medicare bill because he credited the idea for the legislation to Truman,
who had been unable to get a national health insurance program of his own
through Congress. *Photo by Y. R. Okamoto. Courtesy Johnson Library.*

I · *The Triumphs*

It was Harry S Truman by a whisker in 1948 and Lyndon Baines Johnson by a landslide in 1964—two dazzling victories, each in its own way, for two pungent, undaunted presidents. Two gamecocks who had come to the White House originally upon the deaths of two famous presidents had been elected in their own right to show what they could do. Their respective triumphs ushered in the Fair Deal and exalted the Great Society. In the two elections sixteen years apart Democratic Congresses had also been elected. Because of Truman's and Johnson's earlier records and because of promises in their campaigns and in the Democratic platforms of 1948 and 1964, their victories lighted the liberal cause with hopes reminiscent of the heyday of Franklin D. Roosevelt's New Deal.

Cried *The New Republic* on the morrow of Truman's victory over Governor Thomas E. Dewey of New York, "Damn the torpedoes. . . . Full speed ahead!"[1]

"I expect to give every segment of our population a fair deal," Truman wrote on a draft of his State of the Union message, which was to be delivered to a joint session of Congress on January 5, 1949.[2] In slightly different wording the statement was incorporated into the final text, giving his new term its nickname.

"The American people have decided," Truman told the Eighty-first Congress in his message,

> that poverty is just as wasteful and just as unnecessary as preventable disease. . . . We believe that no unfair prejudices or artificial distinction should bar any citizen of the United States of America from an education, or from good health, or from a job that he is capable of performing.

The attainment of this kind of society . . . imposes increasing responsibilities on the government.[3]

Confident and happy over an election that nearly everyone had conceded in advance to Dewey, Truman reiterated his intention of carrying out the Employment Act of 1946. It committed the federal government to use its resources to promote maximum employment, production, and purchasing power. He also advocated extension and strengthening of rent control. He wanted the minimum wage raised. Through strengthening antitrust laws he proposed to halt monopolistic mergers and consolidations in order to intensify competition and give small business a better chance to prosper. Small business, the small farmer, small corporations were regarded by Truman as the backbone of the Republic.

"When there are too many people on relief and too few people at the top who control the wealth of the country then we must look out," he wrote after the election to Charles E. Wilson, president of the General Electric Company.[4]

Eager to use the power of the government to improve health, education, and living conditions, Truman favored extending rural electrification to more communities. He sought to enlarge the benefits of Social Security, "both as to the size of the benefits and the extent of coverage against the economic hazards due to unemployment, old age, sickness and disability." He bucked conservative sentiment, especially strong in the medical profession, to recommend a system of national prepaid medical insurance under Social Security. On another subject, he said in his State of the Union message that he was shocked "that millions of our children are not receiving a good education. . . . I cannot repeat too strongly my desire for prompt federal financial aid to the states to help them operate and maintain their school systems." He called for enactment of a program of low-rent public housing and slum clearance.

Truman also asked Congress to adopt, as it had failed to do earlier, the then daring civil rights program that he had first submitted a year earlier. His "Special Message to Congress on Civil Rights" on February 2, 1948, had been the first request that any president had ever made to Congress for a comprehensive program of civil rights legislation.[5] It took courage to submit that message, which led by stages to the formation of the Dixiecrats, or States' Rights Democrats, who challenged Truman in the 1948 election.

By calling for enactment of the 1948 proposals, Truman asked Congress in 1949 to pass an antilynching bill and an anti-poll tax bill. He requested establishment of a permanent Fair Employment Practices Committee, a permanent Commission on Civil Rights, and a Joint Congressional Committee on Civil Rights to make a continuing study of needed legislation. He called for a voting rights law and action to prohibit racial discrimination on interstate trains, planes, and buses. He proposed home rule for the District of Columbia. In the first three years the administration had been slow in moving against racial inequalities, but on July 26, 1948, Truman issued executive orders to end discrimination in the armed forces and to guarantee fair employment practices in the civil service. The agenda of the civil rights movement of the 1960s was largely laid out in Truman's civil rights message of 1948.

As an offspring of Confederate sympathizers and a politician from the then Jim Crow state of Missouri, Truman had had to pick his way cautiously through the civil rights issue. As a county official in Missouri in the 1920s and early 1930s, his treatment of blacks in public institutions was kind. He believed that blacks should have the right to vote and sensed the danger of racial disorder if the white population persisted in unfairness toward them. He was opposed to what he called the "social equality of the Negro." His standards were those of what would have been considered a broad-minded white in the days before the Supreme Court outlawed racial segregation in the public schools and the civil rights revolution shook the nation.

As was Roosevelt in his final years, Truman was ineffectual in getting domestic reform past the barrier erected in Congress by a coalition of Republicans and conservative southern Democrats. With the approach of the Second World War, New Deal legislation waned. When the war was over, Truman encountered a pervasive disinterest in reform, as surprising prosperity descended on the country. By and large, the best he could do in the domestic field, particularly by the time of his victory in 1948, was to prevent an uprooting of New Deal laws. It was not until the civil rights revolution began in the 1960s and John F. Kennedy's assassination shocked the nation that the impulse for reform revived, and Johnson was able to take advantage of it with his knowledge of legislative maneuver.

Understandably, therefore, Johnson's victory in 1964 encouraged the liberals. "The largeness of Mr. Johnson's majority," said an edi-

torial in *The New Republic,* "frees him for leadership as the small-
ness of John F. Kennedy's inhibited him. The President can self-
confidently get to work on unfinished business of the Kennedy Administration—medicare, an expanded poverty program, aid to education. . . . The 'mandate for unity' will be a mandate for LBJ
programs."[6] When the last dance had ended on the night of the
inauguration of January 20, 1965, Johnson admonished the guests:
"Don't stay up late. We're on our way to the Great Society!"[7]

The theme of Johnson's campaign against Senator Barry Goldwater of Arizona in the fall of 1964 had already been unveiled in a
speech that he made the previous May 22 at the University of Michigan. He told the students that "in your time we have the opportunity to move not only toward the rich society and the powerful
society but upward to the Great Society. . . ." He explained:

> The Great Society rests on abundance and liberty for all. It
> demands an end to poverty and racial injustice. . . . The Great
> Society is a place where every child can find knowledge to en-
> rich his mind and to enlarge his talents. . . . [I]n the next forty
> years we must rebuild the entire urban United States. . . .[8]

Two weeks after the election Johnson discussed with the cabinet
the problems of achieving the Great Society, which he noted would
rquire a "substantial investment."[9] On a post-election visit to Southwest Texas State Teachers College, in San Marcos, from which he
had graduated in 1930, he said, "Today we are at the edge of a new
era of progress toward the American dream."[10]

He could hardly wait to get on with the task, the main blueprint
for which had been drawn in the Economic Opportunity Act of
1964, the vehicle for the "war against poverty." The legislation,
which Johnson had signed into law nine months after succeeding
President Kennedy on November 22, 1963, combined ten different
programs. They were designed to combat illiteracy, unemployment,
lack of training and skills, scarcity of public service, and other man-
ifestations of urban and rural poverty. The most conspicuous agencies brought into being were the "domestic peace corps"—VISTA
(Volunteers in the Service of America)—and the Job Corps, in
which young men and women could enroll for two years.

Six weeks after the 1964 election Johnson spoke separately to
VISTA officials and to members of the prospective National Advisory

Council to the economic opportunity program. He addressed the VISTA representatives as the "first frontline volunteers in our war against poverty." He told them, "This is your job: to guide the young, to comfort the sick, to encourage the downtrodden, to teach the skills which may lead to a more rewarding life."[11] He told members of the advisory group that they were a domestic National Security Council in the war against poverty. "Our objective," he said, "is total victory—and we are going to attain it."[12]

In no small part the near euphoria about social progress that suffused Washington at the start of 1965 was due to Johnson's signal achievement, months after Kennedy's assassination, in getting Congress to pass the Civil Rights Act of 1964. Landmark though it was, liberals saw it as a harbinger of even greater things to come. The 1964 bill finally enacted into law many of the reforms that Truman had been unable to persuade Congress to pass when he was in office.

"Great social change," Johnson observed in a speech to the National Urban League's Community Action Assembly in late 1964, "tends to come rapidly in periods of intense activity and progress before the impulse slows. I believe we are in the midst of such a period of change."[13]

In the best of circumstances Truman would have had a struggle to achieve new liberal reforms, because throughout his final term Congress was dominated, in domestic affairs, by the conservative coalition. Johnson would also have a fight to keep the impulse behind his Great Society programs alive long enough for Congress to vote the necessary heavy funding each year required for their fruition. Still, both presidents had constituencies of considerable power behind them and four years in office ahead. Such were the controversies and costs of the Fair Deal and the Great Society, of course, that those years needed to be a time of peace if domestic goals were to be realized.

War could readily shatter the dreams inspired by the elections of 1948 and 1964. Yet, more than people generally realized in those years, ugly developments affecting American policy were threatening in a distant part of the world.

Even while the election campaign was in progress in the United States in the fall of 1948, Communist-inspired riots ripped through South Korea, where American occupation forces, dispatched at the close of the Second World War, were still stationed. The South

Korean government, a client of the United States, proclaimed martial law in parts of the country. President Syngman Rhee sent a message to his delegation at the United Nations General Assembly session in Paris, warning that the Communist government of North Korea, a Soviet client, might invade the South once a planned withdrawal of all American occupation forces occurred.[14] Nevertheless, the Truman administration proceeded with plans to withdraw since Rhee's government had been established under United Nations auspices and thus could look to the UN for support.

While Lyndon Johnson campaigned in 1964, a war for independence that had been in progress in Vietnam and elsewhere in Indochina since 1946 increased in scope and intensity. In 1950 the United States, under Truman, had taken sides against the native Communist-Nationalist movement in Vietnam, led by Ho Chi Minh. Since 1954, during the administration of Dwight D. Eisenhower, the United States had been dispatching noncombat military advisers to assist the anti-Communist forces of South Vietnam against Ho's North Vietnamese forces. President Kennedy had substantially increased the flow of advisers and broadened the American commitment. On taking office, Johnson carried forward Kennedy's policies. Still, by the time of the 1964 election, the limited American efforts to defeat the North Vietnamese Communists appeared seriously to be losing ground.

Twenty-five days after the election Johnson held a press conference at his LBJ Ranch at Johnson City, Texas, on November 28.[15] From his opening remarks it was obvious what note he wished to strike. "Encouraging evidence" indicated that "the underlying economic forces remain strong." "The coming holiday season," he added, "will find our economy setting new records for production, employment, income and sales." When Johnson had finished his introductory comments the first question by a reporter steered the conference in quite a different direction.

"Mr. President," the reporter asked, "is the expansion of the Vietnam War into Laos or North Vietnam a live possibility at this point?"

The question was prompted by the fact that on November 26, General Maxwell D. Taylor, United States ambassador to South Vietnam, had returned to report to the president and participate in a post-election review of the war. He had arrived in Washington amid reports that to safeguard South Vietnam the administration might adopt a policy of bombing enemy supply routes from North Vietnam and Laos.

On November 28, officials in Washington and Malcolm M. Kilduff, assistant White House press secretary, accompanying the president in Texas, had made a point of telling reporters privately that no drastic changes should be anticipated a a result of Taylor's visit.[16] The question at the presidential press conference, therefore, did not particularly please Johnson. Characteristically in such circumstances, his answer dripped with pain, sarcasm, condescension.

> I don't want to give you any particular guideposts as to your conduct in the matter, but when you crawl out on a limb, you always have to find another one to crawl back on. I have just been sitting here in this serene atmosphere of the Pedernales for the last few days reading about the wars that you have involved us in, and the additional undertakings that I have made decisions on, or that General Taylor has recommended, or that Mr. McNamara plans, or Secretary Rusk envisages. I would say, generally speaking, that some people are speculating and taking positions that I would think are somewhat premature.

The fact of the matter was that Taylor had returned with a briefing paper stating, "If, as the evidence shows, we are playing a losing game in South Vietnam, it is high time we change and find a better way." He proposed undertaking gradually intensifying air strikes against the North.[17]

Johnson returned to Washington for a strategy conference on December 1. Attending were Taylor, Secretary of State Dean Rusk, Secretary of Defense Robert S. McNamara, Vice-President-elect Hubert H. Humphrey, John A. McCone, director of Central Intelligence; General Earle G. Wheeler, chairman of the Joint Chiefs of Staff; McGeorge Bundy, special assistant to the president for national security affairs; his brother, William P. Bundy, assistant secretary of state for Far Eastern affairs; and John T. McNaughton, assistant secretary of defense for international security affairs. As a result of the discussion Johnson approved in principle a strategy of bombing targets in North Vietnam on a rising scale.

After the meeting the White House issued a generally reassuring statement, which did not mention bombing. In fact, the president had not made a commitment to future military operations against

North Vietnam. He had taken a step in that direction, depending on developments. When reporters asked to interview General Taylor, the request was denied. They happened to overhear Secretary McNamara say, "It would be impossible for Max to talk to these people without leaving the impression that the situation is going to hell."[18]

In hindsight, the comment contained the germ of a theme as pertinent to Truman as to Johnson. The elections of the two presidents sixteen years apart were hailed as harbingers of progress in civil rights and rededication to the policy of using federal money to improve the lives of people in cities and on farms. In foreign affairs both presidents were committed to containment of communism, which meant checking the expansion and influence of the Soviet Union and Red China. Relentlessly, events in Asia drew the two presidents, each in his time, away from domestic concerns and toward concentration on what each viewed as challenges to United States vital interests by Communist-led forces in Korea and Vietnam, respectively, abetted by Moscow and Peking. The determination of the two presidents to halt the spread of Communist control led them beyond the capabilities of American conventional military power, barring such massive commitments as might lead to a third world war. Bloody, costly, frustrating, inconclusive limited wars robbed them of public support, crippling their leadership and leaving their presidencies in tatters.

II · *The Traps*

1

Harry Truman and Lyndon Johnson were men of a kind we are not likely to see in the White House again.

Although the foreign policies adopted by Truman remain the matrix of United States foreign policy to this day, he appears, especially in this year 1984, his centennial, as a figure from an age long past. Even when he was president, he was refreshingly old-fashioned in some ways. When Truman was born in the village of Lamar, Missouri, in a four-room clapboard house across a nameless dirt road from a mule barn, Chester A. Arthur was president. Radio had not yet been invented, and the manufacture of the horseless buggies in the United States was still a decade in the future. Truman grew up among people who had experienced the Civil War and who watched wagon trains crossing the frontier. As a politician he became a quintessential party man at a time when political conventions, not primaries and television, determined who would be nominated for president. The only experience Truman had with television was to sit in front of the camera and read his longer, more formal speeches in a flat voice.

As for Johnson, there will simply never be another. All the computers on earth could not put Lyndon together again.

The two came from obscure rural origins—Truman's in the farm-lands of Missouri, Johnson's in the hill country of Texas. They were men of unusual heartiness and earthiness. Certain provincialisms clung to both of them. The barnyard lingered in Truman's humor, incorrigible vulgarity permeated Johnson's. Once when Truman was taking his customary early-morning walk, he stopped at the old Doctors' Hospital on H Street to visit Associate Justice William O.

Douglas, who was a patient. Striding up to Douglas's bed, Truman accidentally kicked over a urinal that lay partially under it. As remembered by a physician, Truman said, "A president can't even go to see a Supreme Court justice without getting pissed on."[1] At a White House gathering during the 1964 campaign Johnson thrust his chin across a table at which he was seated and snorted, "Barry Goldwater doesn't know his ass from his elbow." Johnson then stood up before a group that included a distinguished woman and graphically demonstrated which was which, or, more particularly, which was *not* the elbow.[2] Truman and Johnson were tough, pragmatic, and stubborn. A desire to help the underdog drove them both. In Washington in the 1940s they became lasting friends. Personally, however, they were not alike—no one was like Lyndon Johnson.

More appealing than imposing, Truman was a decent, straightforward, friendly, intrepid man, not given to ruses or sleight of hand. Generally speaking, his character was simple and invigorating, a reflection of nineteenth-century ideals and, of course, prejudices. His recently published letters, written between 1910 and 1959, to his sweetheart and later his wife, Bess, reveal a twenty-seven-year-old's longing in 1911 for a white, Anglo-Saxon, Protestant, agricultural America, undiluted by immigrant laborers. His letters contain passing references to niggers, dagos, "Rooshans," and bohunks, and describe the New York of 1918 as a "Kike town."[3] It was neighborhood language that did not characterize his actions as president, as demonstrated by his civil rights message, his veto of anti-immigration legislation, and his recognition of the new state of Israel, where his name is honored today. "I am the best friend the Jews have had since Moses," he later told his friend Paul Porter, a Washington lawyer.[4]

As an aging former president, he found the demands of blacks during the 1960s and 1970s extreme. The tenor of the feminist movement today would have filled him with indignant disbelief. After Roosevelt's death his renowned secretary of labor, Mrs. Frances Perkins, first woman ever to sit in a cabinet, elected to retire. Truman told his staff that he did not want a woman in the cabinet.[5] The man he chose instead was a calamity. He was Lewis W. Schwellenbach, a slightly prudish person, who was unable to cope with strikes.

Johnson was a tragic political genius of bottomless pettiness, volcanic energy, brilliant intellect, disgusting manners, wild emotions, voracious appetites, habitual mendacity, restless cunning, nagging insecurity, great achievements, and sometimes near lunacy. His worst trait, in utter contrast to Truman, was his relish for humiliating others. Johnson was a bona fide ogre, yet he could be marvelously skillful at doing things to bring help and comfort to others. He was a man of such complexity that it was, and is, often difficult to sort out the good and bad in his motives.

Although congenial and gregarious, Truman was not one who forced himself upon others. In that respect, Johnson was relentless. Once at a White House meeting President Eisenhower stationed his attorney general, William P. Rogers, between himself and the then Senator Johnson with an order to Rogers to keep Johnson from tugging at Eisenhower's lapel.[6]

Johnson had an arsenal of techniques for dominating others. "One," recalled Bryce N. Harlow, a former government official, "was nose-to-nose negotiation, where he'd take that huge head of his, huge corpus, and lean it forward right into your face. And he'd talk to you, nose-actually-to-nose. And he would push people over that way. Dominate them!" As a member of various committee staffs in Johnson's Senate years, Harlow described the ingredients of Johnson's leadership:

> It's a mixture of fear. It's a mixture of reward. It's a mixture of admiration. It's a mixture of being cowed by a much more dynamic personality. It's a mixture of wanting to follow. It's a mixture of greater intellectual force and power and tightness and discipline. It's a mixture of indefatigability. It's a mixture of an endowed energy. It's a mixture of diligence, working harder than the person next to you. It's a mixture of being a good fellow, but reserved simultaneously. You're one of the boys, but you're bigger than any of them. . . .[7]

For all his common sense, Truman was often erratic, usually at times when his indignation got the better of him, as when, in 1946, he proposed drafting striking railroad workers into the army. And Johnson, though instinctively cautious, was given to being carried away by enthusiasms, as when he piled up more social programs than the country could digest or pay for.

When it came to the Korean War, Truman said what he had to say about it, in public or private, which could be considerable, of course, and then said no more. When Johnson turned to the subject of the Vietnam War, there was almost no turning him off. He talked on and on in monologues that might begin in sunlight and end in moonlight. It was not unheard of for him to keep talking almost until dawn. On one occasion he began talking to a group of reporters on the second floor of the White House at 4:00 in the afternoon and was still going strong at sunset. Then nightfall gave him a second wind. He was so absorbed in what he was saying that he forgot to turn on the lights, and the outpouring of words went on in semidarkness, illuminated by one electric light bulb in a corner. It was at the time, early in his administration, when he was making a show of turning off the lights to save the taxpayers' money. When the session finally broke up after 11:00 P.M., the reporters had to use matches to light their way to the stairs.

Truman was not obsessed with ambition either for political power, money, or luxury. His ego would have fit into a corner of Johnson's. Truman kept his troubles in perspective. "Played a little five-cent poker and settled the affairs of the world generally," he wrote in 1946 after an evening of work and relaxation.[8] As best he could, Truman played the hand that had been dealt him in life, though he confided to Bess in 1911, "I've always had a sneakin' notion that someday maybe I'd amount to something."[9]

It is doubtful whether he was ever particularly ambitious to be president before he was faced with running for a full term in 1948. Preferring to remain in the Senate, he had to be dragooned by the Democratic leaders, including Roosevelt, to run as the best available compromise candidate on the ticket with FDR in 1944, a turn that brought Truman to the White House after only eighty-three days in the vice-presidency. Before the 1948 campaign, he had offered twice to step aside for General Eisenhower, if Eisenhower would agree, as he did not, to run as a Democrat. Without doubt, Truman personally would have placed in nomination that year the name of General of the Army George C. Marshall, the then secretary of state and former wartime army chief of staff, if Marshall had displayed the slightest willingness to run. Finally, Truman himself ran with a gusto that sprang in no small part from vengeance against those Democrats, including members of the Roosevelt family, who had tried to dump him before the convention because he looked like a loser. The whistle stops revealed him to be a president with a tart but rarely malicious tongue.

In sharp contrast, playing the hand that had been dealt him, even playing it with ferocity, was not enough for Lyndon Johnson. He clawed and scratched for the deck itself. When he was in the ninth grade, he told a classmate, "Someday I'm going to be president of the United States."[10] His climb to that goal was a marvel of rendering service to constituents, scheming, dissembling, deceiving, tapping the wealth of Texas, mastering the United States Senate, and bending other men to his will. Someone said that Johnson resembled a Mongolian emperor in the way he treated those who worked for him. Members of his staff conceded, however, that he drove himself as hard or harder than he drove them.

As a senator from 1935 to 1945, Truman had won respect and influence and had made contributions to important legislation of the prewar period. After Pearl Harbor he had become a national figure as chairman of the Senate Special Committee to Investigate the National Defense Program. By comparison, however, his career on Capitol Hill was dwarfed by that of Johnson. As the Democratic leader between 1953 and 1961, Johnson had demonstrated such power and control as had not been seen in the Senate's history. He understood, as someone who watched him at close quarters in the White House later said, the sensitive areas in relations between the executive and legislative branches and traversed them skillfully when it came to advancing his own program after Kennedy's death.

As president, Johnson so dominated the political stage that his performance can only be compared with Roosevelt's in the New Deal years. Johnson quickly assembled a coalition of support that enabled him to defeat Goldwater in 1964 by a greater plurality than Roosevelt had amassed in his defeat of Governor Alfred M. Landon of Kansas in 1936.

Making full use of television and the jet plane, instruments of presidential leadership that were unknown to Roosevelt, Johnson became the most ubiquitous president the country has ever seen. He threw himself at the American people with energy so boundless that it was difficult to escape his voice, his face, or his contrails. Certainly Truman never was, nor wanted to be, onstage all of the time in the Johnson style. The elemental force of Johnson tended to lend extra and sometimes extraneous importance to him. Yet it is entirely possible that history will judge Truman as the more important president of the two because of the period in which he served—from 1945 to 1953.

The postwar period was a momentous point of departure, and it was Truman's destiny to hold responsibility for the foreign policy of what was then without question the most powerful nation on earth.

The Second World War, which ended in 1945, had changed the world. The continent of Europe had been laid waste. The resources of the United Kingdom had been drained. An upsurge of Zionism roiled the Middle East. Japan lay in ruins. China was on the brink of civil war. Already weakened by the First World War, the old European empires in Asia and the Pacific were collapsing, with especially grave consequences in Indochina. The world order was suddenly dominated by two superpowers, the United States and the Soviet Union, ravaged yet strengthened. The year 1945 also brought the beginning of the nuclear age. For nearly eight years Truman was the president who had to manage the American adjustment to the changed world. He was the first president who had to decide whether to use the atomic bomb and how to compete with the Soviet Union in the development of nuclear and thermonuclear weapons. It was his decision in 1950 to build the hydrogen bomb. Johnson is renowned for the scores of important domestic bills he got through Congress. What is often forgotten is that in a period of historic activity in foreign affairs Truman, helped by a bipartisan coalition, never lost a major piece of foreign-policy legislation in Congress. It was Truman's policies that established the framework in which all the postwar presidents, including Johnson, shaped their own policies.

On the other hand, an overdue and historic improvement in relations among Americans of different races, as well as better medical care for the poor and the elderly, were accomplished by Johnson's skill and power, as Senator majority leader and as president, in getting civil rights bills and Medicare and Medicaid enacted.

Asia proved to be the snare for Truman and Johnson.

2

"The situation in Korea is . . . disturbing," Truman said in mid-1948.[11]

When the Second World War ended in 1945, Korea was a nation in near anarchy in a vast region of Asia that was itself undergoing one of the great revolutionary upheavals in history. China was approaching a crucial phase of civil war between the Nationalists, led by Chiang Kai-shek, and the Communists under Mao Zedong. Twice seared by atomic bombs, Japan was prostrate. Its collapse opened the way for the Soviet Union, having expanded across Siberia to the Pacific Ocean, to establish itself as a major Far Eastern power contiguous to Korea. Since Japan had annexed Korea in 1910, the destruction of the Japanese empire suddenly set the Koreans free but adrift without a government or a political order and without capable management of their economy. Into this anarchic mess in September 1945 sailed the United States XXIV Corps to occupy the southern half of Korea while the Soviets occupied the northern half. "Pres. Truman anxious to have Korea occupied promptly," noted the "XXIV Corps Journal" of August 25, 1945.[12]

What business did the United States have barging into the chaotic life of a small nation on the other side of the world, to which Americans throughout their own history had paid scant attention? The answer was rooted in the thinking of policymakers in the Roosevelt administration during the war. Roosevelt advocated a postwar temporary international trusteeship for Korea. The State Department thought it was important that the United States participate in the administration of Korea after the Japanese defeat and pending Korean trusteeship, for it did not want the Soviets to control Korean affairs completely.[13] Washington hoped for a Korea friendly to the United States. This policy, this viewpoint, was espoused by the Truman administration. But the Soviets also had a stake. A Korea friendly to them or even a divided Korea with the northern half under friendly rule would provide the Soviet Union with a buffer against attack from the Korean peninsula. In addition, the Soviets, who had entered the war against Japan, and the Americans had a mutual interest in the surrender of Japanese troops deployed on Korean soil.

Soviet forces had begun entering Korea in August 1945. The Truman administration, unprepared for the sudden Japanese capitulation under nuclear attack, flung together its own plans for a Korean occupation. It was fitting that Dean Rusk, then a colonel on the general staff of the War Department, played a major part in writing a Washington proposal, accepted by Moscow, to establish the 38th parallel as an ostensibly temporary dividing line between the Soviet and the American occupation forces.[14] Before long Rusk, as assistant secretary of state for Far Eastern affairs in the Truman administration, was to exert an important influence in the Korean

War. And a decade and a half later, as secretary of state under Johnson, he was to be a powerful voice in United States war policy in Vietnam.

The suddenness of Japan's surrender left American authorities with no available forces trained to manage civil affairs in Korea. In the pinch they called upon the XXIV Corps under the command of Lieutenant General John R. Hodge, an infantry officer without suitable experience for the difficulties that Korea posed. Arriving in the midst of chaos, he muddled along a path that brought right-wing factions into power in southern Korea, even as Communist rule was being imposed in the north. Almost from the start, therefore, the stage was set for a civil war to determine whether the Right or the Left ultimately would govern all of Korea.

The proposal for a trusteeship withered. Instead, as the cold war materialized, the United States and the Soviet Union became rivals for influence in occupied Korea. Efforts to form a provisional government for the whole of the nation, after which the two occupying powers were to withdraw, collapsed in the heat of the rivalry. The 38th parallel became a permanent dividing line. Still, the ultimate American objective remained the establishment of a united, self-governing, independent Korea, friendly to the United States.

In 1946, life in South Korea had degenerated to the point where the United States War Department wanted to end the occupation. Truman, influenced by the State Department, rejected immediate termination. "Our commitments . . . required," he said, "that we stay . . . long enough to see the job through. . . ."[15] The administration decided to continue the occupation for the time being, largely because Korea had assumed an importance beyond the internal affairs of the peninsula.

The Communists were getting the upper hand in the Chinese civil war next door. Another war of insurrection was beginning in Vietnam. The Philippines, Indonesia, Burma, and Malaya were seething with indigenous leftist disturbances. American policy makers were worried about Communist designs on Japan. In Europe and the Middle East, the Soviet Union appeared to be menacing Greece, Turkey, and Iran, and maneuvering to control the Black Sea Straits. With support from Moscow, domestic Communist parties were struggling for power in France and Italy. The worsening cold war was freezing relations between Washington and Moscow. George F. Kennan, American chargé d'affaires in Moscow, had planted in the Truman administration the idea of a policy of containment of imperialistic communism, even though his and the administration's understanding of such a policy may have been divergent, Kennan later contending that he did not mean military containment. Speaking at Westminster College in Fulton, Missouri, Winston S. Churchill declared that "an iron curtain has descended" across Europe. In those circumstances, therefore, Korea became another sector in the cold war, one that the Truman administration was unwilling to yield at once, lest withdrawal adversely affect American influence around the world.

By 1947, however, the prospective heavy foreign aid for Europe under the Truman Doctrine and the Marshall Plan and the worldwide demands on a reduced American military establishment made the Korean occupation too costly a burden. Moreover, the Joint Chiefs of Staff held that in the event of a major war in Asia, the United States would be better off to conduct its operations from a base more advantageous than Korea. Still, the Truman administration did not wish to pull out hastily lest that invite a Communist attack on the South. The administration resolved the dilemma by involving the United Nations in the cause of Korean independence. Since that procedure consumed time, the United States avoided a precipitate withdrawal. On the other hand, by having an independent government established by free elections under the auspices of the United Nations, even if the government ruled only below the 38th parallel, the United States could depart without blatantly abandoning the South Koreans.

After the elections were held in the American zone (the Soviets closed their zone to the balloting), a South Korean assembly was chosen and a constitution drafted. Syngman Rhee was elected president of the Republic of Korea. Yet the lines of international conflict were only drawn tighter. In the northern half of the country, the Democratic People's Republic of Korea was established under the leadership of Kim Il-sung, a former anti-Japanese guerrilla chieftain. A Soviet-style constitution was adopted and a People's Army organized.

Soviet and American occupation troops, in that order, eventually withdrew, the Americans by June 29, 1949. Still, the situation remained volatile. Facing each other across the 38th parallel were a Communist government heavily armed by the Soviet Union and a right-wing regime comparatively lightly armed by the United States.

Each side was determined to conquer the other and gain control of the entire country. Indeed, one of the reasons the United States only lightly armed South Korea was suspicion that Rhee would take advantage of greater power to attack North Korea, thereby threatening to cause a Soviet-American confrontation.

Departing American occupation forces left behind small arms and ammunition, light artillery, mortars, and some vehicles—enough to arm a force of 50,000 South Koreans. Later, equipment for an additional 15,000 men was supplied from American stocks in Japan. Left behind, too, was a 500-man United States Military Advisory Group. Though no longer in occupation, the United States had become the protector of South Korea. United States strategic plans did not include South Korea in the American "defensive perimeter" in the Far East, which was based upon islands. On the other hand, as a United States diplomat explained to a South Korean, the United States had associated itself with other members of the United Nations in support of South Korea. Korea's position, therefore, transcended a definition of interest by a line drawn in any direction.[16] Truman put it forthrightly. In a special message to Congress around the time of the final withdrawal of American occupation forces, he said:

> Korea has become a testing ground in which the validity and practical value of the ideals and principles of democracy which the Republic [of Korea] is putting into practice are being matched against the practices of communism which have been imposed upon the people of the north. . . . The United States has a deep interest in the continuing progress of the Korean people toward these objectives. . . . [W]e will not fail to provide the aid which is so essential to Korea at this critical time.[17]

The implications of the Korean situation were understood in the White House. Three months before the withdrawal was completed, the National Security Council promulgated a top-secret policy paper, NSC 8/2, which Truman approved.* The NSC warned that the Soviets intended to dominate all of Korea, perhaps using the North Korean regime as the vehicle for conquest. Such a move "would

---

* Often cited in this book, the formerly classified reports by the National Security Council on international problems were designated by letters (NSC or NSAM) and numbers. Recommendations in such papers became the policy of an administration when approved by the president, a member of the NSC.

enhance the political and strategic position of the USSR with respect to both China and Japan and adversely affect the position of the U.S. in those areas and throughout the Far East . . . ," the paper said. Defeat of the government established in the South "under the aegis of the UN would, moreover, constitute a severe blow to the prestige and influence of the latter; in this respect the interests of the U.S. must be regarded as parallel to, if not identical with, those of the UN." [18]

On October 1, 1949, a momentous day, Mao Zedong, riding a wave of decisive victories over Chiang Kai-shek, proclaimed the People's Republic of China.

Late in 1949, according to Nikita S. Khrushchev, Kim Il-sung, the North Korean leader, visited Joseph V. Stalin seeking approval for an attack on South Korea. Stalin and afterward Mao Zedong gave Kim a green light, Khrushchev recorded in his memoirs. [19]

When Congress passed the Foreign Assistance Act of 1950, authorizing aid to South Korea and other friendly nations, Truman described the action as "a major contribution to peace and freedom. . . ." [20] The statement was made on June 5, 1950, and reflected the moderate optimism that he appeared to feel at the time about the chances for peace in Asia.

As far as the record shows, none of Truman's advisers went to him that month and told him a dangerous situation seemed to be developing along the 38th parallel. The advisers themselves did not believe it. In retrospect, the misjudgment was astonishing. Intelligence reports to Washington provided an almost classic description of enemy preparations for imminent war. North Korean civilians were being evacuated from the immediate vicinity of the parallel. Nonmilitary freight deliveries in the area had been halted. Transport was being restricted to military purposes, including large shipments of weapons and ammunition. As part of extensive troop movements, heavy armor was moving up. The North Korean radio launched a propaganda campaign against the division of Korea by the "American-Rhee police state."

The intelligence reports were greeted by Washington officials with all sorts of rationalizations. Forgetting the same kind of misjudgment before, at the time of Pearl Harbor, they hoped and believed that the North Koreans were unlikely to do that which they had the capacity to do. Washington was simply not persuaded that the North Koreans intended to involve themselves in armed conflict on a large scale. Perhaps, officials rationalized, the preparations foreshadowed further guerrilla forays of a kind that had been taking place along the parallel for months. The Communists, it was thought, had not exhausted their efforts to overthrow the Rhee government by political pressure and psychological warfare. Why, therefore, should they resort to invasion? Furthermore, or so one argument went, North Korea could not conquer the South without the assistance of Soviet and Chinese military units.

On Saturday, June 24, 1950, Truman flew to his home in Independence, Missouri, to spend the weekend with his family. He and Mrs. Truman and their daughter Margaret were enjoying a late dinner that evening when Secretary of State Dean Acheson telephoned the president from Washington.

"Mr. President, I have very serious news for you," he said. "The North Koreans have invaded South Korea."[21]

3

When the revolution to free Indochina from more than half a century of French colonial rule began in 1946, Lyndon Johnson was a thirty-eight-year-old member of the House of Representatives. Beginning in what was then the second year of the Truman administration, therefore, he was in an advantageous position to observe the procession of shattering events brought about by war in Indochina. As American involvement in those events occurred and as Johnson moved to the Senate, then into posts as Senate majority leader, member of the Senate Armed Services Committee, and, finally, vice-president, he became increasingly involved in the drama. By the time he succeeded to the presidency, he had been learning about Vietnam for seventeen years, conferring with its anti-Communist leaders in Saigon, scrutinizing the growing American role, studying congressional and public moods, and forming his own attitudes.

From the outset of 1946, Washington had viewed Ho Chi Minh's resort to arms against the French as another bad turn in the cold war. The revolt appeared to increase the dangers to the United States position in Asia, already heightened by the outbreak of heavy fighting in the Chinese civil war. Dean Acheson, then undersecretary of state, and a stalwart behind the policy of containment of Communist expansionism, cabled the American mission in Saigon on December 8, 1946, saying that the least desirable outcome of the fighting in Vietnam would be the establishment of a "Communist-oriented state." He also informed Henri Bonnet, the French ambassador in Washington, that while the United States was not then prepared to intervene, it was "ready and willing to do anything which it might consider helpful in the circumstances."[22]

Months of fighting ensued, but the French were still unable to defeat the guerrillas. Meanwhile Mao Zedong's armies, advancing in China, swept south toward the border of Indochina. The Truman administration was alarmed. Mao, it was feared, might invade Vietnam. Or Chinese troops might cross the border in pursuit of retreating Chinese Nationalist soldiers. Or, as proved to be the case, Mao might send arms and technicians to aid the Vietnamese communist insurgents.

From start to finish, fear that Chinese Communist power would spread southward through Indochina motivated American policy in one administration after another. In the Johnson period, Secretary of State Rusk warned of the danger of "a billion Chinese . . . armed with nuclear weapons."[23] From Washington the problem was seen as economic as well as political. Since Southeast Asia was rich in food and natural resources, a 1952 National Security Council statement warned that loss of the region to Communism would be a blow felt from India to Indonesia to Japan. Indeed, the statement declared, the conquest of Indochina would "make it extremely difficult to prevent Japan's eventual accommodation to communism."[24]

Even when battered by the revolt, the French were unwilling to grant Vietnam complete independence. It was clear to the Truman administration that France would, therefore, have a difficult time defeating the insurgents. On the other hand, Truman and Acheson did not want France to withdraw and leave Vietnam under Communist rule. Moreover, the basic thrust of United States foreign policy was to make Western Europe militarily and economically strong enough to contain, with American support, a possible Soviet attack toward the English Channel. France was considered essential to the defense of Western Europe. Hence the French were to be supported and coaxed into standing with their North Atlantic allies. That consideration also became a pillar of continuing assistance for French interests in Vietnam, placing the United States, awkwardly, on the side of colonialism.

As early as 1949, David K. E. Bruce, United States ambassador to

France, warned Washington that if the Communists should conquer Vietnam, Burma and Thailand would fall "like overripe apples."[25] In the Eisenhower administration the overripe apples became dominoes. As one domino fell, President Eisenhower warned at a press conference on April 7, 1954, it would knock over the other dominoes in the row. Thus the application of containment to Southeast Asia would be required to prevent the first domino—Vietnam— from setting off a chain reaction. The domino theory, under one name or another, became an article of faith among American presidents in the 1950s and 1960s, although neither Truman nor Eisenhower nor, to any significant degree, Kennedy used military force to try to keep the first domino from toppling.

Beginning with Truman, however, political support and military and economic assistance were offered in the cause of defeating Ho Chi Minh's forces. In 1949, the French attempted to short-circuit the revolution by installing in Vietnam a puppet regime headed by Bao Dai, a former emperor of the French protectorate of Annam, which later became part of Vietnam. The hope was that he could win the support of a popular majority, which supposedly opposed communism. The Truman administration had no better solution to suggest and was jolted in the winter of 1950 when first Mao Zedong and then the Soviets recognized the Ho Chi Minh regime. In the Western capitals it looked as though international communism was truly on the march in Indochina. Truman formally recognized Bao Dai and offered him an initial $10 million in assistance. "The U.S. thereafter," observed the Pentagon Papers, "was directly involved in the developing tragedy in Vietnam."[26]

In one of the first of an endless series of such presidential statements to be made in the next two decades, Truman said in 1950 that Vietnam was among the most important problems that the United States faced.[27] As in the case of Korea, an area in which the United States had taken little interest before the Second World War, Vietnam had suddenly come to be viewed, largely because of the Communist seizure of China, as vital to American security. The view was to be ever more fervently espoused in Washington as the years passed.

Within weeks of Truman's first grant of aid to Bao Dai came the first of many escalations in American commitment. When South Korea was invaded in June 1950, Washington feared that China might move against Vietnam. Truman increased the amount of assistance to Bao Dai and dispatched a military mission to Vietnam. United States intervention in the Korean and Vietnam wars was cut from the same cloth. Addressing Congress seven months after the start of the Korean War, Truman said: "The threat of world conquest by Soviet Russia endangers our liberty and endangers the kind of world in which the free spirit of man can survive. . . . All free nations are exposed and all are in peril."[28]

In his final budget message to Congress eleven days before Eisenhower was inaugurated on January 20, 1953, Truman deluded himself and, unintentionally, the American people as to the direction of events in Indochina, a legacy that flourished under some of his successors. Speaking only a year before French forces were crushed in the battle of Dien Bien Phu, in northern Vietnam, Truman said that American military assistance had been "a crucial factor in strengthening the troops of France and the Associated States of Vietnam . . . in their fight against a powerful, Communist-led revolt."[29]

As would be the case in future administrations, domestic political pressure had much to do with Truman's intervention in Vietnam with economic assistance, a military mission, and supplies. The fall of China to the Communists had brought a deluge of partisan criticism upon him, though practically speaking there was very little any president in the circumstances could have done to quell the Chinese revolution. After Mao's triumph, conservative Republicans and the China lobby went on a rampage. The latter's articulate allies in Congress, known as the China bloc, in effect forced a large appropriation on Truman to do something to stem the Communist tide in the general area of China. It was because of that appropriation that Truman had the money in hand to give Bao Dai. The intervention in Vietnam caused not a whisper of dissent.

The administration rallied to the support of the French in no small part because it dreaded the political consequences at home of "losing" another country to communism. Truman did as much in Vietnam as he thought necessary to prevent its loss. He was careful not to attempt more, certainly nothing that might embroil him in a wider war with China. When a question was raised about intervening in Vietnam to the degree that he had intervened in Greece and Turkey under the Truman Doctrine of 1947, his reply was "Absolutely not."[30] His intervening to the extent of preventing a loss but not to the extent of risking a larger war was the very prescription that would be followed by Eisenhower, Kennedy, and even Johnson.

Taking office in 1953, President Eisenhower and Secretary of State John Foster Dulles saw the problem in Indochina in much the same light Truman and Acheson had seen it. In his first State of the Union message Eisenhower said that the Korean War, still in progress, was "clearly a part of the same calculated assault that the aggressor is . . . pressing in Indochina. . . ."[31] In the new president's first summer in office the National Security Council concluded in a study that "the loss of Indochina would be critical to the security of the U.S."[32] Dulles charged that Red China was promoting aggression by training and supplying the Communist forces in Indochina. The new administration substantially increased the financial support for the anti-Communists in Vietnam. In January 1954, Eisenhower approved a National Security Council paper that declared that the "loss of any single country" in Southeast Asia would lead to the loss of the entire region, and then India and Japan, and ultimately would "endanger the . . . security of Europe."[33] Illustrative of how American intervention in the Korean War and the Vietnam War was of a piece was the conviction prevalent in Washington that the Communists, having been forced to settle for a truce in Korea in July 1953, had decided to advance in Indochina instead. In accordance with that reasoning, the United States had to be prepared to continue the struggle in Vietnam.

Before long, Eisenhower had moved far downstream from where Truman had disembarked at the end of his term. The reason was twofold. One was the French surrender to the Viet Minh, or League for the Independence of Vietnam, in the battle of Dien Bien Phu. The other was the new order in Indochina that came into being in 1954 after France withdrew, opening the door to a more direct American role in Vietnam. Eisenhower had considered intervening with air power to prevent the French defeat. Congressional leaders, ironically including Lyndon Johnson, opposed the venture without allied participation. His objection was simply to the unilateral aspect of the proposal. Even in 1954, he agreed that the United States had an interest in Indochina that should be upheld, but in collaboration with allies. In a message, Eisenhower appealed to Churchill to join the united action, basing his case on a familiar theme. "[W]e failed," he wrote, "to halt [Emperor] Hirohito [of Japan], Mussolini, and

Hitler by not acting in unity and in time. That marked the beginning of many years of stark tragedy and desperate peril. May it not
be that our nations have learned something from that lesson?"[34] Un-
convinced, Churchill declined. After the French defeat, Eisenhower
weighed the pros and cons of asking Congress for approval to commit combat troops, but the idea languished, especially when the
French indicated that they no longer wanted to fight in Indochina.
As Leslie H. Gelb and Richard K. Betts have written, Eisenhower
kept America out of war but kept America in Vietnam.[35] In fact, the
Vietnam commitment was deepened at the very time when Americans were going about vowing "No more Koreas!"

After Dien Bien Phu, cessation of hostilities between France and
the Viet Minh was arranged at an international conference in Geneva, which adopted the Geneva Accords of 1954. For the purposes
of this narrative the most pertinent provision drew a provisional line
of military demarcation across Vietnam at the 17th parallel, leaving
the future governance of the country to be decided in elections. As
matters stood, meanwhile, Ho Chi Minh and the victors over
France occupied the area north of the parallel, with Hanoi as the
capital, while the area south of the parallel was occupied by Bao
Dai, soon to depart for the Riviera, and his followers, with headquarters in Saigon. In complete accord with the wishes of the
Eisenhower administration, Bao appointed Ngo Dinh Diem premier. A Vietnamese repatriate who had been introduced to influential Washington officials by Francis Cardinal Spellman, archbishop
of New York, Diem was a Catholic who was to become president of
the largely Buddhist South Vietnam.

It had generally been assumed that the Geneva Accords would
soon result in the unification of northern and southern Vietnam under the sovereignty of the northern regime. Diem balked. The
Eisenhower administration did not feel bound by the Accords, of
which the United States was not a signatory. Fearful that they would
lead to eventual Communist control of Southeast Asia, Dulles had
merely taken formal note of them. The United States would act in
its own interest, even though it would contribute to the breakdown
of the Accords.[36]

Determined to check the spread of communism, Eisenhower and
Dulles became increasingly involved in South Vietnam. Most notably, Americans began replacing the departing French and assuming
their functions. American dollars became the life support of the

Diem regime. Instead of going through the French as previously, Eisenhower extended aid, including military equipment, directly to the South Vietnamese government, forging the links of a Washington-Saigon alliance. The Geneva Accords called for elections throughout Vietnam in 1956 to form a national government. As the time approached, the Eisenhower administration worried that the voting would install a Communist government. The administration wanted the elections postponed as long as possible and let Diem know it. He needed no prodding. Acting on a technicality, he refused to hold elections in the South, foreshadowing a shift from political to military struggle. Like the 38th parallel in Korea, the 17th parallel in Vietnam ceased to be a temporary dividing line. It became a fixed boundary between two rival and hostile governments— the Democratic Republic of Vietnam in the North and the Republic of Vietnam in the South. On October 1, 1954, Eisenhower wrote to Diem pledging support for the maintenance of "a strong, viable state, capable of resisting attempted subversion or aggression through military means." While the pledge was premised on Diem's adherence to satisfactory "standards of performance" in matters of state, including reforms, American aid went forward without too fine a point being put upon terms and conditions.[37]

A floodgate of trouble was opened by what proved to be Diem's despotic rule. A rebellion against it began in South Vietnam. In time, with Hanoi's encouragement, the rebels coalesced as the National Liberation Front (NLF). Diem labeled the guerrillas Viet Cong (VC), signifying Vietnamese Communists. For its own ends Hanoi sought to gain control over the NLF by, among other things, infiltrating trained cadres and supplies across the 17th parallel. The Eisenhower administration increased the number of United States military advisers in the small mission sent by Truman to 685. With tension rising, Saigon and Washington reacted by favoring the strengthening of South Vietnamese armed forces.

Raising the American stakes in South Vietnam, the Eisenhower administration sent a new military advisory and assistance group to undertake covert operations against the NLF. The group was headed by a famous CIA agent and antiguerrilla strategist, Colonel Edward G. Lansdale, whose exploits were the inspiration for the leading characters in two novels. *The Quiet American* by Graham Greene and *The Ugly American* by William J. Lederer and Eugene Burdick. The team engaged in paramilitary operations and psychological warfare, including some breathless acts of sabotage, like contaminating the oil supply for Hanoi trams. United States advisers took over from the French the training of the South Vietnamese army, although the administration had been warned by intelligence that Diem was weak and the Communists were strong. The last few years of the Eisenhower administration were a time of rising turmoil and conflict in Vietnam. Yet just one week before the American election of 1960, in which the winner would soon have to shoulder the responsibility for dealing with Vietnam, Eisenhower again wrote to Diem to say that "for so long as our strength can be useful, the United States will continue to assist Vietnam in the difficult yet hopeful struggle ahead." Eisenhower's legacy to his successor, as one later study was to observe, was rich in rhetoric and momentum.[38] In fact, on the eve of leaving office in 1961 Eisenhower, who was particularly concerned at that point with Laos, advised President-elect Kennedy that Kennedy might have to intervene unilaterally to save it.[39]

The commitment in Vietnam that Kennedy had inherited was not, according to his assistant, Theodore C. Sorensen, "one that President Kennedy felt he could abandon without undesirable consequences throughout Asia and the world."[40] Long beforehand, as a senator, Kennedy had stated his conviction that an independent Vietnam was important to American foreign policy.[41] If anything, his determination was strengthened by a speech delivered by Soviet Premier Khrushchev two weeks before the Kennedy inauguration. Predicting the ultimate triumph of communism, Khrushchev asserted that it would come about through wars of liberation in the Third World, specifically mentioning the one in Vietnam. He pledged full support to insurgents, a statement Kennedy seemed to take as something of a personal challenge. Several months later, after Krushchev tried to bully him at a summit meeting in Vienna, Kennedy told James B. Reston of *The New York Times*, "Now we have a problem of making our power credible, and Vietnam looks like the place."[42]

In the early months of his presidency, Kennedy undertook what was to become a 23-fold increase in the American military mission. The escalation breached the limit of 685 advisers, which was then authorized by the Geneva Accords and had been complied with by Eisenhower. For the first time, too, military advisers were individually assigned to roles supporting South Vietnamese in combat. As a result, American casualties rose sharply. Kennedy also ordered a clandestine campaign of sabotage and "light harassment" directed against North Vietnam and conducted by CIA-trained agents of Diem's government. To be targeted were railroads, highways, bridges, and trucks. American pilots were assigned to fly helicopters, airlifts, and reconnaissance missions. Although the issue was nothing like what it was to become in the next administration, the public's credibility about Vietnam was stretched at times under Kennedy as well as Johnson. In May 1961, Kennedy approved the NSC's National Security Action Memorandum 52, stating that the United States objective was "to prevent Communist domination of South Vietnam."[43] He shared the mind-set of his time. During the Cuban missile crisis in 1962 he said, "The 1930s taught us a clear lesson: aggressive conduct, if allowed to go unchecked and unchallenged, ultimately leads to war."[44]

While Kennedy widened the American commitment, he did essentially what Truman and Eisenhower had done, namely, enough to keep the Communists from winning. But the condition facing Kennedy was of a different order of magnitude from that which had confronted Truman and Eisenhower. By the 1960s it became obvious that if Kennedy was to do enough, he would have to do a great deal more than his predecessors had done. By the time of the Kennedy administration the size and effectiveness of the NLF were growing rapidly, and the NLF was receiving ever greater support from Hanoi. As an intelligence estimate warned Kennedy, an "extremely critical period" lay "immediately ahead."[45]

Nevertheless, in the 1960s doing enough merely to keep the Communists from winning was not quite the whole story of American policy. By the time Kennedy was in the White House, as Richard Betts of the Brookings Institution has written, policymakers knew very well that the odds against routing the Communists in Vietnam were poor. In most cases American officials agreed to escalation without genuine expectation of victory. Still, the possibility of good luck was not discarded.

Betts, writing in *The Wilson Quarterly* in the summer of 1983, asked,

> What made the men in Washington believe that they were making efforts that with luck might pan out, rather than marching *inevitably* toward defeat? The answer lies between hubris

and hope. During the early 1960s, both civilian and military theorists of "counterinsurgency" promoted the fateful illusion that American tutelage could reshape the fragile, war-battered South Vietnamese political system, creating a new nationalism among the South Vietnamese that could confront Marxist revolutionary élan with some sort of vigorous Asian Jeffersonianism—through land reform, free elections, better government.

Popular new theories of counterinsurgency—a device for defeating guerrillas with guerrillas and with superior weapons, "pacification" techniques, and enlightened social and political policy—had fascinated Kennedy even as a senator. Counterinsurgency had scored successes in the Philippines and Malaya. On becoming president, Kennedy took a personal hand in strengthening the Green Berets as an elite scourge of Communist revolution and subversion in the Third World. He read Mao Zedong and Che Guevara on guerrilla tactics and instructed the Special Warfare Center at Fort Bragg, North Carolina, to expand its mission.[46] (Twenty years later Fidel Castro revealed that *he* had been influenced in guerrilla warfare tactics by reading Ernest Hemingway's *For Whom the Bell Tolls*.[47]) Kennedy began the expansion of the number of United States advisers in Vietnam with the secret dispatch of five hundred men, most of them CIA-supported Green Berets.

As late as September 9, 1963, he subscribed to the domino theory. "I believe it," he said in a televised interview.

> I think that the struggle is close enough. China is so large, looms so high just beyond the frontiers, that if South Vietnam went, it would not only give them [the Chinese] an improved geographic position for guerrilla assault on Malaya but would also give the impression that the wave of the future in Southeast Asia was China and the Communists. So I believe it.[48]

While broadening American commitment with money, equipment, military advisers, and pilots, Kennedy did not accept proposals from his own advisers for deployment of combat forces. Among other things, he worried that the presence of large American forces in Vietnam might provoke a challenge from China or the Soviet Union. Yet limited though it was, his policy made it more diffi-

cult than ever for the United States to reverse its course and halt a
drift toward war. Meanwhile the situation in Vietnam continued to
deteriorate. Kennedy remained torn over the best road to follow.
Then in brilliant sunshine under a cloudless sky, a radiance that
made violent sudden death the more unbearable to behold, he was
assassinated in Dallas.

When Truman left office, a small American military mission was in
Vietnam, and the United States was bearing between a third and a
half of the French financial burden in the Indochinese war. When
Eisenhower's term ended, American aid ran into the billions, and
685 American advisers were in Vietnam. Upon Kennedy's death, the
number of advisers had risen to 16,000. And no end was in sight.
When Lyndon Johnson took office aboard Air Force One, bound
from Dallas to Washington, he inherited more than a deep-rooted,
publicly supported policy on Vietnam: he inherited a Frankenstein.
Neither Johnson nor Kennedy nor Eisenhower nor Truman nor
Acheson nor Dulles had ever really understood Vietnam, its people,
its culture, its history, its institutions, it politics, its aspirations.
They were aware of the difficult military problems facing them in
Vietnam. But neither Johnson nor his predecessors had ever imagined the infinite suffering and loss the North Vietnamese were prepared to endure to prevent foreign domination.

III · *The Pressures*

1

Truman was shocked by the invasion of South Korea. North Korea's aggression struck him as defiance of the United States and the United Nations. The startling information from Secretary Acheson on the night of June 24, 1950, posed a challenge for Truman so great that it would determine the character of his presidency, the political climate in the United States, and perhaps the future balance of power in the Far East.

New to Truman was the nature of the challenge: open military attack across an accepted international boundary upon an American-sponsored government. It was a government the legitimacy of which had been recognized by the United Nations, and a government to which the people of the United States had sent weapons, advisers, and money.

What was not new to him, as he perceived the source of the attack, was challenge by imperialistic communism, directed from Moscow. The pressures that came to a head for Truman with the North Korean aggression had been building steadily for more than five years. The decisive attitude in which he was to react had been developing, step by step, during those same five years.

From his first week in the White House he had been under unceasing pressure to prevent first the Soviet Union and then the Chinese Communists from making strategic gains disadvantageous to the interests of the United States and its Western allies. On retiring as president in January 1953, he was to reflect: "I have hardly had a day in office that has not been dominated by this all-embracing struggle."[1]

Franklin D. Roosevelt died on April 12, 1945, while in the midst of increasingly acerbic controversy with Stalin over Soviet domination of Poland as the war in Europe drew to a close. When Truman assumed office, the brunt of the dispute fell on him. The Polish issue reawakened old suspicions of and hostility toward the Soviets that had submerged temporarily in the common effort against Adolf Hitler. Americans of Polish descent and the Catholic hierarchy railed against the prospect of a Communist Poland. Republican congressional leaders clamored for a strong policy regarding the establishment of independent governments in Eastern Europe. Influential holdovers from the Roosevelt administration, like W. Averell Harriman, then United States ambassador to Moscow, Secretary of the Navy James V. Forrestal, and Fleet Admiral William D. Leahy, chief of staff to the commander in chief, persistently advised the new president to stand up against perceived Soviet encroachments.

Only eleven days after taking office, Truman received Soviet Foreign Minister Vyacheslav M. Molotov. Believing that blunt talk might set Soviet-American relations on a firmer footing, Truman so sternly demanded of Molotov that the Kremlin live up to its Yalta Conference pledges on Polish independence that the toughest diplomat then on the world scene turned ashen. When the foreign minister tried to get in the last word, Truman snapped: "That will be all, Mr. Molotov. I would appreciate it if you would transmit my views to Marshal Stalin." Pleased with his performance, Truman said afterward, "I gave him the one-two, right to the jaw."[2]

The president had wasted his energy. In the months after the war the Kremlin imposed its authority on half of Europe. In the process, it not only disrupted the foreign policy of the United States but revived long-smoldering anxieties about the Red menace at home. Both circumstances magnified public pressures on Truman. No more "appeasement," his critics demanded.

Doubtless, Stalin was hearing much the same kind of talk. It could well have been occasioned by a number of American acts: building an atomic bomb without telling an ally, Stalin; developing an intercontinental bomber capable of carrying such a bomb; acquiring military bases around the Soviet perimeter; abruptly terminating lend-lease shipments to the Soviet Union after V-E day; and extending postwar financial assistance to other allies but not to the war-ravaged Soviets. The angry talk in the United States about Soviet conduct must have sounded no better in Moscow than some of Stalin's and Molotov's pronouncements sounded in Washington. Thus the cold war grew out of the interaction between two rival superpowers, two different systems of government, two different ideologies, two different cultures, two different sets of ambitions for influence in the world.

Truman was jarred when, at the time of the Potsdam Conference of 1945, Stalin sought the right to exercise with Turkey joint control of the Black Sea Straits and build bases there. The next year the Truman administration was much disturbed by a perceived threat by Stalin to move into the Middle East by taking control of Iran's northernmost province of Azerbaijan. "[T]his may lead to war," Truman told Harriman.[3] The president forced a showdown in the United Nations Security Council even after the Soviets had acted to dispel the threat.

It was not a great exaggeration for Truman to have said that nearly every day of his life as president had been dominated by the cold war. That was the way it appeared to the public at the time, too. Americans were stunned by the revelation of a Soviet espionage ring operating out of Ottawa, spying on the American atomic bomb and other military secrets. When, in August 1946, the Soviets renewed, unsuccessfully, as it turned out, their demands on the Black Sea Straits, Truman sent a naval task force headed by the carrier *Franklin D. Roosevelt* to the Mediterranean to signal American determination to keep the Soviets out of the Middle East. The task force was the forerunner of the United States Sixth Fleet, now on station in the Mediterranean.

The winter of 1947 swept in the beginnings of the most critical phase of the cold war and one that increased Truman's stake in the success of containment. Buried under snow and running out of money, Great Britain could no longer continue its role of supporting Greece and Turkey. In the throes of civil war, the Greek government appeared in danger of defeat by Communist-dominated guerrillas. Turkey felt itself threatened by multiple Soviet pressures, such as the demands on the Black Sea Straits. To head off a possible Soviet breakthrough in the Eastern Mediterranean that would have had nearly global consequences in the view of his national security advisers, Truman decided to assume the British role in Greece and Turkey. The word from the White House was that the president was resolved to show the Soviets that he "meant business" and would let them know "straight from the shoulder" where he stood.[4]

Addressing a joint session of Congress on March 12, 1947, he asked for $400 million for Greece and Turkey and for authority to send them military personnel and military equipment. In a passage that immediately became known as the Truman Doctrine, he said, "I believe that it must be the policy of the United States to support free peoples who are resisting attempted subjugation by armed minorities or by outside pressures."[5]

The statement was the essence of containment, although the Truman administration had no formal global strategy of containment. While the language was open-ended, the Truman Doctrine did not lead the president into support of all peoples who were resisting subjugation—the Nationalist Chinese, for example. Nor was the Truman Doctrine binding on future presidents. Nevertheless, it provided a theme for American foreign policy that was to echo not only through the remainder of Truman's term but down through the years. The overriding concept of helping "free peoples" threatened by armed minorities (meaning Communists) or outside pressures (meaning from the Soviet Union or later Communist China) was undoubtedly a factor in United States involvement in the Korean War and the Vietnam War.

Truman's strong stand on Greece and Turkey was taken by his advisers as a signal to proceed with the defense of Western Europe. With the European economy still paralyzed by the effects of the Second World War, Truman agreed to a historic and unprecedented rescue under the Marshall Plan. While the legislation was being prepared for passage in Congress, a Communist coup in Czechoslovakia in March 1948 shook Washington as it had not been shaken since Pearl Harbor.

In addition to the strategic consequences for the West, the Communist takeover had a great emotional impact on the United States because of President Woodrow Wilson's part in the birth of the Czech republic and the friendly attachment Americans had for Czech Foreign Minister Jan G. Masaryk, son of the republic's first president. Because of the coup, Masaryk either committed suicide or was killed. Truman again went before a joint session and persuaded Congress to restore Selective Service. Dated March 30, 1948, a National Security Council study said, "Today Stalin has come close to achieving what Hitler attempted in vain. The Soviet world extends from the Elbe River and the Adriatic on the west to

Manchuria on the east, and embraces one fifth of the land surface of the world."[6]

Three months after the Czechoslovakian coup an even more alarming situation occurred. As a climax to a currency dispute and other East-West differences over a German settlement, on June 23, 1948, the Soviets imposed a blockade of rail, highway, and water routes to Berlin. Lying deep inside the Soviet zone of Germany, the former German capital was occupied, in respective sectors and for important symbolic purposes, by the United States, Great Britain, France, and the Soviet Union. The blockade threatened the position of the Western powers in Germany. It confronted Truman with a crisis full of danger of a Soviet-American military clash on German soil. The then Secretary of State George C. Marshall notified the American embassy in London on June 28 that Truman had approved a policy. The first point, Marshall said, was, "We stay in Berlin."[7] Repeatedly rejecting forcible challenge to the Soviets on land, Truman elected to rely on an airlift to supply Berlin. It was a decision that both hastened the formation of an independent West German state and forged a historic bond between the West Germans and the Americans. The allies instituted an effective counterblockade against the Soviet sector of Berlin. With Stalin taking the initiative, the blockade and counterblockade were ended nearly a year later, on May 12, 1949.

The disturbing events of 1947 and 1948 had led Western European statesmen to propose a military alliance among themselves, to be joined in time by the United States, as a defense against Soviet aggression. Such a Western European alliance was formed in 1948, and Truman agreed to American participation under the North Atlantic Treaty of 1949. In signing the treaty, the Truman administration endorsed the principle that an attack upon any one of the signatories was to be considered an attack upon all. Acceptance of that provision brought the policy of old isolationism to a complete end.

Great undertakings like the North Atlantic Treaty, the Truman Doctrine, and the Marshall Plan involved the United States deeply as the leader and, in fact, the protector of the non-Communist world. The conduct of such a foreign policy was filled with burdens and responsibilities and depended upon the president's ability to maintain political support for it at home. A challenge—particularly a military challenge—to American leadership and hence to the standing of the president was bound to create a crisis for Truman, personally and politically, as well as for the nation.

When North Korea struck, the lodestar in the outlook of Truman and other American leaders of his generation was the "lesson of Munich." At Munich in 1938, the lesson read, British Prime Minister Neville Chamberlain sacrificed Czechoslovakia to appease Hitler's hunger for conquest only to have the bite whet Hitler's appetite to the point where he sought to devour Britain itself. It was an axiom for Truman and his advisers that the right time to stop aggression was the first time. "Events of this century . . . would indicate," Truman had said in 1945, "that a breach of peace anywhere in the world threatens the peace of the entire world."[8] He and those around him sprang to the conclusion that the North Korean assault had been instigated by the Soviet Union, possibly as a diversion to screen preparations for a still greater attack in Europe and elsewhere. Bending over a globe at one stage and pointing to Iran, Truman said:

> Korea is the Greece of the Far East. If we are tough enough now, if we stand up to them like we did in Greece three years ago, they won't take any next steps. But if we just stand by, they'll move into Iran and they'll take over the whole Middle East. There is no telling what they'll do if we don't put up a fight now.[9]

At a difficult time in the cold war American security seemed threatened and American prestige jeopardized before the world. If Truman would not take the lead in heading off an aggressor, who would? And what would Western Europe think of the value of American guarantees under the North Atlantic Treaty if the United States did not so much as protect South Korea? Years of containment policy came to bear on Truman's instincts at that moment. Years of anti-Communist strategy and rhetoric primed him for decision. Also, Truman was very much concerned that if South Korea, brought into existence under the aegis of the United Nations, were crushed by aggression, the effectiveness of the UN itself might be destroyed. The United States had become a member of the United Nations during his administration. While he understood the limitations of such a body he, like many Americans then, had hopes that it would be a force in keeping peace. He felt a responsibility for supporting it.

With China in Communist hands, Japan had become America's principal partner in the Far East. But what would happen to Japan if the Communists ruled all of Korea, a dagger pointed at the Japanese islands, as a saying went then? Why would the Japanese wish to entrust their future security to American hands if Truman would not even deal with North Korean aggression?

Behind Truman's concerns about the protection of Europe, the Middle East, and the Far East lay political exigencies that resulted from the Communist conquest of China in 1949. Already disturbed by the might of the Soviet Union, the American people generally regarded the passage of the world's most populous nation into alliance with the Soviets as a long-term menace to American interests. Republicans not only trumpeted that view but, still stung by Truman's unexpected victory in 1948, seized upon Mao's triumph as a spectacular issue against the president, the Democratic party, and Dean Acheson, who succeeded Marshall as secretary of state in 1949.

A nasty coincidence for Truman was that Chiang Kai-shek's position had crumbled disastrously at the very time when Alger Hiss was indicted, later to be convicted, of perjury for denying that he had passed classified documents to a Communist underground when he was a State Department official. Before his indictment he had left the department to become president of the Carnegie Endowment for International Peace. Although no one could connect Hiss with the formulation of any major foreign policies while he was director of the special political affairs division, Truman's foes succeeded in establishing Hiss in a great many minds as living proof that the State Department crawled with Communists. The China lobby, Republican legislators, and the right-wing Republican press propagated the insidious line that Truman not only had "lost" China but had let America's traditonal friend fall as a result of Communist penetration in Washington.

Typically, Representative Robert Hale, a Republican from Maine, said, without offering proof, that the State Department was "permeated with Reds and leftists."[10] Endlessly chanted was the Republican theme that the administration was "soft on communism." Truman had "abandoned" Chiang Kai-shek, charged Walter H.

Judd, a Republican from Minnesota and the chief voice for the Nationalists in Congress.[11] Senator Bourke B. Hickenlooper, a Republican from Iowa, accused the Truman administration of "taking us down the road in shaping policies favorable to the Communist party."[12] And practically out of nowhere on February 11, 1950, little more than four months before the North Korean attack, came Senator Joseph R. McCarthy, a Republican from Wisconsin who declared in a speech in Wheeling, West Virginia, that he had the names of fifty-seven Communists (some listeners thought he had mentioned 205) in the State Department. In the short time before the Korean War McCarthy attracted the attention of much of the world with his savage assault on the Truman administration.

The "loss" of China ("[T]he ominous result of the civil war in China was beyond the control of . . . the United States," Acheson argued sensibly but futilely[13]) had done lasting damage to Truman's leadership. The "loss" of Korea on top of it would have meant political torment for him, especially with congressional elections coming up in November, less than five months away.

Though he was not the belligerent man he has sometimes been portrayed as being, Truman instinctively struck back when put on the defensive. The sudden smashing blow in Korea was typical of the kind of situation in which he looked not at the gray area in the center but at the blacks and whites at the extremes. He had had his fill of what he regarded as five years of Communist challenges; he sensed that the American people had had *their* fill. The wrath that was sure to be aroused in Truman by an unheralded military attack against what he considered the righteous interests of the United States in South Korea was captured by his daughter Margaret in her diary. After helping him pack in Independence to return to Washington after Acheson's call, she wrote, "Northern or Communist Korea is marching in on Southern Korea and we are going to fight."[14] It was the beginning of Truman's greatest ordeal, which probably never would have come about if he had not allowed himself needlessly to be drawn into the occupation of southern Korea in 1945.

2

On November 26, 1963, the day after the Kennedy funeral, Johnson approved National Security Action Memorandum 273. The presidential decision it embodied said: "It remains the central objective of the United States in South Vietnam to assist the people and Government of that country to win their contest against the externally directed and supported communist conspiracy."[15]

The previous day he had conferred with Henry Cabot Lodge, Jr., the United States ambassador to Saigon, who had just arrived in Washington expecting to meet President Kennedy. According to information obtained by Tom Wicker, then chief of *The New York Times* Washington bureau, Lodge said that the new president had hard decisions to make on Vietnam, after which the following exchange occurred:

> JOHNSON: I am not going to lose Vietnam. I am not going to be the president who saw Southeast Asia go the way China went.
>
> LODGE: What kind of political support will you have?
>
> JOHNSON: I don't think Congress wants us to let the Communists take over South Vietnam.[16]

For thirteen years Congress had been going along with the escalations undertaken by Truman, Eisenhower, and Kennedy. The meaning of Johnson's reference to China, of course, was that he did not intend to suffer, by "losing" Southeast Asia, the erosion and badgering Truman had suffered over the "loss" of China. "He believed," wrote his former press secretary, George Reedy, in *Lyndon B. Johnson: A Memoir*, "that another Communist victory on the mainland of Asia could open up another 'era of McCarthyism.'"[17]

In one of his last public comments on Vietnam, President Kennedy had said, "[W]e are not there to see a war lost."[18] If there was one pressure that Johnson felt more than another upon succeeding Kennedy, it may have been a compulsion not to be the one to lose a war. The combination of nationalistic feelings and detestation of communism was as strong or stronger in Johnson as in any president the country had yet seen. If what Johnson told Doris Kearns in 1969 was a true reflection of his attitude in November 1963, he had a fear on taking office that an abandonment of his predecessor's policy might bring an attack upon himself, led by Attorney General Robert F. Kennedy, about whom Johnson was paranoid much of the time.[19] "There was not a sparrow fell from a tree," recalled John P. Roche, a Johnson assistant, "but what he was convinced that it was the intervention of a Kennedy."[20] In 1963, he feared that the late president's brother would denounce him as cowardly and unmanly if he turned back in Vietnam. "One of [Johnson's] closest aides from that period told me," wrote another Johnson biographer, Ronnie Dugger, "that as soon as he became president . . . concern built up in his circle that he had to act on Vietnam or be damned by hawks in the press corps and the government. Courage, his courage, was in his mind."[21] On more than one occasion in 1964 President Johnson told General Chester V. Clifton, his military aide, as Clifton recalled the words, "The Russians are going to test me someday, and I am not going to be found wanting."[22]

As Truman had inherited from Roosevelt influential anti-Stalinist advisers, so Johnson inherited from Kennedy advisers who had been pressing for even stronger measures to prevent Communist conquest of South Vietnam. Now they were counseling a president who was unsure of himself in the conduct of foreign relations. Once Johnson decided to persist in Vietnam, the powerful national security bureaucracy swung behind him, and American support for Saigon was renewed. All the inherited advisers had a personal stake in its success. Among them were McNamara, Maxwell Taylor, the Bundy brothers, and Walt Whitman Rostow, a White House and State Department official in the Kennedy administration. Kennedy's secretary of state, Dean Rusk, a man dedicated to stopping further Communist encroachment in Asia, continued in that post under Johnson and in fact became more influential under Johnson than he had been under Kennedy, who had wished to be his own secretary of state.

In an interview for the Lyndon Baines Johnson Library in Austin, Texas, conducted by William J. Jorden, a former newspaperman who worked for the State Department, Johnson was asked which of his advisers had been the most sound day in and day out. He replied:

> I never did divide it up. I had great respect for Rusk's judgment and his evaluations and his demeanor and his manner of presenting things and his unselfishness, as I did for McNamara. No one was ever more respected than Rusk was, and no one was ever supported any stronger than McNamara was at the time they were there.

McNamara left the Pentagon eleven months before the end of

Johnson's term, whereas Rusk had the president's ear all the way. Privately, Johnson was often heard to liken Rusk to the Rock of Gibraltar.

Johnson took office under harrowing circumstances. The country was in shock. Lee Harvey Oswald's bullets had produced an overnight apotheosis of John Fitzgerald Kennedy. Millions of followers of the bright, handsome, cultivated young president could not imagine anyone in his place in the White House, let alone, as they saw him, a crude operator like Johnson. Irish-Americans were in tears. The first Catholic president in American history lay dead. Blacks, having experienced, belatedly, new hope for civil rights under Kennedy, were startled at the thought of a southerner in the presidency. Many liberals, a stronger force then than now, disliked and distrusted Johnson. The Executive Branch was in the hands of Kennedy appointees who were embittered by the assassination in Dallas. Kennedy's following of intellectuals, centered at Harvard, felt lost. An idol of large numbers of the rising new generation was gone. Obviously, the first order of business for Johnson was to rally the people to his own side.

He moved at once in the tradition of vice-presidents succeeding dead presidents. "[L]et us continue," he told a joint session of the Eighty-eighth Congress two days after the funeral.[23] Vice-presidents have no mandates of their own. They rarely have any national following. It is not their function to have their own programs ready at hand. When they take over from dead presidents, they customarily assume their predecessors' mandates and embrace their predecessors' programs, at least in the beginning, as Truman had done.

Johnson, of course, had the authority to terminate the American commitment to South Vietnam after November 22, 1963. In George Reedy's view, disengagement would have been "relatively simple."[24] Johnson could have explained, truthfully, that Saigon was incapable of maintaining a sufficiently stable government to cope with revolution. To be sure, the American Right would have howled that global victory had been won at prodigious cost under Roosevelt but that the peace had been lost under Johnson. Anti-Communist sentiment would have been inflamed; taunts of "losing" Southeast Asia, just as Truman had "lost" China, would have rained upon him. His cherished consensus would have been smaller. Vietnam, however, was still a low-caliber public issue. The people admired the superb manner in which Johnson moved the nation through the trauma of Dallas. The new president could have done a great deal to divert attention from Vietnam by staging a drama over his popular domestic program, as he was to do in any case.

Nevertheless, no consensus has yet been reached as to the option available to Johnson as a practical matter after Kennedy's death. At the other extreme from Reedy's view is the opinion expressed by the scholar and former White House and State Department official Zbigniew Brzezinski. He said that "the option of not going in or the option of rapidly getting out was not a realistic historical option in the mid-sixties, either internationally or domestically."[25]

Given the tenor of the time and the deep anti-Communist bias in the country, it is unlikely that anyone who reached the presidency in 1963 by whatever route would have been motivated to change the policy of containment. Johnson assured Congress that he would pursue Kennedy's commitments from West Berlin to South Vietnam.[26]

Why? In part, he did feel insecure at suddenly finding himself responsible for foreign policy. "Obviously," Reedy said, "he was hoping to be regarded as a man who had emulated Harry S Truman and stood up against communism when it was crucial."[27] Eric F. Goldman, special consultant to President Johnson, wrote,

> What President Truman considered the Munich parallel, was the prime reason for his decision to use American combat power in Korea. In the early period of the Johnson Presidency, on several occasions Harry Truman and Lyndon Johnson talked about the Korean intervention, and the new Chief Executive thoroughly agreed with the retired President's analysis.[28]

In part, Johnson did believe that he must follow Kennedy's policies. With the next presidential election less than twelve months away, he was probably reluctant to flout the reactionary, chauvinistic following forming behind Goldwater by relaxing the stand in Vietnam. In Johnson's mind, too, curiously, defending South Vietnam against communism was essential to the success of his Great Society program.

"The real question," Harry C. McPherson, special counsel to President Johnson, said later, "is . . . whether you would have been able to get a domestic legislative program, a liberal program through, if you had let South Vietnam go down the drain."

According to McPherson, Johnson's experience had taught him

that advocacy of social welfare legislation—"socialism"—was regarded by many in Congress as a concomitant of being "soft" on communism. He quoted Johnson as having said, "I'm not going to be the Democratic president pushing liberal social legislation who's letting go of a part of Southeast Asia that my predecessor John Kennedy and his predecessor Dwight Eisenhower said was critical to the free world."[29] In other words, Johnson believed that in order to get votes for his Great Society programs he had to carry on the Vietnam War, which eventually throttled the Great Society.

No doubt, too, Johnson and others felt the impulse, as Ernest R. May put it, of simply not abandoning friends in Vietnam.[30] Above all, in upholding the aims of Truman, Eisenhower, and Kennedy, Johnson was doing exactly what he believed in. Since the beginning of the cold war he had supported containment. "From 1947 on," Ronnie Dugger wrote, "his positions on international issues were dominated by two words flashing across his mind, 'Munich, Appeasement.'"[31] When the White House proposed funds for Greece and Turkey under the Truman Doctrine, Representative Johnson pitched his supporting speech to the recollection of Chamberlain's capitulation at Munich.[32] When Truman submitted the Marshall Plan, Senator Johnson favored it as a means of preventing "Stalin from overrunning the world."[33]

When, in May 1961, President Kennedy sent Vice-President Johnson to Saigon to urge on Diem the need for political reforms, Johnson returned with a report: "There is no alternative to United States leadership in Southeast Asia." Providing a glimpse into the mind of a man who would become president in two and a half years, the report said that the "fundamental decision required" was "whether we are to attempt to meet the challenge of Communist expansion now in Southeast Asia by a major effort of support of the forces in freedom in the area or throw in the towel." "The battle against communism," Johnson said, "must be joined in Southeast Asia with strength and determination to achieve success there—or the United States, inevitably, must surrender the Pacific and take up our defenses on our own shores." With that acceptance of the domino theory, he went on to assert that "at some point we may be faced with the further decision of whether we commit major United States forces . . . or cut our losses and withdraw. . . ." He told Kennedy, "I recommend we proceed with a clear-cut and strong program of action."[34]

The final months of the Kennedy administration witnessed an episode that made it all the more difficult for President Johnson to withdraw from Vietnam even if he had been inclined to do so. As 1963 advanced, doubts had grown in the Kennedy administration that President Ngo Dinh Diem's government, which was in a state of seemingly rapid decay, could provide a stable base for combating the NLF. Under the influence of his unsavory brother Ngo Dinh Nhu and the latter's powerful wife, Madame Nhu, Diem was becoming increasingly repressive against his people. To Kennedy's embarrassment, as a Catholic and as an ally of Diem, the repression, particularly severe against Buddhists, finally reached unbearable proportions. American television now featured news film of Buddhists burning themselves alive in protest.

As the political crisis in Saigon worsened, a cabal of South Vietnamese generals clandestinely asked the United States for support in a coup d'état to overthrow the Diem regime. With Kennedy's knowledge, Ambassador Lodge and the CIA kept in close touch with the conspirators. Kennedy was aware of the coup and acquiesced in it. His hope was that a new government would bring reform and create conditions in which American assistance would be effective in the war. Diem was overthrown on November 1, 1963, and, to Kennedy's horror, assassinated along with his brother Nhu—exactly three weeks before Dallas. According to Richard M. Helms, Johnson's director of Central Intelligence, Johnson had a mystical belief that Kennedy had been assassinated because he had acquiesced in the coup that led to Diem's death.[35]

Instead of the expected new order and sanity in Saigon, utter disorder ensued as coup after coup erupted for months on end. Consequently, American officials felt obliged to do more rather than less for South Vietnam. As the Pentagon Papers were to put it, United States complicity in Diem's overthrow "heightened our responsibilities and our commitment." "A case could even be made," wrote Gelb and Betts, "that the train of events made direct U.S. intervention inevitable. With Diem's blood at least partially on American hands, it would be even more difficult psychologically to resist further moves needed to shore up the South."[36] The irony of the more intense pressure for intervention exerted upon Kennedy's successor was that Johnson had always opposed the overthrow of Diem as an outrageous mistake.

Tightening the grip on Johnson, Diem's death opened the way to disclosure that the military situation in South Vietnam was much worse than had been realized in Washington. Back from a trip to Vietnam, Secretary of Defense McNamara submitted a gloomy report to Johnson on December 21, 1963, saying that unless trends were reversed within the next ninety days, conditions "would lead to a neutralization at best and more likely to a Communist-controlled state."[37]

Two months into the Johnson administration, on January 22, 1964, McNamara received from General Taylor, chairman of the Joint Chiefs of Staff at that point, a memorandum declaring that the JCS favored "bolder actions." The proposals included commitment of "additional U.S. forces, as necessary, in support of the combat action within South Vietnam" and "as necessary in actions against North Vietnam."[38]

IV · *The Commitments*

1

"By God, I am going to let them have it!" Truman said on returning to Washington from Independence on Sunday, June 25, 1950, to act on the North Koreans' invasion of South Korea.[1]

Acheson's call had reached Truman so late the previous night that an immediate flight from Missouri did not make sense. The president remained at home overnight, meanwhile authorizing Acheson to ask for an emergency meeting of the United Nations Security Council to deal with the North Korean assault. From Washington National Airport on Sunday, Truman went directly to Blair House for a council of war with his highest military and diplomatic advisers. From 1949 to 1952, the Trumans lived in Blair House, which was diagonally across Pennsylvania Avenue from the White House, while the interior of the White House was being rebuilt to correct critical structural weaknesses.

Five days and nights of meetings took place before Truman made his ultimate decision alone, at daybreak on June 30, 1950. As the hours passed on June 25, it became evident that if South Korea were to be saved, help from the outside would have to come quickly or the North Koreans would overrun the whole country. What was not clear at first was the nature of the assistance that would be needed. Specifically, would air and naval support be sufficient to help the South Koreans repel the invaders? The Blair House group, which included General of the Army Omar N. Bradley, chairman of the Joint Chiefs of Staff during the Korean War, did not know what it was up against in the enemy forces. "No one believed," Bradley was to testify, "that the North Koreans were as strong as they turned out to be." None of the group knew how great the consequences of

American intervention were likely to be. "I don't think you can say that any of us knew, to start, when we went into this thing, what would be involved," Bradley testified.[2] Truman and his advisers did not dream, as far as it is possible to judge, that they were stepping into what would be, up to then, the third largest foreign war in American history (it would eventually be displaced to fourth by the Vietnam War). Even if he had realized it, there is no reason to suppose that Truman would have turned back under the circumstances.

By the time of the Sunday night conference, North Korean troops, having crossed the 38th parallel at several points, were approaching Seoul, the South Korean capital. North Korean fighter planes strafed nearby Kimpo Airfield. Throughout Sunday, diplomatic cables poured into Washington, the opinions of their senders reinforcing the conviction that the attack was in reality a Soviet challenge. From Tokyo, John Foster Dulles, the future Republican secretary of state, and John Allison, a State Department Asian expert, jointly cabled their views to Acheson. If the South Koreans could not repulse the attack, Dulles and Allison said, "we believe that U.S. force should be used, even though this risks Russian counter moves. To sit by while Korea is overrun by unprovoked armed attack would start [a] disastrous chain of events leading most probably to world war. . . ."[3]

For nearly twenty-four hours before the Sunday night conference, State Department and Pentagon officials had been working on proposals to submit to the president. From the moment the news of the invasion arrived, the unanimous reaction of those officials was that the North Koreans must be driven back to the 38th parallel. According to Roger W. Tubby, a State Department press officer, Dean Rusk, then assistant secretary of state for Far Eastern affairs, immediately pressed for United States intervention. The architect of the unfolding policy in all its particulars, however, was Secretary of State Acheson.

Nearly a year earlier the Truman administration had withdrawn its occupation troops from South Korea, partly on the assumption that Korea would be of little strategic value to the United States in a general war. Now, however, the thunder of attack aroused in Washington a fear that the balance of power in the Far East was suddenly in danger. As the aforementioned NSC 8/2 had warned in 1949, the Kremlin may have decided to treat the North Korean army as a vehicle for the extension of Soviet control of the area.

As a prelude to the Sunday evening conference Truman asked General Bradley to read aloud a memorandum from General of the Army Douglas A. MacArthur, Far Eastern commander.[4] Bradley had just returned from Tokyo, where MacArthur had given it to him. It dealt with MacArthur's view on the need to keep Taiwan, then usually called Formosa, out of the hands of Communist China. "Unless the United States' political-military strategic position in the Far East is to be abandoned," MacArthur wrote, "it is obvious that the time must come in the foreseeable future when a line must be drawn beyond which Communist expansion will be stopped." While the words had been written before the Korean crisis, of course, the phrase about drawing the line perfectly matched the mood not only of Truman and his advisers but also of the overwhelming number of Americans.

When the conference got under way, General Bradley said that the United States must draw the line somewhere. Truman said he agreed with that statement. Similar comments were to appear over and over in subsequent days in editorials, radio commentaries, and speeches. The North Korean attack and the belief that it was Soviet-inspired created a rare consensus for effective action in the United States. Both parties stood solidly behind Truman at that moment. Practically unanimously, Congress passed a bill extending Selective Service for one year.

Nevertheless, Truman's initial decisions were cautious. Accepting Acheson's proposals on Sunday night, he authorized MacArthur to rush military supplies and equipment from Japan to the South Koreans. Truman directed the air force to prepare plans, but no more at the moment, for destruction of all Soviet air bases in the Far East. He approved orders to the Seventh Fleet to steam north from the Philippines to be prepared to secure Taiwan, where Chiang Kai-shek had fled, turning the island into the last bastion of Nationalist China.

Truman authorized the air force and the navy to go into action to try to prevent Seoul and its environs from being overrun during the evacuation of American dependents. In the discussion around the table Bradley, the then Secretary of Defense Louis A. Johnson, and Secretary of the Army Frank C. Pace, Jr., indicated doubts about committing American ground forces. Subsequently, Rear Admiral Arthur C. Davis, director of the joint staff of the Joint Chiefs of Staff, noted that the chiefs "do *not* want to commit troops."[5] At the

Blair House meeting, however, the subject was not discussed at any length. Later when the orders were going out from the Pentagon, Lieutenant General Matthew B. Ridgway, a deputy chief of staff of the army, asked Bradley if the commitment of air and naval forces to cover the evacuation of dependents was deliberately intended to exclude the use of troops in Korea. "Yes," Bradley replied.[6]

When the first Blair House conference ended, Truman explained to one of his advisers why he had decided on the still-curtailed intervention.

> I believed in the League of Nations. It failed. Lots of people thought it failed because we weren't in it to back it up. Okay, now we started the United Nations. It was our idea, and in this first big test we just couldn't let them down. If a collective system under the UN can work, it must be made to work, and *now* is the time to call their bluff.[7]

Hours before the conference, the UN Security Council had acted along lines proposed by the United States. The council judged that the North Korean attack "constitutes a breach of peace." It called for "the immediate cessation of hostilities" and for North Korean forces to withdraw to the 38th parallel. Finally, it asked all members "to render every assistance to the United Nations in the execution of this resolution and to refrain from giving assistance to the North Korean authorities." The Soviet Union, a member of the Security Council, might have vetoed the resolution and changed the history of the ensuing days. Five months earlier, however, its representative, Jacob A. Malik, had walked out when the council refused to unseat Nationalist China for Communist China, and he was still absent on June 25. North Korea paid no attention to the call of the Security Council; no one expected that it would.

The next day, Monday, June 26, the defense of Seoul was disintegrating. President Rhee and his cabinet fled south. That night a second conference was held in Blair House. Acheson proposed expanding air and naval commitments beyond covering the evacuation of dependents. At his suggestion, Truman ordered the air force and the navy to give maximum support to Republic of Korea (ROK) forces by attacking North Korean planes, tanks, guns, and troop columns. The purpose was to give the disorganized South Korean units a chance to regroup. Truman made it plain that American air and naval forces should not operate north of the 38th parallel. He also approved another recommendation by Acheson that the Seventh Fleet be stationed in the Taiwan Strait to prevent the Chinese Communists from invading Taiwan and to keep Chiang Kai-shek's forces on the island from attacking the mainland. The purpose of the order as far as military strategy was concerned was to restrict the outbreak of fighting to Korea. At that point in the meeting Truman accepted still another Acheson suggestion, previously mentioned, of increasing assistance to Bao Dai and sending a military mission to Vietnam.

General Bradley said that if American ground forces were to be sent to Korea, the United States would not have enough troops available to carry out its other obligations around the world without mobilization. Truman obviously did not believe he was getting into a situation of such magnitude that it would be necessary to discuss mobilization. "I don't want to go to war," he said.[8] Later, however, he told Senator Tom Connally, a Democrat from Texas and chairman of the Senate Foreign Relations Committee: "But don't worry, I'm not going to tremble like a psychopath before the Russians, and I am not going to surrender our rights or the rights of the South Koreans."[9]

On June 27, the president issued a statement saying, "The attack upon Korea makes it plain beyond all doubt that Communism has passed beyond the use of subversion to conquer independent nations and will now use armed invasion and war."[10] Conversely, by Truman's commitment of naval and air forces to action south of the 38th parallel, the policy of containment passed beyond the realm of political and economic action.

Meanwhile, the administration obtained a significant new action in the United Nations Security Council, again with the Soviet representative absent. The council adopted a United States resolution that proposed sanctions for the first time in the history of the United Nations. The council recommended that UN members "furnish such assistance to the Republic of Korea as may be necessary to repel the armed attack. . . ." The clause provided legal grounds for intervention in Korea by the United States and other countries. The council also called for the restoration of "international peace and security in the area." That clause was to take on great importance a few months later when Truman faced the perilous question of whether to end the war by driving the enemy back to the 38th parallel—the president's initial objective—or pursue the enemy across the parallel to end Communist rule of North Korea.

The next day Senator Lyndon Johnson wrote to Truman: "I want to express to you my deep gratitude for and admiration of your courageous response yesterday to the challenge. . . . Having chosen this course, there is no turning back."[11]

At a National Security Council meeting on June 29, Truman learned a lesson about the commitment of even limited air power. The short-range planes and their crews flew from runways in Korea. They depended on seaborne supplies arriving at the port of Pusan on the southeastern tip of the Korean peninsula. The runways and planes had to be serviced and protected. So also did communications, transport, and port facilities at Pusan. Having committed air power, Truman found it necessary to authorize the dispatch of adequate combat troops to keep the planes safe and in operating condition.

In the first few days, the hastily organized American air strikes were powerless to stem the rout of Republic of Korea forces on the ground. Seoul fell to the invaders on June 28. North Korean troops seized Kimpo Airfield. When the ROK Sixth Division was forced to retreat, the South Korean central front collapsed. MacArthur flew to Korea on June 19 to risk a personal reconnaissance. He found that the South Korean troops had been unprepared for the attacks by enemy aircraft and armor. Syngman Rhee's forces had been reduced to 25,000 effective troops at most. They were incapable of counterattack. The fall of the Republic of Korea was threatened by further enemy advances.

In Washington, shortly after 1:30 A.M. on June 30, a message arrived for General J. Lawton Collins, army chief of staff. It was from MacArthur and read, in part:

> The only assurance for holding the present line, and the ability to regain later the lost ground, is through the introduction of US ground combat forces into the Korean battle area. . . .
>
> If authorized, it is my intention to immediately move a US regimental combat team to the reinforcement of [a] vital area . . . and to provide for a possible build-up to a two division strength from troops in Japan for an early counter-offensive.[12]

To MacArthur's disgruntlement, Collins replied in a teleconference with the Far Eastern commander that the president would have to approve such a commitment. "Time is of the essence," MacArthur said "and a clear-cut decision without delay is imperative."[13]

With the military situation as critical as it was, Collins circumvented the rest of the Joint Chiefs of Staff and put the matter directly to Secretary of the Army Frank Pace by telephone. At 4:57 A.M. Pace telephoned Truman, who was already up.

A negative response by Truman would have been hard to imagine. The North Korean invasion was a decisive point in his presidency. His swift reaction to the challenge had so far been applauded abroad and acclaimed at home across a spectrum of opinion from the China bloc to liberal Democrats. Having already committed the air force and navy of the United States, failure to drive forward to victory over a minor power at whatever price would have been a fiasco. Abroad, it would have raised great doubts about American leadership; the domestic scene would have been rocked by political upheaval. Truman probably never even thought of accepting defeat at that point. Without hesitation he made the fateful decision, and he did so without consulting the congressional leaders, without calling the cabinet or the National Security Council into session, without sounding out the Joint Chiefs of Staff as a body. "I told Pace," he recalled later, "to inform General MacArthur immediately that the use of one regimental combat team was approved."[14]

For the moment he reserved decision on the request to commit two divisions also. By the time of a midmorning conference with his advisers, however, he had decided not to restrict MacArthur to two divisions but to authorize him to send, as necessary, the ground troops under his command, which then totaled four divisions. Since the end of the Second World War the United States had maintained tactical forces in Japan pending a peace treaty. No objections to the president's decision were raised around the table. "The fateful events of the 1930s, when aggression unopposed bred more aggression and eventually war, were fresh in our memory," Truman later reported to Congress on the six days of decision making.[15]

At 1:22 P.M. on that June 30, an order of the Joint Chiefs of Staff was sent to MacArthur. On July 1, a Twenty-fourth Infantry Division task force commanded by Lieutenant Colonel Charles B. Smith arrived from Japan at an airstrip near Pusan, South Korea, a port city the United States had to hold in order to support its operations. Brigadier General John H. Church, sent from MacArthur's headquarters in Tokyo, was waiting. "All we need," he told Colonel Smith, "is some men up here who won't run when they see tanks."[16]

Within one week Truman had committed land, sea, and air forces to battle in Korea by executive action. Article I, Section 8 of the Constitution provides that Congress shall have the power to declare war. In those hectic days Truman did not believe that the United States had gone to war, certainly not as war had been thought of in 1861, 1898, 1917, and 1941. He did not want to blow out of all proportion a foray, as he visualized it, by going before a joint session of Congress and asking for a declaration of war.

"We are not at war," he told a press conference on June 29, the day before the commitment of land forces. What was happening, he explained, was that "the members of the United Nations are going to the relief of the Korean Republic to suppress a bandit raid. . . ." As he well knew, presidents as commanders in chief often sent armed forces abroad to suppress piracy, punish offenses, or protect American lives and property. Without congressional authority, for example, President William McKinley had dispatched some five thousand troops to China during the Boxer Rebellion to help relieve the siege of foreign quarters in Peking. At the press conference Truman was asked whether the Korean operation might be called "a police action under the United Nations." Allowing the reporter to put words into his mouth, Truman replied, "Yes. That is exactly what it amounts to."[17]

The idea of simply asking Congress for approval of the emergency steps that the president had been taking was afoot in the White House at an early stage. Unquestionably, Congress would have concurred, overwhelmingly. In the scramble to keep South Korea from collapsing, however, the president and his staff could not come to grips with the question of congressional approval. Senator Connally unwisely advised Truman that a resolution might get tied up in debate, which was the last thing Truman wanted while he was trying to be seen as carrying out a mandate of the United Nations. The chairman of the Senate Foreign Relations Committee assured him that under his powers as commander in chief and because of his responsibilities to the United Nations, he had the authority to proceed as he was. And Truman put too much reliance on the spirit of support he could sense in Congress without giving enough thought to how fickle it might become if the excitement turned to pain.

Without asking for their approval, Truman kept the Republican and Democratic congressional leaders informed of his actions at a series of meetings. While on the Senate floor Robert A. Taft of Ohio and certain other Republican senators questioned the president's right to act on his own initiative, only one person, Senator Kenneth S. Wherry of Nebraska, challenged Truman at one of the meetings. Countering that he was trying to save a situation in a crisis, Truman replied; "If there is any necessity for congressional action . . . I will come to you. But I hope we can get those bandits in Korea suppressed without that."[18]

Congress had previously scheduled a week-long Independence Day recess, and Truman and the Democratic leaders let it stand rather than invite debate. By the time Congress returned, American forces thrown into battle, piecemeal and unprepared, were staggering under the blows of the North Korean army. It was no bandit raid. It was war, and Truman proceeded to conduct it as commander in chief without asking Congress for a declaration. Almost before he realized it, he was faced with a crisis in Korea. On July 9, MacArthur telegraphed the Joint Chiefs of Staff:

> The situation . . . is critical . . . to date our efforts against armor and mechanized forces have been ineffective. . . . Our own troops are . . . fighting with valor against overwhelming odds of more than ten to one. To build up, under these circumstances, sufficiently to hold the southern tip of Korea is becoming increasingly problematical.[19]

2

It was predawn on Sunday, August 2, 1964. A high-priority message rattled into the White House situation room for Lyndon Johnson, who was still in bed. The message read:

Mr. President:

> Early this morning the USS *Maddox* was attacked by three . . . PT boats while on patrol approximately 30 miles off the North Vietnamese coast in the Gulf of Tonkin.
> The Captain of the *Maddox* returned the fire with 5-inch

guns and requested air support from the carrier *Ticonderoga* on station nearby. . . .

The *Maddox* reports no personnel or material damages.[20]

Johnson scheduled a meeting for later in the day to consider a response. He did not want to get involved in a large war in Vietnam. His dream was to rise as high, or higher, if possible, than Franklin Roosevelt by putting through Great Society programs that would complement the New Deal and excel it. Nothing was more urgent in Johnson's eyes, however, than to avoid losing a test of strength and will with communism in an area considered as vital as Vietnam had come to seem. Almost from the moment he had taken office, however, the Communist position had grown menacingly stronger.

While President Johnson was preoccupied in establishing his administration in December 1963, McNamara went to Saigon and returned in a pessimistic mood. To confront a deteriorating situation he proposed exerting "progressively escalating pressure" on the enemy through covert attacks on North Vietnamese targets. For example, air raids on industrial facilities by Thai pilots flying American planes; seaborne commando assaults to blow up rail and highway bridges; gunfire on coastal installations by PT boats; and parachute drops of sabotage and psychological warfare teams. Intensifying the American commitment, Johnson approved the tactics on February 1, 1964, under the code designation OPLAN 34-A. Another ongoing operation in the Western Pacific was the "DeSoto" patrol, on which American naval vessels used electronic devices to gather intelligence along the Asian coast. On August 2, 1964, the destroyer *Maddox* was conducting such a patrol.

A consequence of McNamara's pessimistic report the previous December was a recommendation of the Joint Chiefs of Staff in February and March 1964 for American bombing of North Vietnam. According to William Bundy, Johnson "took a look" at the proposal then and again in April, May, and June but did not act.[21] In the meantime, McNamara had pressed Johnson for a deeper commitment to the defense of South Vietnam. William Bundy proposed a blockade of Haiphong Harbor in North Vietnam. At the suggestion of Walt Rostow, he also worked on drafts of a congressional resolution that would give Johnson the kind of freedom of military action Eisenhower had received from Congress in 1955 when the Chinese Communists threatened to seize the offshore islands of Quemoy and

Matsu as possible steps toward Taiwan. In mid-June, because of the presidential election campaign at home and the uncertainties in Vietnam, Johnson put the resolution aside. He was keeping tight restrictions on direct American military action against the enemy in 1964. At the same time, as the presence of the *Maddox* in the Gulf of Tonkin indicated, he was not altogether backing away from the risk of serious trouble.

The message announcing the PT boat attacks on the *Maddox* banished Sunday tranquillity from the White House. On the "hot line" to Moscow, Johnson sent a personal message to Khrushchev saying that he did not wish to widen the war.[22] One way to narrow the danger, presumably, would have been to withdraw the DeSoto patrol from the Gulf of Tonkin. Johnson did just the opposite. Maxwell Taylor, again ambassador to Saigon, replaced by General Wheeler as chairman of the Joint Chiefs of Staff, immediately recommended retaliation against North Vietnam. According to George W. Ball, then undersecretary of state, Johnson wanted a stronger case for such an action. Rather than divert navy ships from danger, he ordered the Gulf of Tonkin patrols to continue for the time being, with the destroyer *C. Turner Joy* reinforcing the *Maddox*. Having put up both fists, so to speak, Johnson then approved a note to Hanoi warning that "grave consequences would inevitably result from any further unprovoked offensive military action" against American ships "on the high seas."[23] The Joint Chiefs of Staff made ready to deliver, if Johnson's warning were ignored.

Then on August 4, McNamara notified Johnson that the *Maddox* and the *C. Turner Joy* had reported torpedo attacks. Whether or not attacks were actually made remains most doubtful. In poor visibility, overexcited crews, perhaps feeling under pressure to find some pretext, may have imagined what Johnson later called "deliberate" attacks when there were none. In any case, Johnson seemed more than ready to believe the report and ordered retaliation. Planes of the United States Seventh Fleet bombed the North Vietnamese coast, destroying a number of small vessels. In announcing the action on television, Johnson said:

> The determination of all Americans to carry out our full commitment to the people and to the government of South Vietnam will be redoubled by this outrage. Yet our response, for the present, will be limited and fitting. We Americans know, al-

though others appear to forget, the risks of spreading conflict. We still seek no wider war.[24]

Nevertheless, in retrospect the Gulf of Tonkin incident appears to have been a catalyst for a major decision, turning the United States toward more direct participation in the Vietnam War.

Having approved the bombing as commander in chief, Johnson summoned congressional leaders to solicit their support—then and in the future—through a joint resolution. Johnson said in his memoirs,

> I believe that President Truman's one mistake in courageously going to the defense of South Korea in 1950 had been his failure to ask Congress for an expression of its backing. He could have had it easily, and it would have strengthened his hand. I had made up my mind not to repeat that error. . . .[25]

Interestingly, the resolution that Johnson proposed mentioned only unilateral American action, not action in concert with allies, as he had demanded in 1954 in opposing Eisenhower's consideration of giving assistance to the French at Dien Bien Phu.

For Johnson to have asked Congress for a declaration of war over an uncertain PT boat incident would have been excessive. A time was coming when such a request would be fitting, but it had not yet arrived. Nevertheless, Johnson did have precedent for requesting Congress's approval for measures he felt were necessary in a tense international situation that might lead to war. Like so many other things he was to do in Vietnam, however, the way he went about it later aroused distrust of his motives. His proposal of the resolution at a moment when the impression was rife that two American destroyers had been attacked came to seem too shrewd, especially when it also became obvious that the resolution helped Johnson politically. It did so for two reasons. One was that since the involvement in Vietnam was becoming more dangerous, an expression of congressional support facilitated his dealing with it in his own way. The other was that the act of retaliation against the enemy and the winning of congressional support for it played to Johnson's advantage in the campaign against Goldwater, which was then under way. Goldwater had been appealing to the sentiment of numerous Americans who felt that the United States had been pushed around by

Communist powers long enough. The sudden bombing of North Vietnam cut the ground out from under that kind or oratory. And obtaining congressional support for what he was doing portrayed Johnson as a president who was not reckless and militaristic. In the circumstances, furthermore, Congress would have found it difficult to refuse to pass the resolution.

The Southeast Asia Resolution was approved unanimously in the House of Representatives and by a vote of 88 to 2 in the Senate. Opposing it were Senators Ernest Gruening of Alaska and Wayne Morse of Oregon, both Democrats. Morse called the legislation "a predated resolution of war" and the Senate's action a "historic mistake," providing the president "war-making powers in the absence of a declaration of war." That grant of support and the open-ended wording, approving the retaliation against North Vietnam retroactively as well as supporting "all necessary measures" to prevent "further aggression," planted future resentment against Johnson in the Senate. In passing the resolution, Congress approved use of the armed forces to assist any protocol state of the Southeast Asia Collective Defense Treaty (SEATO). A handiwork of Secretary of State Dulles in 1954, SEATO was an ineffectual eight-power pact designed to deter Communist advances in the region of Southeast Asia. A separate protocol extended the treaty's protection, if it could be called that, to South Vietnam, which was not a signatory. In the crises of the 1960s, Johnson and Rusk often invoked SEATO obligations to support United States policy in Vietnam. A painful irony of Vietnam was that one of the purposes of the United States in being there was to prove its dependability to allies who, in turn, not only withheld support but ultimately became critics.

Senator Morse's denunciation foreshadowed later criticism to the effect that under pressure of an emergency, Johnson had duped Congress into rushing through a resolution without an understanding of its implications. Reedy's memoir supports the criticism to an extent. "When [Johnson] presented the text to the congressional leaders on the night of the retaliation," Reedy wrote, "there was no doubt that he left in their minds the unmistakable impression that it would be used only in connection with the specific incident."[26] "I am sure," echoed Frank Church, a Democrat from Idaho, and a member of the Senate Foreign Relations Committee, "that nearly everyone in the Congress thought that he was voting in response to a case of violation of United States rights to freedom of the seas. No one ever thought Johnson was going to use that resolution to justify Americanization of the war in Vietnam."[27] The unassailable fact is that in the debate Senator J. William Fulbright, a Democrat from Arkansas, the chairman of the Foreign Relations Committee and the administration's advocate then, explained the implications of the resolution. Much though he was to regret it later, his explanation was crowned by an exchange with Senator John Sherman Cooper, a Republican from Kentucky.

> COOPER: In other words, we are now giving the president advance authority to take whatever action he may deem necessary. . . .
> FULBRIGHT: I think that is correct.
> COOPER: Then, looking ahead, if the president decided that it was necessary to use such force as could lead into war, we will give that authority by this resolution?
> FULBRIGHT: That is the way I would interpret it.[28]

In the prolonged and bloody hostilities in Korea and Vietnam, Congress never voted a declaration of war. In Johnson's case a declaration would hardly have given him more authority than the Southeast Asia Resolution, as interpreted by him and Fulbright. As General Wheeler observed, the resolution "put the executive branch and the legislative branch in the same bed."[29] A declaration of war by Congress might have contributed, in the Vietnam War as well as the Korean War, to the preservation of national unity. Beyond that, Korea and Vietnam left a cloud over the question of where, no matter what the constitution says, the war-making power in the United States government resides.

The Southeast Asia Resolution proved to be no pretext for immediate escalation. In fact, after the retaliatory bombing ordered by Johnson on August 4, the administration sought to avoid further provocation. Both the DeSoto missions and OPLAN 34-A were temporarily suspended. From the Gulf of Tonkin onward, however, opinion among policymakers gravitated toward a strategy of bombing North Vietnam. In part, bombing was viewed as a means of avoiding commitment of ground forces. In September, Johnson approved a policy to the effect that the United States would retaliate against North Vietnam for any attacks on American units. Yet for months he refrained from resorting to sustained use of air power.

In the fall of 1964, Johnson dove into the election campaign with fervor and loquacity out of all proportion to the requisites for defeating Goldwater. Wafted by his own crowd-pleasing rhetoric and probably believing it himself, he laid traps for his own credibility all over the field. At Eufaula Dam, Oklahoma, on September 25, for example, he said: "We don't want our American boys to do the fighting for Asian boys. We don't want to get involved in a nation with seven hundred million [Chinese] and get tied down in a land war in Asia."[30] In Manchester, New Hampshire, on September 28 he said that "we are not going north and drop bombs at this stage of the game."[31] At Akron University on October 21 he said, "[W]e are not about to send American boys nine or ten thousand miles away from home to do what Asian boys ought to be doing for themselves."[32] On one of the campaign trips, Hugh Sidey of *Time* recalls, Johnson told pool reporters on Air Force One: "I'm not about to send American boys over there. When one little old general in shirt sleeves can come down those trails and take Saigon, do you think I'm going to have American boys go in there and fight those wars? Twenty-two million Chinese sitting up there ready to come in!"[33]

On November 1, two days before the presidential election, the NLF laid a mortar barrage on Bien-hoa airfield near Saigon, killing five Americans and wounding nearly one hundred. Johnson refused to approve retaliatory air strikes, advocated by the military. Almost certainly, caution forty-eight hours before voters were to go to the polls was a large factor in his decision. When his great election victory was won, he ordered a study of what should be done about Vietnam. Though the steps had yet to be approved, the direction was not in question. Johnson gave no more thought to bowing to Communist military pressure in Vietnam than Truman had given to allowing Kim Il-sung to overrun South Korea. The study came to a head when Maxwell Taylor, proposing gradually intensifying air attacks on North Vietnam, arrived in Washington to take part in the conferences. It was at that time that Johnson told reporters at his ranch to expect "no dramatic announcements." At the December 1 meeting in the White House, a two-phased expansion of the war was recommended to him. The first phase, promptly approved, was intensification of air strikes against enemy infiltration routes in Laos and covert action in North Vietnam. The second phase, which he approved only in principle, was sustained bombing of North Vietnam at a rising tempo. The second phase was not ordered in 1964.

Johnson sent a revealing cable to Taylor after the ambassador's return to Saigon. It read:

> Every time I get a military recommendation, it seems to me that it calls for a large scale bombing. I have never felt that this war will be won from the air, and it seems to me that what is much more needed and would be more effective is a larger and stronger use of rangers and special forces and marines, or other appropriate military strength on the ground and on the scene. I am ready to look with great favor on that kind of increased American effort, directed at the guerrillas and aimed to stiffen the aggressiveness of [South] Vietnamese military units. . . . I myself am ready to substantially increase the number of Americans in Vietnam if it is necessary to provide this kind of fighting force against the Viet Cong.[34]

Although scant sign of it showed during the festive time of the inauguration in January, the year 1965 was to set Lyndon Johnson on the road to catastrophe.

The new political season in Washington began with his televised State of the Union message before a joint session of Congress. World affairs, he said, would "continue to call upon our energy and courage." "But," he added, turning the true prospect on its head, "today we can turn increased attention to the character of American life."[35]

Three days later came his special message to Congress on "Advancing the Nation's Health." "I believe," he said, "we have come to a rare moment of opportunity and challenge in the evolution of our society."[36] On January 12, there was a special message to Congress on "Toward Full Educational Opportunity." "We are now embarked," he said, "on another venture to put the American dream to work in meeting the new demands of a new day."[37] And for the inaugural address on January 20: "Let us now join reason to faith and action to experience, to transform our unity of interest into a unity of purpose."[38] If it had been possible to foresee, national unity stood on the brink of its worst crisis since the Civil War.

At the start of 1965, Johnson was not sure that any feasible strategy could save the unraveling South Vietnamese government. In growing number, North Vietnamese soldiers were appearing in the South to bolster the NLF. Nevertheless, Johnson was convinced that American interests demanded an effort to prevent a Communist victory. The number of American advisers in South Vietnam had risen to 23,000. On January 14, the president notified Taylor that immediately upon any "spectacular enemy action," the ambassador should propose a fitting reprisal. "I am determined," Johnson said, "to make it clear to all the world that the U.S. will spare no effort and no sacrifice in doing its full part to turn back the Communists in Vietnam."[39]

On February 7, the awaited spectacular action, the worst Communist attack yet against an American military installation, occurred at Pleiku in the central highlands of South Vietnam. An advisers' barracks was attacked with a fury that killed 8 Americans and wounded 109 more. According to William Bundy, Senator Mike Mansfield, a Democrat from Montana and a friend of Johnson's, urged him to negotiate with Hanoi instead of retaliating. The president brusquely replied that the United States could not, as Bundy recalled his words, stand still for that kind of attack.[40] Pleiku was a critical point of departure toward dramatic further escalation.

Johnson called an evening cabinet meeting. McGeorge Bundy, who happened to be in Saigon at the time, telephoned the White House to urge immediate air strikes against North Vietnam. In the cabinet room Johnson solicited the views of George Ball, the senior State Department official present. As Johnson later recalled his words, Ball replied, "We are all in accord that action must be taken."[41] Johnson had been pressing for removal of American dependents, and now he decided on prompt evacuation and authorized a retaliatory bombing attack against the North. He said, as he has related, "I can't ask our American soldiers out there to continue to fight with one hand tied behind their backs."[42] Obviously a new phase of the war was at hand. "We have no choice now," he said in a statement announcing the removal of women and children, "but to clear the decks and make absolutely clear our continued determination to back South Vietnam and its fight to maintain its independence."[43]

McGeorge Bundy returned with a report warning that defeat of South Vietnam appeared inevitable within a year or two. "The stakes are extremely high," he told Johnson. "The American investment is very large, and American responsibility is a fact of life which is palpable in the atmosphere of Asia, and even elsewhere. The international prestige of the United States and a substantial part of our influence are directly at risk in Vietnam." He recommended a "policy of *sustained reprisal*," adding, "Once such a policy is put in force, we shall be able to speak in Vietnam on many topics and in many ways, with growing force and effectiveness."[44] The memorandum was in tune with Johnson's convictions and the North Vietnamese made things easier for him with a violent attack on February 10 on Qhi Nhon, killing twenty-three American servicemen. Johnson's formal approval of a sustained air offensive, called "Rolling Thunder," was given on February 13. Vice-President Humphrey had the temerity to send him a memorandum raising doubts about the political effect of the bombing at home. That was the last anyone heard of Hubert Humphrey in Johnson's war councils until the vice-president became an ardent enthusiast in the cause months later.

The Rolling Thunder offensive did not begin until March 2. William Bundy, the assistant secretary of state for Far Eastern affairs, was made aware of one thing by his younger brother, McGeorge Bundy, the special assistant to the president for national security affairs. "Look, get this straight," McGeorge Bundy said. "The president does not want this depicted as a change in policy." William Bundy and his colleagues had supposed, he recalled, that Rolling Thunder "would, in effect, *have* to come out as clearly stated upgrading of our resolve and our whole scale of action and be depicted in that light." Johnson, Bundy said, "got into a very firm set of mind that . . . this was just a couple of new things we were doing, but it wasn't a change in policy. He wanted, in effect, to mute the whole thing."[45] Johnson's deception undermined his relations with McGeorge Bundy. "He did pretend that he really wasn't changing policy," Bundy told reporters at a breakfast in Washington on May 21, 1984. Bundy said: "We had a great row over the initial processes. We had a continuous disagreement. You can't just start . . . Rolling Thunder. . . . You really have got to have a speech. You have got to say what you are doing." Johnson was concerned, Bundy explained, with "passing two bills a day." More admiring of John Kennedy than of Johnson, Bundy resigned early in 1966, the timing hastened by his appointment as president of the Ford Foundation. "I left the White House because I got the feeling," Bundy said, "that it was not easy for me to understand and repond to what the president really wanted, partly because of this disagreement on public presentation explaining . . . policy." To the end of his term, however, Johnson called upon Bundy as one of his outside advisers.

Even though rolling Thunder was a change in tactics, it was accorded small chance in the White House of bringing about an American victory. Bombing was ordered to prevent defeat, in part by heightening the morale of the South Vietnamese.

When the air attacks on the North began, it was Johnson's turn to face the lesson that Truman had been forced to learn when he authorized air combat in Korea. With Rolling Thunder gaining momentum, the planes, supplies, communications, and runways in South Vietnam had to be protected by United States troops against enemy interference. Where bombing had once been considered a means of obviating the use of ground forces, ground forces were now requested to facilitate bombing. And the expected failure of air power to turn the tide would redouble the pressure to use large numbers of ground forces.

Like Truman, Johnson acted to protect air-force installations. On March 8, 1965—nearly fourteen months after he had become president—3,500 marines were put ashore in full battle dress in South Vietnam to guard the air base at Da Nang. They were the first American combat units to stand on Asian soil since the Korean War.

Taylor had warned Johnson against such a deployment. Once the policy against committing ground forces had been breached, the ambassador cabled, it would be "very difficult to hold the line on future deployments. . . . [I]ntervention with ground forces would at best buy time and would lead to ever increasing commitments until, like the French, we would be occupying an essentially hostile foreign country. . . ."[46] Johnson also had been reminded in late February by Undersecretary of State Ball, who opposed escalation, that if an air offensive were pursued, the enemy might retaliate with heavy ground action that would require the United States to send adequate combat troops to save the situation.[47]

The marine battalions were described by government officials as being on limited duty; Rusk and McNamara gave public assurances that their role was defensive.[48] In speeches and press conferences Johnson asserted that his policy was simply an extension of the respected President Eisenhower's pledge of support to the late President Diem in 1954, a time when the United States had fewer than seven hundred military advisers in Vietnam. As Johnson told reporters on March 13, 1965, his own policy in Vietnam "is the policy that was established by President Eisenhower."[49]

The bombing of the North did not ease the situation below the

17th parallel. NLF troops were sweeping through the countryside smashing South Vietnamese forces. Johnson wanted the situation retrieved while there was still time. Even before the marines landed, he had poked his huge forefinger into the chest of General Harold K. Johnson, army chief of staff, who was a survivor of the Bataan Death March and had been a stalwart in the defense of Pusan, in Korea, and said, "You get things bubbling, General."[50] General Johnson had called at the White House before leaving on a trip to Saigon. By then, under Hanoi's direction, the NLF was developing well-equipped regiments and divisions that were a deadly menace to isolated towns and South Vietnamese strongholds. Upon General Johnson's return, the president urged the Joint Chiefs of Staff to do something to "kill more VC."[51] The chiefs knew an order when they heard one. Five days later, on March 20, they recommended for the first time that American units be committed to combat. When General Johnson sought instructions on how much more strength should be applied to the security of South Vietnam, McNamara, with his customary efficiency, replied, "Policy is: Anything that will strengthen the position of the GVN [government of South Vietnam] will be sent."[52]

A failure of the United States to make the point of saving an ally from Communist assault was an image that Lyndon Johnson and those who sided with him were not willing to accept. For Rusk, it seems, making the point was important enough to go beyond limited war if necessary. In a memorandum to Johnson on July 1, 1965, the secretary of state said that "the central objective of the United States in South Vietnam must be to insure that North Vietnam not succeed in taking over or determining the future of South Vietnam by force. We must accomplish this objective without a general war if possible." He added: "The integrity of the U.S. commitment is the principal pillar of peace throughout the world. If that commitment becomes unreliable, the Communist world would draw conclusions that would lead to our ruin and almost certainly to catastrophic war."[53] The viewpoint was one that Johnson fully accepted.

By army tradition a good defense requires a good offense. The American commander in the field, General William C. Westmoreland, head of the Military Assistance Command, Vietnam (MACV) urged a strategy relying on advance by his ground units and called for more and more of them. In early April the National Security Council promulgated National Security Action Memorandum

328, which declared, cautiously, that the president "approved a change in mission for all Marine battalions deployed to Vietnam to permit their more active use under conditions to be established and approved by the Secretary of Defense in consultation with the Secretary of State." Again, Johnson demanded that it be kept secret that military policy was being changed. "Premature publicity" was to be avoided through "all possible precautions," the NSC document said. Statements "on these troop movements" were to be made only with McNamara's personal approval "in that these movements and changes should be understood as being gradual and wholly consistent with existing policy."[54] NSAM 328 authorized another increase of from 18,000 to 20,000 marines. On June 16 McNamara announced the planned deployment in Vietnam of from 70,000 to 75,000 men in all. Then on July 2, the Joint Chiefs of Staff submitted a new recommendation for a total troop strength of 179,000, which Johnson took under consideration.

"These deployments," McGeorge Bundy said in a memorandum to the president, "did not give us bad reactions, and it became easier for Westmoreland to propose, and for us to accept, additional deployments."[55]

While the dispatch of marines and the subsequent sharp increases in American troop strength in Vietnam did cause surprisingly little commotion at home in the spring of 1965, dragon's teeth were being sown, to use William Bundy's expression, and serious warnings sounded in the inner circle in Washington. Because of his background in European affairs, George Ball was more knowledgeable and certainly more articulate about the French disaster in Indochina than any of Johnson's other advisers. Ball's memory of Dien Bien Phu led him to oppose escalation in language that was often clairvoyant yet never decisive when it came to influencing presidential decisions on Vietnam. In April, Ball warned Johnson against rising American casualties. Ball said that "we must face the hard fact that large and articulate elements of the intellectual community and other segments of United States opinion do not believe in our South Vietnamese policy."[56] He argued in favor of new efforts to establish a coalition government in Saigon and obtain a cease-fire, to be followed by American withdrawal.

The outgoing director of Central Intelligence, John McCone, warned against the evolving strategy from an opposite point of view. He argued that unless American offensive operations on the ground were accompanied by much heavier bombing of North Vietnam, ever larger numbers of troops would have to be sent without material improvement in the chances of victory.

Since his days in Congress, Johnson had frequently looked outside the government for counsel from certain old friends with distinguished reputations. One was Clark M. Clifford, a renowned Washington lawyer and influential Democrat who had been special counsel to President Truman. Privately, Clifford, who was to play a cardinal role in the Vietnam drama at a later stage, had been kept abreast of the drift to escalation. On May 17, 1965, he wrote to the president:

> I believe our ground forces . . . should be kept to a minimum. . . . My concern is that a substantial buildup . . . would be construed by the Communists, and by the world, as a determination on our part to win the war on the ground.
>
> This could be a quagmire. It could turn into an open end commitment on our part that would take more and more ground troops, without a realistic hope of ultimate victory.
>
> I do not think the situation is comparable to Korea. The political posture of the parties involved, and the physical conditions, including terrain, are entirely different.
>
> I continue to believe that the constant probing of every avenue leading to a possible settlement will ultimately be fruitful. It won't be what we want, but we can learn to live with it.[57]

The man who then exercised the greatest influence over Johnson was McNamara, who favored escalation combined with intense political effort to begin negotiations. Yet even the new director of Central Intelligence, Vice-Admiral William Raborn, Jr., (ret.), questioned whether the one would lead to the other. Moreover, he asked, how could South Vietnam fend off an illegal resumption of Communist pressure after a formal settlement and withdrawal of American forces? "There is little point," he said in a memorandum, "in spending US lives and treasure to obtain a conference or a settlement which, in the absence of a viable non-Communist state, must lead either to U.S. re-intervention or a subsequent Communist takeover."[58]

Also critical of McNamara's plans for escalation, McGeorge Bundy sent the secretary of defense a memorandum. "If," Bundy inquired,

we need 200 thousand men now . . . may we not need 400
thousand later? . . . Is there any real prospect that U.S. regular
forces can conduct the anti-guerrilla operations which would
probably remain the central problem in South Vietnam? . . .
Still more brutally, do we want to invest 200 thousand men to
cover an eventual retreat?[59]

Another insidious problem grew out of the shift from defensive to
active combat operations by American troops, with Johnson insisting
that no change be acknowledged. American reporters in Saigon discovered what was happening and said so in their stories. The somer-
saults in Washington over explanation of the deceit, Philip L.
Geyelin wrote, "opened up another crack in the Administration's
credibility."[60] William Bundy commented later,

I think you'd have to say, that the president's policy of not bit-
ing the bullet at any point in a public sense and saying, "This is
what we're doing and why we're doing it" . . . sowed the
dragon's teeth in terms of the credibility gap charge. He played
the cards so *very* close to his chest . . .[61]

Secrecy bedeviled Johnson's relationship with the press and the
public.

Open dissent appeared with increasing frequency. On April 2,
Canadian Prime Minister Lester B. Pearson spoke at Temple University in Philadelphia, calling for a pause in the bombing. Johnson
bridled at the spectacle of a foreign leader questioning presidential
policy on American soil. When the two men met the next day at
Camp David, Maryland, the presidential retreat north of Washington, Johnson evidently gave Pearson a piece of his mind. On April
17, under the sponsorship of Students for a Democratic Society,
more than 15,000 demonstrators picketed the White House to protest the bombing. The next day Senator Fulbright came out for a
bombing pause. "The president was in a very intense He-who-is-
not-with-me-is-against-me kind of mood in that period," Bundy recalled.[62]

The month of July 1965 was a great turning point in the Vietnam
War and in the presidency of Lyndon Johnson.

NLF forces were growing in number and extending their sway

over a widening area of South Vietnam. South Vietnamese cities stood isolated from surrounding countryside controlled by the NLF. The desertion rate in the South Vietnamese army was increasing at a pace that prevented much-needed enlargement of Saigon's combat forces. The economy of South Vietnam was ruptured. North Vietnam was not only withstanding Rolling Thunder but, despite the air attacks, still infiltrating a rising number of troops into the South.

Dilemmas beset Johnson. To cut and run, with some 75,000 servicemen in Vietnam, would cause, he feared, a storm of opposition from conservatives at home, producing political stalemate. To employ the might of the Strategic Air Command against North Vietnam was thought to risk intervention by China and the Soviet Union. To declare a state of national emergency and mobilize a large expeditionary force at a cost of billions would jeopardize the Great Society. To stand his ground in Vietnam with just the 75,000 men already there would be for Johnson to witness casualties mounting and NLF control spreading. To send more troops would result in still more casualties while providing no guarantee of a satisfactory settlement. From time to time, especially when he had been drinking, according to Reedy, Johnson had visions that Vietnam would eventually destroy him.[63]

How many troops would be needed to wear down the NLF and Hanoi in a long struggle and force them to negotiate? Opinions differed as Johnson grappled with the problem throughout July. Having lost his case against escalation, Ball urged Johnson at least to limit the commitment indefinitely to 100,000 men. General Westmoreland wanted from 175,000 to 200,000 in 1965 alone. McNamara informed Johnson that "it should be understood that the deployment of more men (perhaps 100,000) may be necessary in 1966 and that the deployment of additional forces thereafter is possible but will depend on developments."[64] General Wheeler told the president that it might take from 700,000 to one million men up to seven years to achieve victory in terms of crushing the Communist forces and pacifying South Vietnam. In supporting Westmoreland's request, McNamara also recommended a call-up of about 235,000 reserves and national guard units. It should be noted, he advised Johnson, "that in mid-1966 the United States would, as a consequence . . . have approximately 600,000 additional men . . . as protection against contingencies."[65] William Bundy, seeking a course between extremes, recommended that deployment taper off at 85,000 men for the next two months "to test the military effectiveness of U.S. combat forces and the reaction of the Vietnamese army and people to the increased U.S. role." McGeorge Bundy wanted the president to reject Ball's advice and discuss "the narrower choice between my brother's course and McNamara's."[66]

Johnson conferred for days with various sets of advisers. Some writers have viewed the sessions as window dressing to convince the public that the president was doing his best to reach a statesmanlike decision when in reality he had already decided. Others have suggested that the meetings were typical Johnson contrivances for gathering military and civilian advisers in a consensus in support of his own ultimate decision. "If a decision is to go ahead, I am committed," Ball said, according to the minutes of one session.[67] On the other hand, the meetings were vehicles in which many points of view were offered. Standing still or pulling out was never in prospect, not when Johnson, in his frame of mind, had recommendations for going on from the secretary of state, the secretary of defense, the Joint Chiefs of Staff, and the field commander, General Westmoreland. Later, the historian Herbert Y. Schandler put his finger on the crux of the problem.

> From 1965 on, U.S. involvement grew in slow stages, with each step preceded by an agonizing policy review at the highest levels. . . . Throughout the course of this involvement, however, none of the policy makers involved in these reviews and decisions seemed capable of looking ahead to the long term, of developing an overall, coherent, long-range strategy for the achievement of specific U.S. objectives.[68]

At the end of the discussions in July 1965 Johnson decided in his own way what was to be done.

His decision can best be understood by bearing in mind that he acted within the context of the Vietnam War *and* the Great Society. He wanted the best of both worlds. His decision, as William Bundy later recalled, "was his way of trying to get the best of both." No great debate, no going to the country for a mandate for making the war America's war, no call-up of reserves, Bundy observed.[69] The need for men would have to be met through Selective Service. Truman had called up the reserves in the Korean War. Such an act, however, is politically unpopular, as Johnson had observed close at hand when Kennedy called up some reserves during the Berlin crisis of 1961. Furthermore, Johnson would have had to ask Congress for large appropriations for reserves at a time when Medicare and the voting rights bill were being debated. Despite the requests of McNamara and the Joint Chiefs for reserves, Johnson elected not to risk his domestic legislation in a surge of controversy over such costs. He ordered McNamara to plan the new escalation with no more than $400 million in new funds, although McNamara thought it would be more candid and responsible to ask for $1 billion for the remainder of the 1965 calendar year. His deputy, Cyrus R. Vance, estimated that $8 billion would be needed in the next twelve months. But Johnson refused to create an impression that the country might have to adopt anti-inflation controls or that guns might displace butter. Available funds could be scraped together to pay for the war at least until the start of 1966.

Since early 1961, when John Kennedy started the practice, presidential press conferences were often held in the evening when television attracted the maximum audience. But Johnson went to the other extreme and scheduled the press conference to announce his decision during the lunch hour on July 28, 1965. He began in a low key by reading a letter from a woman asking why her son was in Vietnam. He gave a detailed answer, embracing, essentially, the lesson of Munich, the domino theory, the policies of Eisenhower and Kennedy, the menace of China, and the importance of the sanctity of a United States commitment. He said that Westmoreland had told him what was needed to deal with aggression. (That Westmoreland had asked for a force of from 175,000 to 200,000 men in 1965 alone, the president did not divulge to the public.) "We will meet his needs," Johnson said. Then he stated his decision:

> I have today ordered to Vietnam the Air Mobile Division and certain other forces which will raise our fighting strength from 75,000 to 125,000 men almost immediately. Additional forces will be needed later, and they will be sent as requested.
>
> This will make it necessary to increase our active fighting forces by raising the monthly draft call from 17,000 over a period of time to 35,000 per month, and for us to step up our campaign for voluntary enlistments.[70]

In the previously mentioned 1969 interview with William Jorden, Johnson said of the July 1965 decision:

I knew that if I ran out, that I'd be the first American president to ignore our commitments, turn tail and run, and leave our allies in the lurch, after all the commitments Eisenhower had made, and all that SEATO had made, and all that Congress had made and all that the Tonkin Gulf [resolution] said, and all the statements that [President] Kennedy had made, and Bobby Kennedy had made, and that everybody had made. I'd be the first American president to put my tail between my legs and run out because I did not have the courage to stand up and support a treaty and support the policy of two other presidents. . . . I chose to stand.

Before Johnson left office, United States forces in Vietnam approached 543,000, the maximum commitment.

In June 1950, Truman had committed the United States to combat in Korea. In the spring and summer of 1965, Johnson committed the United States to combat in Vietnam. Each president knew what he was doing even though he could not foretell the disasters that lay ahead. Johnson and Truman acted to preserve their respective foreign policies, which called for denial of Communist control over particular corners of Asia. Both presidents went to war in order to maintain what they considered to be the political balance needed to sustain their foreign policies at home. In other words, both felt required to placate strong, articulate sentiment in the United States against further Communist expansion abroad while doing so on a scale and for objectives that did not arouse fear of a new world war.

V · *The Caldrons*

1

In the days after the task force of the Twenty-fourth Infantry Division landed in Korea on July 1, 1950, the threat of calamity hung over American troops in battle, while shock and incredulity gripped Americans at home. Death, confusion, retreat after retreat—could this be the army that only yesterday had thrilled the nation by its victories at Normandy, the Bulge, the Rhine, Guadalcanal? What had Truman done? American soldiers chased across rice paddies by North Koreans? What was the matter?

From the outset catastrophe spread. Lacking land mines, the task force was routed and bled by the first enemy tank column it encountered, near Osan, midway between Seoul to the north and Pusan to the south. As reinforcements arrived, they were rushed, unprepared, into battle at places with unheard-of names like Pyongtaek, Chonan, Konju, Taejon. Only a small fraction of the American soldiers had ever been in combat before. Yanked from a comfortable life of occupation duty in Japan, they were thrust into the dusty hills and heat of a totally strange terrain to cope with relentless attack by a foe estimated to have 80,000 men in the field. Ambushes took a high toll on the Americans. Their mortars and machine guns were often abandoned in fright; communications were chaotic. YAK fighters dispersed American observation planes. Some infantrymen trudged up roads, never to be seen again. Others were found dead, shot in the head, with their hands tied behind their backs.

The high rate of casualties among officers multiplied the confusion in the American ranks. One colonel was cut in two by a shell from a tank. When a retreating convoy scattered, Major General William

F. Dean, commanding general of the Twenty-fourth Division, was separated from his troops, knocked unconscious in a fall, captured, and held prisoner for three years. Such was the turmoil that in the first week of action fifteen hundred men of the Twenty-fourth Division were missing. It was roughly at that point that MacArthur informed the Joint Chiefs of Staff that he was doubtful whether his forces could hold the southern tip of Korea.

The next two divisions to arrive from Japan were the Twenty- fifth Infantry and the First Cavalry (entirely infantry by then), but both were quickly demoralized, sometimes to the point of panic, in action in the central mountains and along the east coast, where Republic of Korea forces were already in retreat. A message was sent from the field to MacArthur in Tokyo requesting permission at that desperate juncture to move the headquarters in Korea from the central mountains all the way south to Pusan, the last possible stronghold. MacArthur ignored the request.

The American occupation force in Japan had been designated the Eighth Army; it was commanded by General Walton H. Walker. When Truman responded to the Communist attack, the Eighth Army's jurisdiction was extended to Korea, and MacArthur appointed Walker commander of United States ground forces. It was Walker who had requested permission to move his headquarters farther to the rear. Instead of replying, MacArthur, starting his last war and one that throughout history was to compromise his great reputation, flew to Korea on July 27. Erect and agile at seventy, he told Walker that retreats must cease. Two days later Walker went to the Twenty-fifth Division headquarters and gave an order to the highest officers to hold the line—"stand or die," the press described it. "There will be no more retreating, withdrawal, or readjustment of the lines or any other term you choose. . . ." Walker said, according to notes paraphrasing his remarks. "There will be no Dunkirk, no Bataan; a retreat to Pusan would be one of the greatest butcheries in history. We must fight to the end."[1]

Nevertheless, in the latter part of July American troops, battling courageously by all reports, were still being forced back everywhere. Only an extraordinary effort by the Twenty-fourth and Twenty-fifth divisions halted a North Korean flanking attack on Pusan, which, if successful, might have made the enemy victorious.

Before the first week of fighting in July had passed, MacArthur had been compelled to ask for reinforcements over and above the four divisions in his command. Truman approved. Shortly afterward, within a space of two days, MacArthur practically doubled his estimate of the ultimate force he would require—eight divisions instead of the four originally authorized by Truman. The president and the Joint Chiefs of Staff strove to give him what he requested. MacArthur's calls bared a difficult situation into which Truman had drifted. The United States was unprepared to fight a large conventional war in one area of theretofore minor strategic importance and still stand ready to protect its interests in regions of vital importance, such as Europe and the Middle East.

At the close of the Second World War in 1945, the United States had a stunning military force of nearly 12 million men and women. Popular demand, frightened congressional acquiescence, and ineffectual resistance by Truman, new in office, combined to bring about helter-skelter demobilization even though the war had multiplied American interests around the globe. By the summer of 1947, the armed forces had melted down to 1,564,000, and the Selective Service Act had expired. To compensate, Truman proposed universal military training, a program under which young men, as civilians, would receive a year of basic training. In time, therefore, the country would have had a reserve "citizens' army" that could have been mobilized quickly by act of Congress. UMT, as it was called, proved a thoroughly unpopular idea, and Congress would not pass it.

Although the national security establishment judged the objective of the Soviet Union to be the domination of the world, the Soviet state had been so devastated by war that Washington did not expect a new outbreak of major hostilities. The danger of brushfire wars attracted little attention in the administration. Throughout Truman's first term, therefore, the administration opposed the spread of Communism abroad essentially by economic and political means. Concern over the inadequate armed forces was offset by the United States monopoly on the atomic bomb, still intact four years after Hiroshima and Nagasaki.

Truman appeared to be more concerned about the national debt, which stood at $252 billion at the start of his second term, than about military preparedness. Up to that point he had managed the popular feat of keeping the federal budget balanced, or nearly so. He had achieved it by reducing the military establishment. The total defense budget for the fiscal year 1950, in the last week of which the

Korean War erupted, was $14.4 billion. The global demands of an expanding foreign policy, the North Atlantic Treaty included, simply outran the protection of conventional American military power. In July 1950, when MacArthur was appealing for reinforcements, the United States had a total of ten divisions. One was on occupation duty in Germany, four—all below strength and inadequately supplied—were under MacArthur, and five were in general reserve in the United States. It was out of those five, including the Second and Third Infantry divisions and parts of the First Marine Division, that MacArthur was reinforced. When MacArthur requested the Eighty-second Airborne Division, the army chief of staff, General Collins, declined, informing him that it was the only effective infantry unit left in the United States. The air force chief of staff, General Hoyt S. Vandenberg, characterized his domain as a "shoe-string air force."

General Omar Bradley, the JCS chairman, said that fall,

> It is a bruising and shocking fact that when we Americans were committed in Korea, we were left without an adequate margin of military strength with which to face an enemy at any other specific point. Certainly, we were left without the strength to meet a general attack . . . except for the atomic bomb.[2]

In the cruel harvest of July, Americans at home got a taste of the sour side of low defense budgets, as they had after Pearl Harbor and Bataan. In Korea, however, the situation probably would not have been much different at the outset if Truman had added a couple of billion dollars to the defense budgets of 1949 and 1950 unless, of course, he had been more responsive to North Korean threats and had hastened to build up American armed forces in Japan before the June attack. Otherwise, because of the strategic priority for Europe, the extra money would probably not have been spent on Far Eastern ground forces, which had to meet the attack. It would still have taken weeks to get adequate forces into Korea. On the whole, of course, American military strength would have been greater without the Truman budgetary restrictions. Criticism of past policy poured from columnists like Joseph and Stewart Alsop and from Republicans. "The Korean death trap," Senator Joe McCarthy said, "we can lay at the doors of the Kremlin and those who sabotaged rearming, including Acheson and the president, if you please."[3]

However justified the criticism, the first summer of the Korean

War brought to fruition a profound change that had been in the making in the Truman administration for a year. It was a change that has affected American history down to the present day in the form of huge military appropriations, expansion of the nuclear arsenal, and the stationing of American troops in Europe in peacetime.

Worried about their inadequate conventional forces, the Joint Chiefs of Staff requested in 1949 a substantial increase in the then small number of atomic bombs. A special committee of the National Security Council, appointed by Truman to advise him, still had the question under consideration in September 1949 when the awesome news broke that the Soviets had exploded a nuclear device, ending the American monopoly on the bomb. Then, on October 1, Mao Zedong proclaimed the People's Republic of China, causing fear in the United States of a monolithic Sino-Soviet Communist bloc. On October 10, the special committee advised Truman to accelerate the building of atomic bombs. On October 19, he gave the order. On January 31, 1950, informed by scientists that the Soviets had the capability to build a hydrogen bomb, Truman again accepted a recommendation of the special committee and initiated a program to build a "super," as the H-bomb was referred to in the government.

As part of that decision he also approved a recommendation of the special committee for a reassessment of America's military posture. Under the auspices of the secretaries of state and defense, the review was carried out by a group headed by Paul H. Nitze, director of the State Department's Policy Planning Staff, a former Wall Street investment banker who was very close to Secretary of State Acheson. On April 7, 1950, slightly more than three months before the Korean War, the chilling report of the group was submitted to Truman in a paper designated NSC 68.[4] The gist of it was that the defense budget should be increased from $14 billion a year to perhaps $40 billion a year. The report warned that Moscow was "developing the capacity to support its design for world domination," while "our military strength was becoming dangerously inadequate." Containment was not necessarily enough any longer. Action was needed to foster a "fundamental change" in the "inescapably militant" Soviet system. With Moscow launched on a program of building nuclear weapons, the United States could find itself in a "disastrous situation" as early as 1954. The "survival of the free world is at stake," the report said. The administration must set about to rearm not only the United States but its allies as well.

Truman temporized. NSC 68 could have been implemented only through a massive reversal of administration policy. The cost would have been so great that Truman almost certainly could not have marshaled public and congressional support for such a vast rearmament program without the shock of a grave international crisis. It is questionable whether he would have tried. Weeks passed. Then, in rain and darkness along the 38th parallel, the crisis was born in the flashing of North Korean artillery fire.

At a cabinet meeting on July 14, two weeks after American forces began their retreat in Korea, Acheson appealed for what amounted to a start on implementing NSC 68. On July 19, Truman finally sent Congress his first message on the war. He requested new funds totaling $11.6 billion for military purposes for the remainder of the 1951 fiscal year. Heavy new requests were to follow. He asked Congress for more men, equipment, and supplies for MacArthur; for a substantial increase in the size of the armed forces over and above the increase needed for Korea, and for assistance to "the free nations associated with us in common defense to augment their military strength." "The attack upon the Republic of Korea," he said, "makes it plain beyond all doubt that the international Communist movement is prepared to use armed invasion to conquer independent nations. We must, therefore, recognize the possibility that armed aggression may take place in other areas."[5]

In their concern over that menace—especially in their fear that West Germany might prove as vulnerable to Soviet attack as South Korea had been to the North Korean army—Truman and Acheson discussed the situation in Europe at a meeting in the Oval Office on July 31. The upshot was their determination to strengthen the North Atlantic alliance, particularly in two ways that were remarkable at that point. One was by an unprecedented and lasting deployment of United States troops in Europe in peacetime as part of a collective force. The other was by rearming West Germany, a breathtaking thought only five years after the death of Adolf Hitler. Work on both of these undertakings went forward to fruition. On September 9, Truman announced his approval of "substantial" increase in American troops in Europe. Because of French resistance, however, the rearming of West Germany did not begin until the Eisenhower administration. The consequences of the Korean War stretched around the globe. As the German historian Hans W. Gatzke was to write, the single most important event affecting the future of Germany after the Second World War was the invasion of South Korea.

That same invasion, meanwhile, had convinced Truman that the conclusions of NSC 68 were valid. He asked the National Security Council for a recommendation on it by September 1. At that time, with Truman presiding, the NSC adopted the conclusions of NSC 68 "as a statement of policy to be followed over the next four or five years. . . ." The total budget for defense and international affairs was to rise from $17.7 billion in the 1950 fiscal year to $53 billion in fiscal 1951. A point of departure in postwar American history, the approval of NSC 68 was one of the great and lasting consequences of the Korean War. It contributed heavily to the militarization of the cold war.

A week after Truman had committed troops, an event occurred that made the Korean War unique in American history. It was a vote in the United Nations Security Council that substantiated to a degree the long-sought goal of collective security under a world organization to halt aggression and punish the aggressor. At the urging of the United States, the council adopted a resolution welcoming support of all members of the United Nations in the Korean War. Member states were called on to furnish military forces for a unified command to be exercised by the United States under the blue-and-white flag of the United Nations. Since Americans bore the brunt of the fighting, the Security Council asked the United States to designate a commander of United Nations forces. On the recommendation of the Joint Chiefs of Staff, Truman named MacArthur. Under the circumstances, no other choice was conceivable.

When Truman decided to go to the defense of South Korea, his talks with friends indicated that he envisioned a mightier array of United Nations forces fighting, side by side, with the United States than ever materialized. Fifteen other nations contributed troops to combat: Australia, Belgium, Canada, Colombia, Ethiopia, France, Greece, Luxembourg, the Netherlands, New Zealand, the Philippines, South Africa, Thailand, Turkey, and the United Kingdom. All of them sent forces in at least battalion strength, except Luxembourg, which dispatched a single company, and South Africa, which sent an air unit. Only the British Twenty-seventh Infantry Brigade from Hong Kong arrived before mid-September 1950 and helped in the defense of Pusan. While several of the contingents furnished by other United Nations members proved outstanding in combat, their aggregate strength, aside from that of the British Commonwealth Division, was insufficient to exert significant effect on the course of the war, according to military historians. A number of United Nations members that did not send troops contributed medical supplies, food, and other nonmilitary items. But to an overwhelming degree, the burden of the war was carried by the United States. The substantial army of the Republic of Korea operated under the command of the Eighth Army. Because of the Soviet veto, the Republic of Korea was not a member of the United Nations.

When offers of help from allies first began arriving, Truman told his subordinates to "take everything" in the way of ships, planes, troops, and supplies. "We may need them," he said. He wanted each contribution, beginning with some British naval vessels and crews, promptly reported to Congress. His eagerness to let the country know that he was obtaining help was later matched by Johnson's demands to his officials to get "more flags" in Vietnam. The sorry lack of success in that case was due partly to the fact that the United Nations was not carrying out sanctions against North Vietnam, as it had, in very different circumstances, against North Korea.

For all but the earliest days of the fighting, the war against North Korea was waged by United Nations forces, of which the forces of the United States were dominant. That arrangement added a certain complexity to Truman's responsibility for decisions that was not present for Johnson later. The United Nations Command, under MacArthur, had its headquarters in Tokyo. Control of military operations was in the hands of the United States as executive agent of the United Nations. It meant that control was exercised by Truman as commander in chief of United States forces. The United Nations might provide general guidance in war policy, but it did not control events on the battlefield. From Tokyo, MacArthur dealt with the Joint Chiefs of Staff through General Collins, the army chief of staff, and the chiefs reported to the secretary of defense and ultimately to the president.

For Truman to be, in effect, the executive agent of the United Nations and at the same time dependent on Congress for appropriations and other legislation related to the war placed him in a crosscurrent that no other president has experienced. A time would come, for example, when the United Nations allies wanted to consolidate gains that had been made in South Korea and seek a truce, whereas an articulate faction in Congress, responsive to MacArthur's views, wanted not only to advance but to extend the war to China. By concurring with his allies, Truman was to incur the anger of the Republican Right. As for MacArthur, he and the generals in his headquarters were contemptuous of the United Nations, as was a faction in Congress, and itched to conduct the war free of UN political pressure.

Truman was carefully briefed on the progress in Korea. That war was of a more familiar nature and easier for the president and the people to follow than the amorphous guerrilla war in Vietnam was to be. American troops in Korea fought much as they had in Europe after Normandy, with similar field dispositions up through the levels of division, corps, and army. Lines of advance followed highways or sea routes. Advances and retreats were relatively simple to plot on maps. The large helicopter gunships and troop carriers used in great numbers in Vietnam had not yet been developed. As in the European Theater of Operations, infantry was supported by armor, artillery, and tactical aviation. Americans used napalm, as they were to do in Vietnam, and civilian casualties were caused by destructive American bombing attacks on cities, towns, and villages. And as was to be the case in Vietnam, too, the enemy was capable of great cruelty. A cardinal advantage the United States enjoyed in Korea in contrast to Vietnam was that the government under the autocratic and sometimes unpredictable Rhee was relatively stable, purposeful, and widely supported by the population in the war. With such a base, American soldiers did not find themselves menaced by South Korean guerrillas indistinguishable from the rest of the people.

Usually once a week Truman invited General Bradley to the White House for a late-afternoon drink and discussion of the war. Periodically, Truman met with all of the chiefs. In contrast to Roosevelt's personal and informal approach to strategic decisions during the Second World War, Truman relied heavily on the regular government organizations, such as the Departments of State and Defense, the JCS, CIA, and the National Security Council. The council is the highest agency of the government concerned with diplomatic and military policy. It consists of the president, the vice-president, the secretaries of state and defense, the chairman of the Joint Chiefs of Staff, and the director of Central Intelligence. At Truman's request the NSC had been established by Congress in the National Defense Act of 1947, but until June 1950 he held only infrequent formal NSC meetings. He began to rely on the NSC regularly after the Korean War started. Nevertheless, he was determined to preserve presidential prerogative and insisted on treating NSC deliberations as advisory. The final decision, set forth in NSC papers, was always the president's.

Compared with the White House since the 1960s, the presidential staff in the Truman administration was a mere handful, a dozen or so mostly first-rate assistants. Their job was to serve the president, not, as was to happen in certain later administrations, to try to run the government. Apart from Averell Harriman, who came to the White House as a trouble shooter and adviser immediately after the Korean War began, Truman had no specialists in foreign policy on his staff. It was Eisenhower who established the post of special assistant to the president for national security affairs, an office that has since become almost a bureau. It has been headed by a succession of conspicuous figures, including McGeorge Bundy, Walt Rostow, Henry Kissinger, Brent Scowcroft, Zbigniew Brzezinski, and Alexander M. Haig, Jr. Unlike any member of Truman's staff, such men came to play important parts in the making of national security policy. There were three men whom Truman used as conduits to National Security Council information and, to an extent, as his own staff in the conduct of the war. The principal one was Admiral Sidney W. Souers, executive secretary of the NSC. Another was James S. Lay, Jr., his successor. The third was Admiral Robert L. Dennison, the president's naval aide and later commander of the NATO Atlantic fleet. It was not because of a title but because of his competence that Truman used him as part of the White House–NSC liaison.

Truman almost always followed the practice of dealing directly, rather than through his staff, with the responsible cabinet officers. In the war, that meant dealing with Acheson as secretary of state and with General Marshall, the former secretary of state, who assumed the post of secretary of defense three months after the war began. Those two men, and often Undersecretary of Defense Robert A. Lovett, were his main reliance. They served him loyally. Their influence was very great. Major decisions were made by Truman on their advice, which usually took the form not of lists of possible options but of positive recommendations that the president could accept, reject, or alter in conference. In the Vietnam War, Lyndon Johnson had a mania for information, almost hour by hour, and had officials in spasms trying to satisfy him at any time of the day or night. Truman did not feel that he had to know everything at once. He trusted his advisers to give him whatever information he needed when he needed it. At night he went to bed and, unlike Johnson during Vietnam, slept until he was awakened at 5:30 A.M. by what he called his "reveille habit." Truman made the major strategic and diplomatic decisions. In contrast to Johnson, he left tactical decisions to his commanders. It proved to be a matter of high importance that once he had made the decision to fight a limited war in Korea, he had the support of the Joint Chiefs of Staff. Such basic differences as were to develop between Johnson and the chiefs over Vietnam never occurred in the case of Truman.

A crucial time in Korea began on August 1, 1950, when Eighth Army headquarters ordered the hard-pressed ground forces to withdraw behind the Naktong River for an ultimate stand in a rectangle in southeastern Korea that became known as the Pusan Perimeter. For weeks the defenders fought off enemy attacks. As long as the United Nations' lines held, the battle had the effect of drawing the bulk of the North Korean army into the southern reaches of the peninsula. The movement, of course, increased the threat to the stability of the perimeter. It also put the North Korean army in peril of entrapment. As the summer wore on, two interlocking developments took place that not only were to change the nature of the Korean War but would also open the door to events that, years later, contributed significantly to drawing the United States into war in Vietnam.

One development was a plan by MacArthur for a large amphibious landing at Inchon, on the west coast just south of the 38th parallel, to trap the North Korean army deployed below around the Pusan Perimeter. The other was a momentous decision by Truman to alter the original war aim and send United Nations forces across the 38th parallel to wipe out the remaining military power of North Korea.

The developments were interlocking in the sense that the Inchon landing, which a daring MacArthur carried out skillfully on September 15, 1950, did bring the United Nations forces surging north to the parallel in position for an invasion of North Korea. And Mac-

Arthur's triumph, filling the American people with elation and sudden hope of victory, made it very difficult for Truman to deny the popular general the chance to go north and end the division of Korea once and for all. Indeed, the momentum of administration policy had by the time of Inchon swung clearly in the direction of crossing the parallel.

When the United States Tenth Corps went ashore at Inchon, commanded by Major General Edward M. Almond, North Koreans broke off the battle at the Pusan Perimeter and fled north to escape encirclement. The Eighth Army at last burst out of the perimeter and chased its tormentors toward the poised Tenth Corps. MacArthur's plan was to catch them between the two forces and destroy them. The plan was only partially successful; an estimated 25,000 enemy soldiers somehow escaped the trap and made their way to North Korea, where in time they could be readied to fight again.

The decision to cross the parallel was one of the two or three most significant ones Truman made as president. The problem was difficult in the extreme. The original war aim in June was to drive the enemy out of South Korea, restoring the 38th parallel as the boundary. That would have been a notable achievement in the name of collective security. The permanent objective of the United States and the United Nations, however, was the far more ambitious one of establishing a free, independent, united Korea.

If Truman had decided to halt at the parallel, where United Nations forces stood at the end of September, vast dissatisfaction would have risen from the public and from Congress only weeks before the off-year elections. The Communists would have remained in power in North Korea and, with Soviet assistance, rebuilt their army. American troops would have had to stay in South Korea indefinitely to secure the parallel against renewed aggression.

But if Truman elected to cross the parallel, enormous gains might be realized. All of the North Korean army might be crushed. The Kim Il-sung regime might collapse. The United Nations might at last unify Korea and take a festering burden off Washington's back. In the process the Soviet orbit in Asia would have been retracted, a crown of diamonds for the policy of containment. Such an outcome, seemingly within easy reach now, would have been regarded as one of the greatest achievements of Truman's presidency. Balanced against such a prize, however, was a danger. If United States troops invaded North Korea, China or the Soviet Union might intervene to save a Communist state.

Soon after the war began, Rhee informed Truman that he would not be bound by any settlement that left Korea divided. The implication was that he might have ordered the ROK army across the parallel even if the Americans came to a halt. Dulles, then in the State Department as a Republican consultant and negotiator of the Japanese peace treaty, argued that it would be foolish to allow the North Koreans to retire behind the parallel and regroup. All summer, John Allison, director of the State Department's office of Northeast Asian affairs, pressed for a policy of occupying North Korea and holding elections under the United Nations to unify the country. In meetings in Tokyo with members of the JCS, MacArthur said that he intended to pursue the enemy across the parallel and might have to occupy all of North Korea in order to defeat its army. The members of the JCS agreed that he should be authorized to go north. Dwight Eisenhower, then president of Columbia University, independently suggested that it might be necessary to destroy Kim Il-sung's army in combat in North Korea. The more the question was studied in the government, the stronger became the lure of a victory that would end Communist rule of North Korea and thereby shorten the shadow of Soviet power in the Far East. Harriman recalled afterward: "It would have taken a superhuman effort to say no. Psychologically, it was almost impossible not to go ahead and complete the job."[6]

Pressure to "complete the job" built up rapidly in the press and in Congress. David Lawrence, a conservative columnist, wrote that if United Nations forces "are not permitted to go beyond the 38th parallel to disarm the government which has committed the aggression, the Republicans will certainly make capital out of that policy" in the forthcoming congressional elections.[7] A former Republican national chairman, Representative Hugh D. Scott, Jr., of Pennsylvania, wasted no time in charging that the State Department was ready "to subvert our military victory" by "cringing behind the parallel."[8] Unquestionably, conservative Republicans would have attacked Truman ferociously if he had ordered an unwilling MacArthur to halt at the North Korean border.

Lure of victory, the drama of Inchon, political pressure, public opinion, and the recommendation of his highest advisers all influenced Truman's decision. On September 9, the National Security Council promulgated, and the president promptly approved, NSC 81/1, a document that was to be the basis of future directives to MacArthur. It recommended unification of Korea if it could be accomplished without risk of war with China or the Soviet Union. Barring such an eventuality, the document said, it "would be expected that [MacArthur] would receive authorization to conduct military operations . . . in pursuance of a rollback in Korea north of the 38th parallel, for the purpose of destroying the North Korean forces." NSC 81/1 said that "there is a clear legal basis for taking such military actions north of the 38th parallel as are necessary" to accomplish the mission. The basis was the United Nations Security Council resolution of June 27, calling on members not only to repel the North Koreans but also "to restore international peace and security in the area."[9]

Having got into Korea in the first place, defeating Kim Il-sung's forces in the North was the way Truman chose to get out of it. Technically, MacArthur's mission was not the political one of reuniting Korea. That task involved a number of nonmilitary steps, particularly elections, and was under the jurisdiction of the United Nations General Assembly. MacArthur's role was to restore peace and security in the area by defeating the remaining North Korean troops. But the idea of unification lay behind his mission. At an NSC meeting Truman recalled that in the Second World War the German army disintegrated after the Allied crossing of the Rhine. He was counting on a similar end of the North Korean army after MacArthur's forces drove north of the parallel. The way would then have been opened for reunification of Korea and withdrawal of American troops.

The Joint Chiefs of Staff prepared a directive to MacArthur. Truman, Marshall, and Acheson approved it. Sent on September 27, it said, "Your military objective is the destruction of the North Korean Armed Forces." In the absence of intervention by major Chinese or Soviet forces or threat of it, MacArthur was authorized to conduct military operations in North Korea.[10] Both in Washington and at United Nations headquarters, officials wanted to avoid making an issue of the crossing of the parallel. At a State Department meeting Assistant Secretary Rusk was asked why the United States did not inquire of the Soviets how they would like to see the Korean problem settled. The Soviet reply, he said, probably "would be to stick to the 38th parallel and with the military situation moving as rapidly as it is, we don't want to have to negotiate with them on that point."[11] Policymakers did not want a vote on the question in the United Nations. They preferred that MacArthur proceed, unostentatiously, and do whatever he found to be a military necessity. Hence officials were annoyed at news stories from the Eighth Army that called attention to preparations for an advance to the north. With Truman's approval, Secretary of Defense Marshall notified MacArthur, "We want you to feel unhampered tactically and strategically to proceed north of the 38th parallel."[12] MacArthur was not one to place a narrow interpretation on his instructions. "Unless and until the enemy capitulates," he replied, "I regard all Korea open for our military operations."[13] On October 2, he reported to the Joint Chiefs that elements of the ROK army were across the parallel and had advanced from ten to thirty miles, meeting practically no resistance.

At 5:35 A.M. on October 3, a secret cable arrived at the State Department for the secretary of state from the American chargé d'affaires in London bearing the code letters NIACT. The code indicated that the message was to be called to Acheson's attention at any hour of the day or night. The message reported that the British had just shown the United States embassy a telegram from Peking. It stated that Chinese Foreign Minister Zhou Enlai had summoned the Indian ambassador, K. M. Panikkar, and informed him that if United States troops should cross the 38th parallel, China would intervene in the defense of North Korea. The warning did not apply to a crossing by South Koreans only.[14] Zhou's words were the most direct in a series of similar statements out of Asia from Chinese sources since the Inchon landing. They were taken with various degrees of seriousness in Washington. Yet, as with the signs in early June that the North Koreans were preparing to invade South Korea, the Chinese rumblings were largely wished aside on the strength of one rationalization or another.

Zhou Enlai was subjecting India to a "war of nerves" because China was excluded from the seat in the United Nations still held by Chiang Kai-shek. Peking was bluffing, trying to scare the United Nations out of taking a stronger stand in North Korea. Panikkar was a leftist, willing to help Zhou play a game. The intimations out of China were not "solid." China could realize no material gain from intervention. On the contrary, such an adventure might weaken Mao's regime.

Truman's reaction was ambivalent. On the one hand, after listening to his advisers, he surmised that China might indeed be indulging in propaganda. On the other, anxiety nagged him. In a speech on September 1, he had appealed to the Chinese people not to be "misled or forced into fighting against the United Nations and against the American people, who have always been and still are their friends." After the rumblings over Inchon and various reports about a massing of Chinese troops in Manchuria and the movement of some of them into North Korea as "volunteers," he asked the CIA for a reassessment. All known factors, the CIA responded on October 12, led "to the conclusion that barring a Soviet decision for global war, such action [Chinese intervention] is not probable in 1950."[15] The report had to be transmitted to the president. On October 12, he was flying westward by stages to meet General MacArthur on Wake Island on the fourteenth (fifteenth on Wake). By then, the full-scale invasion of North Korea had begun. On October 9, the First Cavalry and the Twenty-fourth Infantry Division, the ROK First Division and the Twenty-seventh British Brigade had advanced north of the 38th parallel. Opposition was light. The whole venture was merely a "mopping-up operation," MacArthur told John J. Muccio, United States ambassador in South Korea.[16]

"Have to talk to God's righthand man. . . ," Truman wrote to his cousin on the way to Wake Island for the meeting that had originally been concocted by his staff as a political tactic in the 1950 election campaign.[17] Truman and MacArthur had never met previously. Twice after Truman had taken office MacArthur had declined, on the grounds of urgent responsibilities in Japan, requests by Truman to visit Washington. Neither man admired the other, but up to that point no serious and substantive differences over Korean strategy had arisen between MacArthur, on the one hand, and the president and his senior advisers on the other. Truman had come to the White House skeptical of the brass in general and MacArthur in particular, referring to him as a "stuffed shirt." Decidedly, Truman was suspicious of the general's presidential ambitions. In 1944, the year Roosevelt and Truman ran on the Democratic ticket, MacArthur had allowed his name to be entered as a candidate for president in the Republican primary in Wisconsin. Although Governor Dewey won it, Truman still suspected that MacArthur would seek the Republican nomination in 1952.

When Truman's plane *Independence* rolled to a stop on Wake Island, the president espied MacArthur sitting in a Jeep behind a small crowd. Remembering stories about how MacArthur had seemingly tried to upstage President Roosevelt at a similar wartime meeting in Honolulu on July 26, 1944, Truman refused to budge from his seat until MacArthur finally came to the ramp of the *Independence*. Only then did Truman descend, and in the few hours allotted they had a friendly visit.

The first thing Truman asked the general when they climbed into a car was whether he thought that China would enter the Korean War. "I have been worried about that," Truman was overheard to say by a Secret Service agent riding in the front seat.[18] MacArthur replied that his intelligence reports indicated that the Chinese would not intervene. He made the point again at the formal meeting in a Quonset hut. "It is my belief that organized resistance throughout Korea will be ended by Thanksgiving," he told the president.

Elated, Truman stopped in San Francisco en route back to Washington and said in a speech, "We know now that the United Nations can create a system of international order with the authority to maintain peace."[19]

An exciting moment in MacArthur's drive in North Korea came on October 26 when the reconnaissance platoon of the Seventh Regiment of the ROK Sixth Division reached the Yalu River at Chosan, opposite the silent Manchurian shore. The news was thrilling. Men of the First Cavalry had visions of a Thanksgiving Day parade in Tokyo. *The New York Times* said in an editorial that "except for unexpected developments along the frontiers . . . we can now be easy in our minds as to the military outcome." Almost no one then recalled Chinese Foreign Minister Zhou Enlai's public warning on September 29: "The Chinese people absolutely will not tolerate foreign aggression, nor will they supinely tolerate seeing their neighbors being savagely invaded by the imperialists."[20] The more intimate warnings, of course, had reached Washington through top-secret diplomatic cables, of which the public knew nothing. Like Truman himself, however, the public was apprehensive about recurring reports of Chinese "volunteers" in North Korea.

Even as the small group of ROK soldiers stood at the Yalu, a disturbing occurrence was reported.

Not all of the ROK Sixth Division had been as fortunate as the reconnaissance platoon in reaching the river. Short of the Yalu, another unit had been halted near the village of Onjong by fire, supposedly from North Koreans. In the ensuing engagement the enemy turned out to be Chinese. To the east, another ROK regiment came upon a Chinese roadblock. Fighting broke out. A captured Chinese soldier said that nearly five thousand Chinese troops were deployed in the vicinity of the roadblock. In the next day or two, Chinese forces startlingly appeared, forcing the Eighth Army to retreat across the Chongchon River, sixty-five air miles south of the Yalu.

On November 7, Korean time, MacArthur staged a massive bombing attack on the Yalu River bridges. The consequences beyond the destruction were significant. As the boundary between Manchuria and Korea, the Yalu was the most sensitive area in the war. Yet MacArthur had ordered the attack without Washington's knowledge. Word that it was being readied reached the Joint Chiefs of Staff at the last moment through Lieutenant General George E. Stratemeyer, commanding general of the Far East air forces. With Truman's assent, the chiefs ordered the raid postponed. MacArthur replied with a message intended for Truman's eyes, saying that Chinese troops and equipment were "pouring" across the bridges from Manchuria. The invasion, he declared, was threatening the destruction of United Nations forces. Faced with an apparent crisis, Truman authorized the bombing of the spans on the Korean side of the river. But the realization in Washington that MacArthur had attempted to confront the administration with a fait accompli had a bearing on great events to follow. MacArthur's act incurred the distrust of Truman, Acheson, and the Joint Chiefs of Staff. In the delicate situation at hand in the war as well as in relations with the allies, concern lurked that MacArthur might at any time confront Washington with some still graver fait accompli. At the moment, he made plans, explicitly known to the Joint Chiefs of Staff, for a sweeping advance to the Yalu to finish off the North Korean army.

2

Search and destroy. That was the new and costly American strategy on the ground in Vietnam approved by President Johnson. "Now we were committed to major combat. . . ." he said, looking back on his decision of July 28, 1965, immediately to increase American forces from 75,000 to 125,000 and to send more later as needed.[21]

When the major American escalation began after the Communist attack on Pleiku in February 1965, an enclave strategy was in effect, seemingly befitting the objective of forcing the Communists to negotiate by denying them victory. The strategy involved the occupation by limited American forces of certain important areas, most of them near the coast. With the United States navy supreme, supplies could flow and men could be readily taken in and out. Presumably the enclaves could be defended with moderate casualties. Meanwhile, South Vietnamese troops were supposed to overcome the enemy in other areas in the South. The drawback, as painfully demonstrated later in the spring, was that the forces of North Vietnam—"that raggedy-ass little fourth-rate country," as Johnson called it—were inflicting such severe defeats on the South Vietnamese that the whole South was likely to collapse around the enclaves if strategy were not changed. Furthermore, American military leaders viewed the enclaves as a negative strategy that left the initiative in enemy hands. In army tradition Westmoreland wanted to take the offensive and win the war in the field. Hence the pressure on Johnson for more troops.

The shift from the enclave strategy was underscored in June when Westmoreland was authorized to use American ground forces wherever he needed them to bolster the staggering South Vietnamese army. An effect of the aggressive search-and-destroy tactics was that towns and villages were bombed and burned, and crops and vegetation destroyed by herbicides, sending hordes of refugees into overcrowded cities and thereby corrupting Vietnamese society in hideous fashion. Along with the war came drugs, prostitution, the black market, filthy housing conditions, stifling, fumy traffic, and almost uncontrollable inflation.

Once the major escalation began in 1965, fundamental differences developed between Johnson and the Joint Chiefs of Staff that had never existed between Truman or Roosevelt and the JCS in the two preceding wars. In the simplest terms, the Joint Chiefs wanted Johnson to grant them the authority to hurl the conventional might of the United States against the North Vietnamese in whatever amounts were necessary to force Hanoi to settle matters as quickly as possible. Merely defeating the enemy in the South was not the chiefs' conception of how to deal with the issue. They wanted to roll over North Vietnam with ground forces. "If you are going to fight a war," as General Wheeler, chairman of the JCS during most of the Johnson administration, said afterward, "you shouldn't fight it in South Vietnam. You'd better fight it in North Vietnam because that's where the problems arose. . . . [North Vietnam] was the source."[22] To that end, and for other reasons as well, the JCS wanted Johnson to call up the reserves.

For the United States to have been in a position to meet all its worldwide commitments then would have required standing forces of a size impractical for a democracy to maintain in peacetime. Thus all the services had reserve units. All contingency plans, as Wheeler was to note, assumed that if sizable forces were committed anywhere, "we would immediately reconstitute the strategic reserves . . . by a call-up of reserve units." In the Vietnam War, he said, the services discovered that by relying solely on the draft and the regular forces, there was a shortage of officers and noncommissioned officers. In fact the services were using "the United States regular units [and] NATO units in Europe as a replacement pool"—a foolish business in Wheeler's view.[23]

Once the decision to launch an air offensive was made, the JCS also wanted to bomb Hanoi intensively—a strategy that, in retrospect, has made sense to some students of the war. Douglas Pike, an outstanding authority particularly on the situation in North Vietnam, has written recently that the start of Rolling Thunder frightened the leadership in Hanoi. Yet as North Vietnam proved capable of absorbing the limited blows, the leaders came to believe that the country was withstanding the worst that the United States could deliver—a belief that was to be rectified by President Richard M. Nixon's all-out Christmas bombing in 1972. If the United States had launched such an attack early in 1965, Pike said, Hanoi might have negotiated "an agreement, then sought by Lyndon Johnson, providing for a cease-fire and mutual withdrawal of Northern forces and U.S. troops from South Vietnam. Such an accord, of course, would not have ended Hanoi's quest for unification; it would simply have brought a change in tactics and a new timetable."[24] In short, the political problem at the heart of the Vietnam dilemma would have reasserted itself despite a military onslaught.

The chiefs were also turned down on their recommendations for bombing North Vietnamese sanctuaries in Cambodia and closing the port of Haiphong—in short, as Wheeler later put it, for conducting air and naval warfare against the North Vietnamese on a scale "that would teach them what war was all about [so] they wouldn't be so damned eager to indulge in one." The chairman of the JCS was convinced that the United States misused its air and naval power, with the result that Hanoi, aided by technical personnel and construction workers supplied by China, was able to persist.

Another reason the Joint Chiefs of Staff wanted the reserves mobilized, Wheeler explained later, was psychological. "[W]e felt," he said, "that it would be desirable to have a reserve call-up in order to make sure that the people of the United States knew that they were in a war and not engaged in some two-penny adventure."[25]

It is an arresting fact in military annals that in the third-largest foreign war in American history the Joint Chiefs of Staff, officially the military advisers to the president, failed to persuade Johnson to approve any of these strategies, except for minor concessions later in his term. To this day it rankles the military establishment that the chiefs did not resign in protest, supposedly to spare the armed forces the lasting embarrassment of Vietnam. What would have come from such an act is impossible to say. Certainly, the resignation of the Joint Chiefs of Staff in the intense political pressures of the Vietnam War would have brought an upheaval in the United States, with Congress compelling a reexamination of strategy. But as matters stood, it was civilian control with a vengeance.

In the beginning, no serious public issue arose over differences between the president and the JCS. Discussions on strategy took place in the privacy of the White House. Publicly, the chiefs remained loyal to the president. No one can be sure, of course, what pitfalls may have lurked along the path that they preferred. It is probably true that moderate, informed opinion in the country in the period after the 1965 escalation would not have favored an American invasion of North Vietnam or massive bombing of Hanoi or, in all likelihood, mining the port of Haiphong, where Soviet ships might have been sunk. Johnson pursued a course contrary to that recommended by the chiefs because he feared, on the basis of the Korean experience, intensification of the war; because he hoped that limited war might force a settlement; and because he did not want to put the country on a war footing, shelving domestic reforms. For all these positions there was strong middle-of-the-road support.

Johnson's strategies, disastrous though they turned out to be, had a rather firm historical and political base.

13The entry of China into the Korean War against United Nations forces in 1950 exerted a long and profound influence on American policy and thought. By the time of the Eisenhower and Kennedy administrations, for example, China had become in many respects a more feared adversary than the Soviet Union because the Chinese seemed more warlike. Truman's shocking experience in the fall of 1950 inhibited Eisenhower and Kennedy from sending troops to Indochina. Surely, one of the most crucial effects of the memory of the massive Chinese offensive against Truman's armies was the inhibition it placed on Johnson in using the armed forces to their full potential in Vietnam. The Chinese offensive of 1950 drastically altered not only the Korean War drastically but the Vietnam War as well. Yet whereas Truman had paid far too little heed to threats out of China, Johnson, ironically, may have been overly affected by the putative Chinese menace fifteen years later, though that is easy to say in hindsight.

A recently declassified eight-volume, army-sponsored study by the BDM Corporation of McLean, Virginia, raises the question whether fear of a wider war growing out of Vietnam may not have constrained the Chinese even more than the Americans. *The Strategic Lessons Learned in Vietnam*, as the study is titled, notes that in the Cultural Revolution of the mid-1960s China may have had all it could handle. Moreover, according to the study, the Johnson administration consistently underestimated the restraint on Peking caused by a growing political rift between China and the Soviet Union. The study also questions whether North Vietnam would have been receptive to the presence once more of large numbers of Chinese on their soil.[26] China had once controlled Vietnam for more than one thousand years, and long and deep enmity festered between the two peoples. What, then, if it was unrealistic to think that China would intervene? In that case, were the Joint Chiefs of Staff right? Could Johnson have moved in with great strength in 1965 and 1966 and crushed the North Vietnamese forces? The speculation will always linger, only to raise further questions. How could the United States ever have fostered a permanent, stable, independent, non-Communist Vietnam? Would the American people still be struggling with the task, now and perhaps for years to come?

Another historic base of Johnson's strategies was the universal anxiety about nuclear war that had been mushrooming since Truman ordered the atomic bombing of Japan in 1945. The early years of the Eisenhower administration had produced the doctrine of "massive retaliation." It implied the use by the United States of nuclear weapons in case of aggression. The doctrine was conceived as a way of lessening the economic burden on the United States and its allies in supporting the policy of containment with large standing armies. In the mid-1950s, policymakers judged that no conventional defense could contain the manpower of the Communist nations. A more practical way to deter aggression, Dulles and others argued, was for the non-Communist countries to be prepared to respond to aggression at times, places, and with means of their own choosing. In the universities and among some military leaders, notably General Taylor, massive retaliation was rejected in favor of the concept of flexible response to aggression. In this view, the United States would use its power in a limited and gradual way to force its will on an enemy. Conventional rather than nuclear weapons would be employed to make the enemy see the handwriting on the wall. Signals (in the Vietnam War they often took the form of bombing pauses) would be sent to coax him to negotiate. As an alternative to possible nuclear war, the concept seemed sensible and made its way into the Kennedy administration. McNamara, the Bundy brothers, and other holdovers carried it into the Johnson administration after Kennedy's assassination.

Deputy Secretary of Defense Cyrus R. Vance recalled:

> We had seen the gradual application of force applied in the Cuban missile crisis [of 1962], and had seen a very successful result. We believed that if this same gradual and restrained application of force were applied in South Vietnam that one could expect the same kind of result; that rational people on the other side would respond to increasing military pressure and would, therefore, try and seek a political solution.[27]

Ironically, the war in Vietnam the liberals came to hate and denounce was fought in futility with the strategy they had conceived. As Harry McPherson said afterward,

> . . . they were the ones who were most upset over the

Eisenhower-Dulles massive retaliation policy. They were the ones who called for a capacity to meet limited wars and keep them limited. They were the ones who wanted the helicopters and the Green Berets, who thought that by a combination of this skillfully applied military power and economic resources and a commitment to political democracy . . . we could settle just about any problem anywhere in the world. And McNamara was so good at it, at producing the kind of military weaponry that was fit to fight a war like this, that we assumed, I suppose, that we also had the techniques and the understanding that was fit to fight.[28]

Unfortunately, Vietnam, with its difficult terrain, civil war passions, and logistical assistance to the enemy from the Chinese and the Soviets, was the worst place imaginable for testing the concept of gradual response.

As the number of Americans in Vietnam grew and battle deaths rose, with no settlement in sight, Johnson clung to a middle-of-the-road course—the "eyedropper approach," General Wheeler called it—despite the Joint Chiefs of Staff. While raising the pressure in gradual doses, he insisted on keeping in his own hands the power to lower it if he perceived danger of Chinese intervention. Time and again he sought to tempt Hanoi into peace talks with bombing pauses and endless diplomatic approaches of one kind or another. His political instincts told him that sooner or later he could make a deal with Ho Chi Minh, as he had done countless times in other situations on Capitol Hill, but every attempt withered.

While the president was fighting a limited war more than nine thousand miles away, the North Vietnamese were waging total war on their own soil with tactics suited to their jungles and mountains and perfected over centuries of fighting foreign domination. Meanwhile, according to the BDM study, the policy of gradual escalation gave the North Vietnamese time to replenish men and materials, augmenting their own resources with those provided by China and the Soviet Union. Yet Johnson still refused to call up reserves. Furthermore, to try to lower discontent at home the administration limited military tours of duty in Vietnam to one year at the expense of efficiency in the field.

At the outset, Johnson rejected several possible offensives, any of which, he feared, might have brought Chinese or Soviet intervention. As Wheeler mentioned, the president would not invade North Vietnam. Neither would he attack Cambodian sanctuaries, mine North Vietnamese ports, bomb Hanoi and other North Vietnamese population centers, nor attack lines of communication near the Chinese border. Out of the same fear, he would not destroy the North Vietnamese dike system. To reduce the risk of wider war, Rolling Thunder was limited. The usual targets were supply dumps, barracks, roads, and bridges. Because of the uncertainty of China's response, according to the BDM study, air strikes against enemy power stations, airfields, surface-to-air missile sites, and oil-storage tanks were postponed.

While fear of a wider war was manifest in the discussions, memorandums, and cables within the government, other considerations came into play. The United States did not seek a total victory. Johnson and his advisers realized that all-out bombing and mobilization would create dissension at home—the last thing the president wanted while his Great Society program was moving through Congress. The price of all-out warfare and the resulting controversy over appropriations were prospects that Johnson was determined to avoid. In a speech at Johns Hopkins University on April 7, 1965, he pledged that in Vietnam "we will do only what is absolutely necessary."[29] That meant trying to convince Hanoi that it could not conquer a South Vietnam backed by American military power.

Johnson was not sympathetic to the Joint Chiefs' proposal to call up reserves partly as a means of impressing the public with the gravity of the war. George E. Christian, the last of his press secretaries, said that the president did not want Vietnam "to crowd out other things he was trying to do." Christian added:

> He didn't want a war messing up his domestic programs, and he was determined to go ahead with full funding of everything he wanted to do and just was determined not to let the war disfigure his administration. . . . [T]o him we were going to defend South Vietnam and that was that, and he didn't try to rally the country. . . . He didn't have any desire to lead a crusade in Vietnam. He wanted to do the job and stand by our commitment.[30]

To adopt the larger strategies of the Joint Chiefs of Staff Johnson would have had to confront the public and arouse active support for such a war. Instead he preferred to edge into the conflict as unobtrusively as possible without creating a war psychology. Johnson's decision against mobilizing the reserves, the BDM study noted, narrowed the public's perception of the United States involvement for a time. Hence it was easier for the administration to pursue a guns-and-butter policy. A particular concern of Johnson's was that the war not loom large enough to give conservatives in Congress an excuse to vote against his liberal program.

When the news from Korea turned sour after China's intervention, Senator Wherry and other conservative Republicans, all of whom had favored the president's intervention in the beginning, seized on the opportunity for political gain by calling Korea "Truman's war." Vietnam was indeed Johnson's war, at least as a description of executive direction.

Johnson practically turned the White House into a command post. As we've seen, his mode of operation was different from Truman's conduct of the Korean War in several respects. Moreover, Johnson was tormented by doubts, steeped in ambivalence, and caught up in assorted emotional episodes, all characteristics from which Truman was remarkably free. In contrast to Truman, for example, Johnson asserted his leadership in tactical military decisions, specifically and broadly. He made his principal decisions not in the setting of the National Security Council but at luncheons in the White House on Tuesdays with an informal group having no statutory existence and a membership that changed from time to time. Wheeler was to recall,

> His method of doing business was contrary to that of President Kennedy, who liked to see things in writing. He [Kennedy] read very fast. He absorbed things quickly in writing. President Johnson preferred to use, I imagine, the system that he developed when he was majority leader on the Hill—that of getting people in a small, smoke-filled room and boring into a subject until he had picked your brains. . . . There was nothing unusual at all for him to say, "Well, I called so and so, and so and so, and so and so last night." These would be people all around the country.[31]

It was Johnson's war, too, because of the megatonnage of his personality forever pressing on policymakers, advisers, and administrators. The intense pressure was felt not only in Washington but in the Mission Council in Saigon, on which sat representatives of the various American agencies in Vietnam dealing with the war. One of the representatives, Barry Zorthian, then head of the Joint United States Public Affairs Office, believes that no one has ever measured the effect of Johnson's personal weight on his subordinates. Zorthian said, "The intensity and the pressures and the nature of those pressures on the Mission Council and, through the members of it, on the agencies working out there I think has not really been probed enough."[32]

After the war, Willian Bundy criticized Johnson's conduct of it as lacking in day-to-day coordination. Bundy complained that Johnson took everything into his own hands and, as Bundy put it, all the threads ran only to the president without reaching some policymakers who needed to be informed. Not a regular participant, Bundy called the Tuesday luncheons an "abomination," unstructured to the point where no one knew in advance what subjects were to be discussed and what papers might be needed. Not only was there no preparation, as Bundy saw it, but no written statement on what had emerged from the discussions. "I think his style generally carried the lack of system and structure way too far," Bundy said.[33]

When, to cite an example of Johnson's methods, he received reports of an attack on the *Maddox* and the *C. Turner Joy*, he discussed them with the NSC without reaching a decision. Then he conferred over luncheon with McNamara, McCone, and Rusk, who were NSC members, and McGeorge Bundy and Vance, who were not. There the decision to retaliate against North Vietnam with bombs was made, whereupon Johnson reconvened the NSC for a discussion "in detail," as he later put it. Many NSC meetings were "simple recitals," William Bundy recalled. "You knew nothing was going to be decided. . . ." But when Johnson held important informal meetings with senior advisers, sometimes including men outside the government, then, Bundy added, "you felt the president had already started to formulate."[34]

Because of his experience as a dissenter, George Ball is entitled to be heard when he describes Johnson, as he does in his memoirs, as a listener, not a characterization easily accepted by those who had to endure the president's interminable monologues. William Bundy said,

[M]y recollection is very clear that the quality of men President
Johnson had around him and the way that he dealt with them
on the whole created an atmosphere in which you did level. It
was tough to level. . . . This was a very, very big and tough
mind. You felt he was latching on to every word you said and
that you'd better measure your words, because if you got a fact
wrong, he would remember.[35]

On Christmas Eve, 1965, Johnson declared a bombing pause that
lasted for thirty-seven days. The hope was that it would lure Hanoi
into talks, but apparently there was something more to the decision
than that. Rusk told Lodge:

The prospect of large-scale reinforcements in men and defense
budget increases of some twenty billion for the next eighteen-
month period requires solid preparation of the American public. A crucial element will be clear demonstration that we have
explored fully every alternative but that [the] aggressor has left
us no choice.[36]

The bombing pause took on a slightly comic aspect when Johnson
sent his highest officials flying all over the globe, heralding America's wish for an end to the war. "Fandangle diplomacy" David
Kraslow and Stuart H. Loory dubbed it.[37] Hanoi, of course, did not
respond, and Johnson had to shoulder the burden of resuming
bombing at a time when dissent from a bombing strategy was a
highly emotional issue at home.

Johnson regretted the pause and, according to the recollections of
William Bundy and Clark Clifford, resented the advice of those who
had advocated it. "He became," Bundy said afterward, "extraordinarily wary . . . and . . . a little more inclined to think in terms of
where did this guy stand when the chips were down on that
blankety-blank pause that I was euchred into. . . ." "You did use up
a great deal of credit if you advised him something that he came to
feel was not the right thing to do."[38] Evidently, according to Bundy,
the stock of Clifford and Associate Justice Abe Fortas of the Supreme Court, longtime friends and unofficial advisers to Johnson,
rose in his eyes because they had counseled against the Christmas
bombing pause. Johnson told Brzezinski, who was a member of the
State Department's Policy Planning Staff in 1966 and 1967, that the

only persons he could trust for sound and solid advice in international affairs were Clifford and Fortas, neither of whom had had a career in making foreign policy.[39] McNamara had been in the forefront of advocacy of the bombing pause.

If Johnson was a listener, sometimes he was perhaps too good a listener for comfort. In a late phase of the war McPherson conveyed his own doubts about it to Johnson in the form of memorandums purporting to summarize what the political opposition was saying. If McPherson had revealed himself as a dove, he said, "I would [have been] aced out of the whole Vietnam thing."[40]

Throughout the early period of the war Johnson's contact with the Pentagon was largely through McNamara, to the resentment of the Joint Chiefs of Staff. They were annoyed by the business management approach to the Department of Defense taken by the former president of the Ford Motor Company. They considered him and his brainy staff of "Whiz Kids" arrogant. In the chiefs' opinion McNamara assumed a professional knowledge of military matters that lay in their sphere of competence. His, too, was a restraining hand on their strategy of heavier attack. Only in time did Wheeler become close to Johnson and a member of the Tuesday luncheon group. Protégé of his predecessor, Maxwell Taylor, Wheeler's forte had been as a staff officer. He was a diplomat in his field, polished and attractive, and a warm friendship appears to have developed between him and the president, though it was not one that changed Johnson's course. While trusting individual military officers, Johnson retained a good deal of skepticism about the military bureaucracy and the fact that it resorted to military power for solutions.

As special assistant to the president for national security affairs, McGeorge Bundy had a thriving shop by the time of the Johnson administration. He had about a dozen professionals working for him, including two very able public servants, Chester L. Cooper and Michael V. Forrestal, son of James V. Forrestal, the first secretary of defense.* Bundy and his staff coordinated a great deal of material, including intelligence, for Johnson. A crisp, articulate former Harvard dean who did not leave all the mannerisms of the deanery behind him in Cambridge, Bundy made fact-finding trips to Vietnam.

---

* In the Truman administration in 1947 the Department of Defense was established to consolidate the old War and Navy Departments and the newly formed Department of the Air Force.

He wrote numerous memorandums to Johnson, advised him, kept him abreast of options being discussed, and suggested which options the president might prefer. Bundy was one of the principals in making war policy, a man who favored defending South Vietnam with the commitment of troops and bombers to compel the North to negotiate.

When Bundy resigned in February 1966, he was succeeded by Walt Rostow, a former professor of economics at the Massachusetts Institute of Technology and no less articulate than his predecessor. In the worst of situations Rostow could see the light at the end of the tunnel when few others could even find the tunnel. Said McPherson,

> Walt has a kind of rugby player's view of a lot of international events. It's sort of a "pull up your socks—let's get going, let's put our shoulder to the wheel, let's bow our necks and it's going to be okay" point of view. You feel, for God's sake . . . that he's not aware of the degree of shake and shiver in the situation. . . .[41]

Rostow had little trouble getting Johnson's ear. The best measure of Rostow's hawkishness may have been his word of caution to Johnson one day that Henry Kissinger "may go a little soft when you get down to the crunch."[42]

By and large, the members of the Tuesday luncheon group were the president, the secretaries of state and defense, the chairman of the JCS, the director of Central Intelligence, the special assistant to the president for national security affairs, the White House press secretary, and Tom Johnson of the White House staff, who took notes on the discussions. "It was there," Wheeler recalled, "that we thrashed out . . . the details of and the decisions as to what was going to be done in regard to the war in Vietnam. . . . It was from these meetings, I think that [Lyndon Johnson] derived the information that gave him the bases for many of the decisions that he took."[43] Illustrative of the fundamentals in which Johnson dealt at the luncheons was the fact that Wheeler usually brought maps showing the targets the military wished to bomb in North Vietnam. Johnson insisted on approving each target, when it would be hit, and with what kind of bombs, just as he decided how many troops would be sent, regardless of what the military recommended. He always kept such tight control over targets in North Vietnam that he said "they can't even bomb an outhouse without my approval."[44] "He placed political constraints on the war," wrote Schandler, "in effect determining strategic guidance himself."[45]

The role did not rest easily on Johnson. Sometimes he lashed out at his tormentors, as when, speaking at a Democratic dinner in Chicago on May 17, 1966, he lambasted "nervous Nellies." At other times he muttered. Or grumbled. Or snarled. Or cried out in anguish. Or bellowed. Flashlight in hand, he wandered through darkened White House corridors in the middle of the night, passing to and from the situation room in the basement for a check on the results of bombing raids on targets he had approved and on the fate of bombing crews. He recalled instances in which he awoke spontaneously at the precise hour he knew bombers would be over a certain target. "He felt a deep responsibility for the wounded and the dead," Reedy said, "and translated this into a determination that their suffering should not be in vain. To him, this meant that the United States had to 'win' in order to vindicate its casualties. . . ."[46] At breakfast, when he was visiting the White House, Sam Houston Johnson, the president's brother, said that he could tell by Lyndon's appearance when the night's news had been bad. "There would be dark hollows under his eyes, his face appeared somewhat gray and drawn, his shoulders slumped forward, his voice was slightly raspy."[47] On June 24, 1965, Johnson made a night flight from Washington to speak in San Francisco at the commemoration of the twentieth anniversary of the founding of the United Nations. He invited several legislators on the trip, including Senator Church as chairman of a subcommittee concerned with United Nations affairs. Presently, an aide brought the president a radio message. Johnson read it, flushed, and threw it across the desk at Church, who had recently made an appeal in the Senate for negotiations instead of bombing. The message reported the death of some American soldiers in Saigon from plastic bombs.

"What would you do?" Johnson demanded of Church. "I suppose you would turn the other cheek."

"Mr. President, I am as shocked and disturbed as I know you are," Church said, later recalling the incident. "After all, we are the ones who sent those Americans out there. American bombers are dropping napalm on families, and they have no way to reply. I suppose if I were one of them, I would fight back any way I could, including using plastic bombs."

Johnson turned his back on Church. The next day a photographer lined up all of the president's guests except Church on the plane for a photograph. The senator had gone off to another part of the cabin by himself. "Come on, Frank," Johnson summoned him. "I think it would be good for me to have my picture taken with a peacenik."

Church was quick to add later that the incident showed only one side of Johnson. At one of their next meetings in the White House, Johnson gently escorted him around the Truman balcony for a view of the gardens. "He either put his arms around you and squeezed the air out of you or he relegated you to the dungeon," Church said.[48] Johnson was wracked by the frustrations of Vietnam. "I can't get out," he once exclaimed to his wife in 1966. "I can't finish it with what I've got. So what the hell can I do?[49]

Month in and month out, he directed tirades at newspapers, magazines, and television. At a meeting in the White House in 1965 attended by, among others, Barry Zorthian and Frank Stanton, president of CBS, Johnson piled abuse on Stanton, who was his friend. According to Zorthian, Johnson was infuriated by a CBS news report from Vietnam by Morley Safer that showed Americans in the field setting fire to a Vietnamese hut with a Zippo cigarette lighter. In Stanton's presence, Johnson questioned the loyalty of Safer and other CBS correspondents and threatened to make public derogatory information about them. When asked whether Johnson attributed Communist backing to American reporters, Zorthian replied, "Oh, yes. He'd just fulminate against them he'd get so goddamned mad."

On another occasion when Zorthian was in Washington for consultations, he was summoned to the president's bedroom after lunch. As he often did, Johnson had put on his pajama top and gone to bed to take a nap before starting what he called his "second day" in a twenty-four-hour period. When Zorthian entered, Johnson began thundering against the news media and demanding to know why Zorthian, who had no authority to take such action, did not prevent reporters in Saigon from filing the things they filed. Johnson would not stop talking to listen to whatever Zorthian might have had to say.

Recalled Zorthian,

But in the middle of this monologue—nonstop monologue—[he] threw off his bedcovers, got out of bed, walked around the room, not missing one word—he still kept talking—walked over to the john where the door was open, left it open, relieved himself loudly, still talking, came back, got into bed, put the covers over him again, never stopped talking. And all the talk was about the press.[50]

No chart can depict how Johnson was briefed on the war. He was on the telephone incessantly, day and night, to senators, cabinet officers, generals, and, as he once recalled, "some little fella tucked away in one of those agencies."[51] He surrounded himself with news tickers, televsion sets, maps, captured documents, and reports that must have run into the thousands, which he demanded around the clock from exasperated military officers. Their despair did not bother him in the least. "If they can sit around and talk to newspapermen," he's known to have said, "they can keep their president informed."[52] Johnson's obsessive need for a continuing flow of information of all shades of importance was fueled in part by his intolerance of being surprised by any development of any kind.

The year 1965 had witnessed a proliferation of teach-ins at colleges across the country, in which opposition to the war was cultivated quietly but effectively. It was the year of a form of protest that was startling to older Americans who had lived through two world wars and the Korean War without having seen anything like it. Draft cards had been burned by many men of military age. The White House was enmeshed in threads of criticism being spun by emerging schools of thought. One, for example, cautioned that the economy was approaching capacity, raising the prospect of shortages in certain skills and materials and thus suggesting the need for economic controls, which were abhorrent to Johnson. Another held that between the war and the Great Society, the American economy was already overextended and could not withstand further military escalation. In that connection, severe inflation in South Vietnam, stimulated by the deluge of American dollars, aroused concern in Washington that South Vietnamese society might disintegrate. The situation militated against deployment of as many more troops as Westmoreland wanted.

The year did not end without reminders that twenty-four months earlier McNamara had said that December 1965 would be the point at which the major part of the American military task in Vietnam would be completed. Instead, 184,300 Americans were in Vietnam, and McNamara proposed a still greater buildup. In a memorandum to Johnson on December 7 he recommended a total of 400,000 servicemen to be in the field by the end of 1966 and warned that another 200,000 might be needed in 1967. Even then success would not be assured. As the number of American troops rose, he said, the North Vietnamese, regarding "their own staying power . . . superior to ours," would increase their forces proportionately.[53] Characteristically, the president agreed to send fewer men than the Pentagon had requested—385,500 were to be in the field by the end of 1966 and 425,000 by the end of June 1967.

Johnson's troubles were coming in battalions. In the *Washington Post* of December 5, 1965, Murrey Marder wrote: "Creeping signs of doubt and cynicism about Administration pronouncements, especially in its foreign policy, are privately troubling some of the Government's usually stalwart supporters. The problem could be called a credibility gap." A new term had been introduced into the language—one that, upon endless repetition, drove Johnson wild. "To touch Johnson off," said his assistant John Roche later, "just mention the word credibility. [H]e would go right up the wall. Bang! Just like that. Gone! Vanished!"[54]

The friendly relationship that had developed between the influential columnist Walter Lippmann and Johnson after the latter became president collapsed during 1965 over Johnson's war policy. Lippmann now wrote trenchant antiwar articles and urged his friend George Ball to resign and denounce Johnson's course in Vietnam. Instead, Ball departed quietly in the fall of 1966.

In November and December 1965, the First Cavalry, back in action on the Asian mainland again after fifteen years, this time riding to combat in helicopters, fought a battle in the Ia Drang Valley. As was usually to be the case, the "kill ratio" was in favor of the Americans. Still, more than three hundred of them died. Typical of what was in store, not much was changed by the action. The reality of the war was caught by McNamara's friend and most influential adviser, Assistant Secretary of Defense John McNaughton, a former Rhodes Scholar and graduate of Harvard Law School who afterward became a Harvard law professor. "We have in Vietnam," McNaughton wrote at the time, "the ingredients of an enormous miscalculation." What was being "escalated" was military stalemate, said McNaughton, once an advocate of a military buildup. The American objective in the war had degenerated, in his words, to one of avoiding humiliation, of preserving the United States' reputation as a guarantor of an ally's security.[55] More significantly, doubts had begun to assail Robert McNamara himself, particularly on the effectiveness of the American air offensive but, beyond that, on the ultimate question of whether the United States military effort could bring Ho Chi Minh to terms.

While the 173rd Airborne Brigade units and the First Infantry Division were in action in Hua Nghia and Binh Tuong provinces, Johnson went before a joint session of Congress on January 12, 1966, to deliver his State of the Union message. He conceded that the cost of the war was such that the administration could not do "all that we would like to do." But, he added, "I believe that we can continue the Great Society while we fight in Vietnam."[56] A fortnight later William Fulbright, former friend turned archcritic, used his position as chairman of the Senate Foreign Relations Committee to turn hearings on a foreign aid authorization for South Vietnam into a debate on the war. Part of the hearings were televised nationally and hence were an effective vehicle for airing dissent. George F. Kennan, a distinguished former diplomat, testified that the United States should liquidate its military involvement in Vietnam "as soon as this can be done without inordinate damage to our own prestige or to the stability . . . in the area." The tone of the hearings reflected some of the burgeoning hostility to Johnson's war policies in the Senate. In an exchange with General Taylor, Senator Morse predicted that "it isn't going to be too long before the American people as a people will repudiate our war in Southeast Asia." That would be good news for Hanoi, Taylor observed. "I knew," Morse retorted, "that that is the smear artist that you militarists give to those of us who have honest differences of opinion with you, but I don't intend to get down in the gutter with you to engage in that kind of debate, General."[57]

In the midst of the hearings, Johnson suddenly called a press conference on February 4 and announced that he was about to leave for Honolulu to confer with the leaders of South Vietnam. He had talked with his assistants earlier about such a meeting, but his hasty announcement plunged them into helter-skelter planning. For the

next few days Hawaii became the stage for one of the great side-
shows of the world that season, starring the president of the United
States, who towered in height over the chief of state and the prime
minister of South Vietnam—respectively, General Nguyen Van
Thieu and Air Vice-Marshall Nguyen Cao Ky. Johnson's performance of course grabbed the top headlines from Fulbright, as the
president began the occasion with a thinly disguised attack on General James M. Gavin (ret.), former airborne commander, director of
war plans and operations for the army, and United States ambassador to France. Now a business executive, Gavin had indicated in
the February 1966 issue of *Harper's* that the United States ought to
return to an enclave strategy in Vietnam. Johnson branded the suggestion a "retreat."

The Honolulu conference concentrated largely on a plan of
Johnson's for luring all Vietnamese away from hostilities by extending Great Society benefits to their country, as Texas had been en-
riched by dams, irrigation, and rural electrification during the New
Deal. Nearly a year earlier in his Johns Hopkins speech, Johnson
had said that he was willing to ask Congress for a billion dollars to
start a Mekong River hydroelectric development "on a scale to dwarf
even our own TVA."[58] The undertaking, Frances FitzGerald wrote,
would have been "the greatest piece of pork barrel legislation in
history—except that the Mekong River does not run through North
Vietnam. But perhaps that could be fixed, too."[59] Such thoughts did
not diminish Johnson's hopes. "Uncle Ho can't turn that down," he
told his assistant Bill D. Moyers on the flight back to Washington.[60]

The Hawaiian respite was brief. Hard decisions awaited Johnson
in Washington. The Joint Chiefs of Staff, frustrated by political restraints against dispatch of the troops they thought they needed,
pleaded for more than Johnson had recently approved. Reluctantly,
he met them halfway. Doubts were assailing his advisers. For a
meeting of a group of them on April 16 William Bundy presented
the draft of a paper that read, in part:

> As we look a year or two ahead, with a military program that
> would require major further budget costs—with all their im-
> plications for taxes and domestic programs—and with steady or
> probably rising casualties, the war could well become an al-
> batross around the Administration's neck at least equal to what
> Korea was for President Truman in 1952.[61]

The albatross was overhead again in a few weeks when the disappointing progress of the war brought recommendations from the military for expansion of Rolling Thunder, despite pessimistic CIA forecasts as to its effectiveness. In June 1966 Johnson yielded and authorized the bombing of oil tanks in the Hanoi-Haiphong area. As controversy over bombing continued to spread, he intimated at a press conference on June 18 that public criticism in the United States was encouraging Hanoi to persevere. Chester Bowles, United States ambassador to India, called on him in the summer of 1966 while on home leave. "Literally half our time together," Bowles wrote later, "was taken up by almost paranoic references to Bobby Kennedy, Wayne Morse, Bill Fulbright and others." Bowles thought that Johnson was "headed for deep trouble, with the probability of an increasing obsession with his 'enemies.'"62

Johnson relished referring to Fulbright as "Half-bright." The senator, a former Rhodes Scholar and former president of the University of Arkansas, had fared worse under Truman, who became so irate at him for investigating alleged improprieties in the Truman administration that he referred to him as an "overeducated s.o.b." As for Bobby Kennedy, Johnson in charitable moods called him an "upstart." In the previous administration Kennedy had taken no large part in his brother's policies on Vietnam, but he was in favor of them. After Dallas he did not seem to dwell on the war until he was disturbed by the beginning of Rolling Thunder in the spring of 1965 and sensed a change in the political mood of the country. In April of that year Kennedy, then a United States senator from New York, called on Johnson and urged a bombing pause. Johnson said he had been considering one and did institute a pause in May, but only briefly, because Hanoi did not respond. By the time of the Fulbright hearings several months later, Kennedy was fully aroused about the war. Veering from his late brother's course, he issued various comments and suggestions about a settlement that angered Johnson. "Bobby wouldn't be talking that way," he complained to Chalmers M. Roberts of the *Washington Post*, "if Jack Kennedy were still president. I kept faith with Jack Kennedy on Vietnam."63 Such tolerance as lingered in the Johnson–Bobby Kennedy relationship was shattered early in 1967 by an otherwise unimportant incident.

Invited to England to deliver an address, Kennedy extended his stay to confer with British Prime Minister Harold Wilson and, on the Continent, with Charles de Gaulle, German chancellor Kurt Kiesinger, Pope Paul VI, and other leaders. Johnson, in the midst of frustration over dead-end probes for a formula to persuade Hanoi to negotiate, was annoyed no end by the well-publicized excursion. Annoyance does not describe what happened next. While in Paris, Kennedy, accompanied by a United States embassy official, talked with Etienne Manac'h, director of Far Eastern affairs in the French foreign ministry. Manac'h related that the head of the North Vietnamese mission in Paris had made a statement to him that seemed to soften Hanoi's previous conditions for negotiations. Kennedy merely listened, then moved on in his journey, while the American diplomat cabled the gist of the Manac'h report to the State Department. The cable was leaked to *Newsweek*, and the way the story came out, loudly, in the press was that Hanoi had directed a peace feeler to Bobby Kennedy while Lyndon Johnson sat in the dark in the White House.

Returning from Europe, in February, Kennedy felt obliged to pay what is known in Washington as a courtesy call on the president, however inappropriate the description in that case. *Time* afterward reported that Johnson called Kennedy a son of a bitch to his face. The story, apparently, was wrong in detail but not in spirit. Kennedy later gave members of his staff the following account of the meeting. Kennedy told Johnson that he had not been aware of any peace feeler—the report had been leaked by Johnson's own State Department. Johnson thundered, "It's not *my* State Department, God damn it. It's *your* State Department." Johnson declared that the war would be over by June or July. Then he said, "I'll destroy you and every one of your dove friends [mentioning Fulbright, Church, and some others] in six months. You'll be dead politically in six months!" Johnson shouted, Kennedy said. Kennedy volunteered an opinion as to what should be done, the steps to include a halt in the bombing, a cease-fire by stages, and permission for the NLF to participate in the choice of a new government in Saigon. "There just isn't a chance in hell that I will do that," Johnson snapped, according to Kennedy's account. Johnson went on to say that Kennedy and his friends were responsible for the prolongation of the war and American deaths in Vietnam. "Look," Kennedy remembered having said, "I don't have to take that from you." Finally the storm blew itself out and Kennedy departed.[64]

At the time Johnson was little moved by the noisy showmanship of hippies, radicals, campus vandals, and draft-card burners who, whatever the degree of their idealism, were patently as much a special-interest group acting to avoid Selective Service, retain graduate school deferments, and so on, as any other special-interest group. Quietly and secretly, however, a small company of intellectuals not identified with campus protests did in the course of 1966 effectively reinforce McNamara's growing doubts about the war, with results that were to ripple throughout the remainder of the administration.

In March 1966 two Harvard scientists, Dr. George B. Kistia-kowsky, formerly science adviser to President Eisenhower, Dr. Carl Kaysen, and two MIT professors, Dr. Jerome B. Wiesner, former science adviser to President Kennedy, and Dr. Jerrold R. Zacharias, suggested to McNamara a seminar of scientists and academic specialists to study technical aspects of the war. McNamara agreed to provide necessary information to the group, which included scientists who had contributed to the development of the country's most advanced weapons systems since the end of the Second World War. After meetings throughout the summer in Wellesley, Massachusetts, under the auspices of the Institute for Defense Analysis, a think tank serving the Pentagon, the group submitted a report to McNamara on August 29.

It found that American bombing of North Vietnam had had "no measurable direct effect on Hanoi's ability to mount and support military operations in the South at the current level." Even if the administration had not exerted political restraints on the scope of the bombing, the air offensive would not have won the war because "North Vietnam has basically a subsistence agricultural economy that presents a difficult and unrewarding target system for air attack," the report said. Little of military value was produced by North Vietnam's industry. Most of the essential supplies for the Communist forces were "provided by the USSR and Communist China."

Neither intensifying the bombing nor mining Haiphong Harbor and other North Vietnamese ports would remedy the situation, the report said. The scientists challenged the administration's assumptions that bombing would convince Hanoi that its losses would exceed its possible gains and hence impel Ho Chi Minh to a peace conference. The report held that "there is currently no adequate basis for predicting the levels of U.S. military effort that would be required to achieve the stated objectives—indeed there is no firm basis for determining if there is *any* feasible level of effort that would achieve these objectives."[65]

McNamara, protagonist and architect of the early military commitment, returned to Saigon for an assessment in October, 1966. Popularly regarded as a human computer, he was, and is, a man of great breadth of mind, civility, and grasp of the troubles afflicting the human race in the twentieth century. He was endowed with a microchip memory and a capacity for absorbing technological and scientific data. President Kennedy had given him unprecedented authority over the American missile buildup of the early 1960s. The nub of contemporary criticism of McNamara was that he used quantitative techniques of systems analysis to arrive at conclusions in matters involving the spirit and motivations of the North Vietnamese that were not susceptible to such methods. Yet he was an independent thinker and not given to self-delusion. When he went to Vietnam this time, he was sobered by what he learned, and his report to Johnson on October 14 reflected it.

In a pessimistic vein, McNamara suggested that the number of American forces in Vietnam should be leveled off for the long haul at 470,000, which was 100,000 fewer than the military was requesting. He proposed stabilizing Rolling Thunder at its existing intensity and even suggested consideration of halting all bombing of the North, if, after careful judgment, such a course seemed to offer hope of drawing Hanoi into negotiations. On the other hand, he foresaw little chance of ending the war on satisfactory terms for the next two years. He urged concentration on defense in order to help the South Vietnamese to rally. He did not think the current bombing was accomplishing much. He pictured South Vietnam, high and low, as being awash in corruption. After having tried for years to enlist the full support of the South Vietnamese against Communist inroads, the United States was, if anything, losing ground in the attempt, as McNamara saw it. He proposed that a barrier, partly electronic, be built near the 17th parallel and across the trails in Laos to curb enemy infiltration and thereby lessen the need for more American troops.[66] At the base of McNamara's discouragement was the capability of the enemy to continue building up forces in the South despite the bombing and American ground operations.

When his report was shown to the Joint Chiefs of Staff, they would not swallow it, especially the proposed ceiling of 470,000 troops. The chiefs had little faith in an electronic barrier and defended bombing as a "trump card" for bringing Hanoi to negotiations. They were still resentful of the constraints that had prevented them from bombing with full force when America took over the war in 1965.[67]

Thus the conflict around Johnson continued. He made no significant change in strategy at the moment. The same war went on. The First Cavalry began a forty-day search-and-destroy operation in Binh Dinh province. The 196th Brigade launched a large search-and-destroy operation in Tay Minh province. Elements of the Fourth and Twenty-fifth Infantry divisions and the First Cavalry opened a seventy-two-day operation in Pleiku province. No claims were made that these actions were decisive.

Johnson flew to Manila in late October, shortly before the 1966 American congressional elections, to confer with what he once termed "my prime ministers"—leaders of Asian and Pacific nations that had modest forces helping the South's cause in Vietnam. These nations were South Korea, Australia, New Zealand, the Philippines, and Thailand. The president saw to it that the communiqué pledged that allied forces would be removed from Vietnam "not later than six months" after Hanoi "withdraws its forces to the North, and ceases infiltration, and as the level of violence thus subsides." The Democrats retained control of Congress in the elections, while losing forty-seven seats in the House, a high yet not abnormal figure for off-years. During the conference Johnson flew to the American base at Camranh Bay, South Vietnam, for a review of troops and an officers' club reception. There he had to say something. He wished his hosts good luck and told them to nail the coonskin to the wall. Thereafter, it was obligatory for members of the antiwar movement to shudder upon hearing an allusion to coonskins.

The predicament in which Johnson found himself at the start of 1967 was a classic case of a president left to conduct a war without a substantially united country behind him. While, until well into 1967, a majority of the public continued to approve of his policy in Vietnam, it was a cool majority that provided a thin shield against the heat of antiwar sentiment. Johnson was working without a solid mandate. Perhaps even if he had attained one through a declaration of war by Congress, it would have eroded under the stress of Vietnam. However, the lack of strong, broad support now, nearly three years after the Gulf of Tonkin, with no end of the war yet in prospect, had a paralyzing effect. Caught in a fierce crossfire between hawks and doves, Johnson was unable to move decisively in any direction. The wearying president was running a government wracked by internal conflicts, particularly the ever-widening differences between the secretary of defense and the JCS, and external quarrels, centering on a counterattack by the Right in Congress against liberal antiwar influences.

The occasion for renewed internal turmoil rose on March 18, 1967, when, in hope of bringing the war to an end in two more years, Westmoreland asked for 200,000 new troops over and above the existing ceiling of 470,000. The field commander came to the United States and, accompanied by General Wheeler, called on the president to solicit his approval. "When we add divisions," Johnson asked, "can't the enemy add divisions? If so, where does that leave us?"[68] The manpower situation had reached the point where implicit in Westmoreland's request was a requirement that the reserves be mobilized.

William Bundy quickly spotted trouble: A call-up would ignite, he said, "a truly major debate in Congress." With dissent spreading, "we should not get into such a debate this summer."[69]

The situation in the Pentagon was extraordinary. The highest civilian official, McNamara, drifting deeper into discouragement over the war, moved farther and farther from the thinking of the highest uniformed officers, the Joint Chiefs of Staff. Hence the president was getting divided counsel on the prosecution of the war. McNamara, for example, was opposed to Westmoreland's request for troops; the secretary of defense favored 30,000 more troops, not 200,000 more.

Then, on May 19, McNamara showed Johnson a draft memorandum he had prepared that was drastic and controversial and seems to have caused downright alarm among the chiefs. The secretary recommended a deflation of American war aims and a willingness to accept a coalition government in Saigon, including non-Communist members of the NLF. Pricking a live nerve in the military and their hawkish friends in Congress, he proposed a further limitation on the bombing of the North. His idea was to concentrate air attacks on infiltration routes below the 20th parallel in North Vietnam (an "aerial Dien Bien Phu," Wheeler protested). McNamara based his proposal partly on the heavy losses of American pilots and planes in operations over the Hanoi-Haiphong area above the 20th parallel. He also said:

> [A]n important but hard-to-measure cost is domestic and world opinion: There may be a limit beyond which many Americans and much of the world will not permit the United States to go. The picture of the world's greatest superpower killing or seriously injuring 1,000 noncombatants a week, while trying to pound a tiny backward nation into submission . . . is not a pretty one.[70]

McNamara recommended that, as soon as feasible, the United States "move" the Saigon government toward a political settlement with non-Communist members of the NLF in search of accommodation and a cease-fire. Such persons would be accepted as members of an opposition political party and, if necessary, as individual participants in the Saigon government—"in sum, a settlement to transform the members of the [NLF] from military opponents to political opponents," McNamara said.[71]

When Bobby Kennedy had suggested in February 1966 that the NLF be admitted to a share of the political process in Saigon, the Johnson administration was so angry that Vice-President Humphrey publicly likened the proposal to "putting a fox in the chicken coop." And, as noted, when Kennedy a year later recommended to Johnson during their row over the Manac'h affair that the NLF be allowed to participate in the choice of the Saigon government, Johnson retorted that there was not a "chance in hell" that he would agree to it.

McNamara's ideas on a coalition were not accepted by Johnson. The fact that Kennedy had suggested something along the same lines was not likely to have been the main barrier. The basic policy of the Johnson administration, echoing the aspirations of Eisenhower and John Kennedy, had been enunciated in NSAM 288, of March 17, 1964: "We seek an independent non-Communist Vietnam."[72] For Johnson to have consented to a coalition, including members of the Hanoi-supported NLF, would have been politically treacherous. All that apart, Johnson seems to have resented McNamara's continuing warm and close friendship with the Kennedys. While acknowledging McNamara's loyalty to him, Johnson told Doris Kearns afterward that the secretary was more the Kennedys' "cup of tea."[73]

As for troops, Johnson still clung to the middle of the road rejecting McNamara's and Westmoreland's proposals. He agreed to raise the authorized level from 470,000 to 525,000—outrageously too high to the doves and dismayingly low to the hawks, some of whom suspected that Johnson was yielding to concerns about world opinion. The very thought of it exasperated them. Representative L. Mendel Rivers, a Democrat from South Carolina and chairman of the House Armed Services Committee, had already demanded that the administration "flatten Hanoi, if necessary, and let world opinion go fly a kite."[74] Where Johnson encountered most serious resistance, however, was in the Senate Armed Services Committee, or rather its Preparedness subcommittee, both chaired by the powerful Senator John C. Stennis, a Democrat from Mississippi.

Since the Second World War, military and congressional advocates of air power, backed by a wealthy air lobby, had been a moving force in Washington. The Preparedness subcommittee was loaded with senatorial advocates of increased bombing, among them a kingpin, Senator W. Stuart Symington, a Democrat from Missouri whom Truman had appointed as the first secretary of the air force in 1947. For months the Pentagon had fed the subcommittee complaints about political restrictions on air operations in Vietnam. Ever-louder rumbles had been coming from Stennis. Then he counterattacked. In August, three months after the McNamara memorandum, the senator called hearings and scheduled testimony by the hierarchy of officers concerned with the use of air power in Vietnam. At least from the start of the Second World War through the time of the Stennis hearings, Congress was impressed, in some cases awed, by and brimming with cordiality toward the Joint Chiefs of Staff. No one knew better than Lyndon Johnson as a former member of the Senate Armed Services Committee the latent power in Congress for brewing a storm over a politically imposed, inadequate usage of American military power in the war. The danger that the hearings might trigger it was not inconsiderable. Some of the dissatisfied legislators, Johnson wrote afterward, "held key positions in Congress, and we needed their backing. . . . I knew that a unilateral bombing halt would run into fierce opposition from these powerful men. . . ."[75]

On the day the hearings opened, August 9, 1967, Johnson rejected McNamara's recommendations for new limits on bombing and approved a wider range of targets, six of them within a theretofore forbidden area encircling Hanoi. Nine others were on the northeast rail line in the so-called China buffer zone, only eight miles from the Chinese border.[76]

The hearings were held in executive session, but the testimony was released promptly and made big news, giving the public for the first time a perspective on the differences between the secretary of defense and the Joint Chiefs of Staff. The witnesses in uniform provided an encouraging account of what air power had supposedly accomplished in the war already. They attacked the "doctrine of gradualism" and assured senators that the bombing could have been much more effective if civilian officials had accepted professional military advice and lifted restrictions. Then came McNamara's crackling reply.

The cost of bombers lost in raids, he said, was three times that of the value of enemy property destroyed. Despite the bombing, more enemy trucks were operating than before, more traffic was moving along roads, more roads had been built. Air attacks had had negligible effect on the rate of enemy infiltration into South Vietnam. The most important targets remaining were Haiphong Harbor and two other ports. But, McNamara argued, even if they were attacked at the risk of sinking Soviet shipping, enemy supplies could be brought in aboard lighters along four hundred miles of North Vietnamese coast or overland across the five hundred miles of border between North Vietnam and China.

"The bombing of North Vietnam," he said, "has always been considered a supplement to and not a substitute for an effective counterinsurgency land and air campaign in South Vietnam."

To the anger of the hawks, McNamara had simply blown away the dreams of Capitol Hill that the war would be rather cheaply won by air power. The subcommittee issued its report on August 31, 1967. Noting the conflicting views between McNamara and the JCS as to whether Haiphong Harbor could be closed effectively by air power, the report contained a message for Johnson. Calling for "hard-hitting" military tactics, it said:

As between these diametrically opposed views, and in view of the unsatisfactory progress of the war, logic and prudence requires [sic] that the decision be with the unanimous weight of professional military judgment.

It is not our intention to point a finger or to second guess those who determined this [current] policy. But the cold fact is that this policy has not done the job and it has been contrary to the best military judgment. What is needed now is the hard decision to do whatever is necessary, take the risks that have to be taken, and apply the force that is required to see the job through.[77]

Johnson called a press conference on September 1, the day after the Stennis report, and lauded the chiefs. He said that while they, McNamara, Rusk, and Johnson "are not in complete agreement on everything, there is no deep division."[78] Johnson was in a tough mood that summer of 1967. Henry Kissinger, who was advising the administration on the quest for negotiations with the enemy, later related to Arthur Schlesinger, Jr., a scene in the cabinet room, in which Johnson kept asking McNamara, "How can I hit them in the nuts? Tell me how I can hit them in the nuts?"[79] One target that had figured in the hearings was Cam Pha, the third-largest port in North Vietnam. Against the advice of the military, McNamara opposed bombing it. Ten days after hailing the JCS at his press conference for having "acted very ably," Johnson approved the bombing of Cam Pha.[80]

At the end of October 1967, according to Johnson, McNamara told him that to go on as they had been in Vietnam would be dangerous. Johnson asked him for a memorandum on the subject, which McNamara submitted on November 1. The secretary questioned whether, with rising costs and casualties and slow progress at best, "it will be possible to maintain our efforts in South Vietnam for the time necessary to accomplish our objectives. . . ." McNamara, therefore, proposed, among other things, a halt in all bombing of the North by the end of 1967. Hanoi's position was that no negotiations could take place until the bombing of North Vietnam had ceased unconditionally.

"We would hope," McNamara said, "for a response from Hanoi, by some parallel reduction in its offensive activity, by a movement toward talks, or both."

Johnson solicited comments on the memorandum from Rostow, Taylor, Fortas, Clifford, and Rusk. In varying degrees they opposed an unconditional halt in bombing. Johnson agreed with their advice. Essentially, he feared that a bombing halt would be interpreted "in both Hanoi and the United States as a sign of weakening will. It would encourage the extreme doves; increase the pressure for withdrawal from those who argue 'bomb and get out;' decrease support from our most steady friends; and pick up support from only a small group of moderate doves."[81]

Suddenly, on November 28, the news broke in London that Johnson had nominated McNamara as president of the International Bank for Reconstruction and Development (World Bank) and would name a new secretary of defense. To the American public the word came as a surprise and a sensation. Bobby Kennedy rushed to the Pentagon. His friends and followers, who regarded McNamara as a shining figure, were beside themselves. Many of them interpreted McNamara's fate as signifying that Johnson had deposed him to clear the way for a new escalation of the war. The interpretation was not necessarily correct.

Along with the proposal for a bombing halt, McNamara had recommended in his memorandum certain alternative moderating measures. He urged stabilization of American military operations in South Vietnam; no new ground forces beyond the level already approved would be sent. In that connection, he wanted the South Vietnamese to be given a greater responsibility for their own security. If bombing of the North were not halted, he advocated at least holding air operations at the existing intensity. Johnson said that those proposals struck him as cogent. He did not, he said in a memorandum for the record six weeks later, want to announce a policy of stabilization, lest it signal a weakening will. On the other hand, "at the moment I see no basis for increasing U.S. forces above the current approved level." He still opposed an American invasion of North Vietnam. While continuing to bomb the North, he would scrutinize significant military targets so that air strikes "would not involve excessive civilian casualties, excessive U.S. losses, or substantial increased risk of engaging the USSR or Communist China in the war. . . ."

McNamara's memorandum and Johnson's response foreshadowed, with variations, many elements of the policy Johnson was to follow in Vietnam for the remainder of his term.

What words were exchanged when Johnson and McNamara finally came to a parting of the ways will probably never be known. Johnson is dead, and McNamara cannot recall whether he ever said, "I quit," or Johnson ever said, "You're fired." One of the standard interpretations is that their relationship finally foundered on the

Stennis hearings, during which McNamara did not submit his testimony to the White House for clearance. McNamara did not sense that the hearings exacerbated his relations with Johnson. He saw no point in having his testimony approved, because he had said the same things countless times in White House conferences. He was clear in his own mind that the president's power came from the people, that a cabinet officer had no power of his own, serving only at the will of the president. McNamara believed that once he disagreed with Johnson, the proper and honorable thing to do was resign. He felt that it would be wrong for him to persist in making things difficult for Johnson after Johnson had decided on a policy and equally wrong to try to use his own influence in Washington to bring pressure on Johnson to change that policy.

As the differences between McNamara and the chiefs increased throughout 1967, Mcnamara made no attempt to hide them in the councils of the government. Decision making became more difficult for all concerned, not the least for Johnson, who could anticipate McNamara's dissent. McNamara was simply convinced that too much was being asked of military power in the Vietnamese morass. He was convinced that the United States could not win a military victory there, that it could not weaken the will of the North Vietnamese or substantially reduce their capacity to make war, least of all by bombing, which was costly in lives and money. Mainly, McNamara was concerned with how military operations might be fashioned to facilitate diplomacy. Under that broad subject was the question of what military tactics would be most effective. For months, every time the matter of targets came up, these issues were hashed over and rehashed until the situation became very difficult for Johnson and McNamara. Long friendship and mutual respect had thrived between them, but now both were unhappy over their impasse. McNamara stayed into the fall, feeling that he should leave yet reluctant to go with the war in the state it was in.

In the nuclear age the position of secretary of defense is one of the world's most difficult jobs. McNamara had held it for six and a half years by midsummer of 1967. He was nearly exhausted, perhaps in danger of a breakdown. His wife was ill in a hospital. Johnson was worried about McNamara's health and reminded members of his staff how Secretary of Defense James Forrestal had gone to pieces in 1949, finally committing suicide. The time had come when Johnson, too, was ready for a change at the Pentagon. As much as he trusted McNamara, he distrusted a group of high-ranking advisers to the secretary, all with Ivy League backgrounds or connections. Among them were McNaughton, Paul C. Warnke, successor to McNaughton as assistant secretary of defense for international security affairs and later law partner of Clark Clifford, Adam Yarmolinsky, deputy assistant secretary of defense for international security affairs, and Alain Enthoven, assistant secretary of defense for systems analysis. In his previously mentioned post-presidential interview with Jorden, Johnson explained, "I thought all of them were pretty soft." Doubtless, the meaning of this is that all of them became skeptical of the war.

Late one summer afternoon in 1967 Johnson and McNamara had a drink together in the sitting room off the Oval Office. As he had before, Johnson asked McNamara what he wanted in life. Johnson let McNamara know that he felt he owed him a good deal for his loyalty and labor, as well as for some difficult chores McNamara had, with his business background, done for the president in respect to policy outside the Pentagon. The presidency of the World Bank was to be open soon. McNamara wanted it. Johnson had known that, and the subject came up again in the sitting room. McNamara never thought that differences between him and Johnson on the war were personal. Johnson could easily have given the prestigious World Bank nomination to someone else. He had other loyal friends and advisers who coveted it. Historically, the bank presidency had been held by an American. When it came time for nominations, Secretary of the Treasury Henry H. Fowler asked the president for his choices. His choice, Johnson said, was McNamara. Fowler reminded the president that it had been customary to recommend three Americans to the bank. "McNamara, McNamara, and McNamara," Johnson replied.[82] McNamara was aware of what was going on. He remained at his post in the Pentagon until February 19, 1968.

The day McNamara's resignation was announced, Chalmers Roberts and Benjamin C. Bradlee of the *Washington Post* were in Johnson's office at the moment when McNamara happened to call. They could not hear what McNamara said, but they heard Johnson reply, "Yes, Bob, I'm sitting here with tears in my eyes, too." "LBJ," Roberts wrote afterward, "was as dry-eyed as any human being could be."[83]

In the fall of 1967 the country was permeated by rising doubts about the war. For what was to prove a very stiff price, Johnson set about to dampen them.

On November 13, Ellsworth Bunker, then United States ambassador to Saigon, called on Johnson and later told reporters that 67 percent of the population of South Vietnam was under the control of the South Vietnamese government. At his own press conference four days later, Johnson heartily expressed his pleasure with the "progress" that was being made. Recalling Eisenhower's pledge to Diem in 1954, he said:

> We said we would stand with those people in the face of common danger.
> The time came when we had to put up or shut up. We put up. And we are there. We don't march out and have a big battle each day in a guerrilla war. It is a new kind of war for us. So it doesn't move that fast. . . .
> We are making progress. We are pleased with the results. . . .
> We are inflicting greater losses than we are getting.[84]

On "Meet the Press" on November 26 Vice-President Humphrey said: "I do think it is fair to say that there has been progress on every front in Vietnam—militarily, substantial progress, politically, very significant progress. . . . There is no military stalemate. There is no pacification stalemate."[85]

Meanwhile, Westmoreland made a trip to Washington to sing the leading role before television cameras, Congress, and the National Press Club. At a club luncheon on November 21 he declared that it was conceivable that "within two years or less, it will be possible for us to phase down our level of commitment and turn more of the burden of the war over to the Vietnamese armed forces."[86]

Yet Westmoreland and the administration were already in possession of intelligence that the Communists were planning an extraordinary offensive. It was expected to begin around the time of Tet, the lunar New Year's observance in Vietnam at the end of Janaury 1968, although no indication had been obtained that an attack would come on the holiday proper. Much to his later regret, Johnson did not take the American people into his confidence and prepare them for what might be coming.

ight: Thirteen-year-old Harry
ruman. *Courtesy Truman
ibrary.*

elow: Truman, the young
armer in his mid-twenties,
ding on a cultivator, about
910. *Photo by Harry Vieth, Jr.
ourtesy Truman Library.*

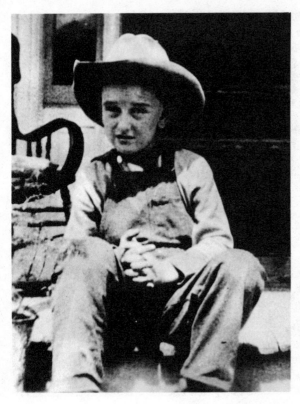

Left: Lyndon, the boy, in Johnson City, Texas. *Courtesy Johnson Library.*

Below: Johnson at the time of his graduation from high school, about May 1924. *Courtesy Johnson Library.*

Opposite, above: Vice-President Truman being sworn in as president in the Cabinet Room of the White House immediately after the sudden death of Franklin D. Roosevelt, in Warm Springs, Georgia, on April 1 1945. *Photo by Abbie Rowe, Nation Park Service. Courtesy Truman Library.*

Opposite, below: President Truman later in his term, addressing a joint session of Congress. *ACME-UPI photo.*

Vice-President Johnson being sworn is as president aboard Air Force One, in Dallas, after President Kennedy had been shot by Lee Harvey Oswald on November 22, 1963. *Photo by Cecil Stoughton. Courtesy Johnson Library.*

President Johnson addresses a joint session of Congress on March 15, 1965, to urge enactment of the voting rights bill. *Photo by Cecil Stoughton. Courtesy Johnson Library.*

Truman during the Korean War with the two men on whom he placed his greatest reliance, Secretary of State Dean Acheson *(left)* and Secretary of Defense George C. Marshall. *Courtesy Truman Library.*

Truman with some other members of his staff and cabinet at Washington National Airport in about 1950. *Courtesy Truman Library.*

Above: Johnson on September 15, 1967, during the Vietnam War with the two men on whom he placed his greatest reliance, Secretary of State Dean Rusk *(left)* and Secretary of Defense Robert S. McNamara. *Photo by Geissinger. Courtesy Johnson Library.*

Right: Johnson and his *bête noir* and Democratic challenger, Robert F. Kennedy, meet in the Oval Office on June 22, 1966. *Photo by Y. R. Okamoto. Courtesy Johnson Library.*

Above: Truman and his Korean War commander, General of the Army Douglas A. MacArthur, meet for the first and only time on October 15, 1950, on Wake Island. Six months later, Truman relieved MacArthur of his command on the grounds of insubordination. *State Department photo. Courtesy Truman Library.*

Left: Of all the improbable pairs, Robert F. Kennedy and General Douglas MacArthur were leaders of dissent—MacArthur against Truman's policies in the Korean War and Kennedy against Johnson's policies in the Vietnam War. Here, in 1962, they meet in the more tranquil setting of a national football dinner in Washington. *Photo by Bill Mark. Courtesy MacArthur Library, Norfolk, Virginia.*

Johnson and his Vietnam War commander, General William C. Westmoreland, meet in the Oval Office on November 16, 1967, while Westmoreland was in Washington for consultations. *Photo by Y. R. Okamoto. Courtesy Johnson Library.*

Johnson and Westmoreland review American troops at Camranh Bay, South Vietnam, on October 26, 1966. *Photo by Y. R. Okamoto. Courtesy Johnson Library.*

VI · *The Disasters*

1

The situation in which the United States found itself on November 24, 1950, with tens of thousands of its troops poised to attack far above the 38th parallel in wintry North Korea, was disastrous.

MacArthur had blithely discarded the anxiety he had revealed on November 7 when he bombed the Yalu bridges because Chinese forces, he said, were "pouring" into North Korea and threatening destruction of the United Nations command. Then, unexpectedly, the Chinese vanished almost as suddenly as they had appeared and had driven back the Eighth Army. No one in Washington or Tokyo knew where they had gone, or why, or what China's ultimate intentions were. In any case, MacArthur's fears evaporated along with the Chinese. Disdaining the worries that had by then been aroused in Washington, partly as a result of his own messages, he made ready for his grand advance to the Yalu.

Some of Washington's apprehensiveness sprang from the displeasure of the Joint Chiefs of Staff with the disposition of MacArthur's forces. Rather than mass all his troops, he had divided them. The Eighth Army under Walker—the main force—was deployed on the western side of the peninsula. The Tenth Corps under Almond had made an amphibious landing around Wonsan on the east coast. As the two forces struck north, they would be separated by the Taebaek Mountains, which created a gap of some fifty miles between them. One would not be able to reinforce the other in an emergency. The tactical reasons MacArthur had advanced for the arrangement drew only doubts from Bradley, but the chiefs were both caught up in the traditional rule of latitude for a theater commander and uncomfortable about overruling MacArthur. While he was under their jurisdiction, he was senior to all of them. The army chief of staff, General Collins, later admitted that he and his colleagues were "perhaps somewhat overawed" by MacArthur's success at Inchon, a risky venture that had also incurred the chiefs' doubts. They approved his plans for a separated Eighth Army and Tenth Corps, but took care to have their action endorsed by Truman, Marshall, and Acheson.

At the time of the first Chinese attacks on United Nations forces below the Yalu the JCS had suggested to MacArthur that his objectives should be reconsidered, the implication being that he ought to go on the defensive. MacArthur was adamant. Confident that his air power could interdict Chinese reinforcements, he replied that a change of objectives "would completely destroy the morale of my forces" and undermine the policy of disposing the remaining North Korean forces. He insisted that "there be no weakening at this crucial moment and that we press on to complete victory which I believe can be achieved if our determination and indomitable will do not desert us."[1]

Tremors reached United Nations headquarters in New York. The British suggested that MacArthur pull back far enough to create a demilitarized zone south of the Yalu to calm China's fears. But military plans were in place, and Acheson, who was not likely to have made such a decision without consulting Truman, replied that withdrawal would have an adverse effect on American public opinion. MacArthur chimed in with a warning that establishment of a demilitarized zone would be interpreted throughout Asia as appeasement of China.

Despite the uncertainties, the administration made no move to prevent MacArthur's offensive. "General MacArthur," Acheson commented at a National Security Council meeting, "is free to do what he militarily can . . . without bombing Manchuria."[2] The administration was both apprehensive and optimistic about the offensive. The crowning mischief was that no American official had the slightest valid idea how many Chinese might be in Korea. Partly, this ignorance may have been due to an otherwise praiseworthy policy of Truman's. He would not allow American planes to cross over the Yalu into Manchurian airspace, even in hot pursuit of enemy aircraft that had attacked MacArthur's forces. The restriction was ordered to avoid any episode that might lead to hostilities with China. The drawback was that the Americans were unable to photograph daylight Chinese troop movements, if any, at the Manchurian approaches to the river. The lack of intelligence itself became an incentive for advancing. Marshall and Acheson favored MacArthur's push, if only to ascertain how many Chinese troops were deployed and where. The thought of negotiations with the enemy was not absent in Washington, but the general feeling was that negotiations should come after MacArthur's advance.

The information that reached Truman and his advisers was bewildering. Four days after the first clashes with the Chinese on October 25, Everett F. Drumright, United States chargé d'affaires in Seoul, cabled the State Department that reports about Chinese "volunteers" in North Korea were exaggerated. "Eighth Army headquarters," he said, "states its units have not reported coming into contact with any sizeable number of Chinese troops. On basis current information Eighth Army is not inclined to accept reports of substantial Chinese participation in North Korean fighting." The next day Drumright sent a contradictory cable. This time he gave a higher estimate of Chinese strength and suggested that Chinese forces might be "instrumental in checking advance to the Yalu."[3]

Then the Chinese disappeared. In mid-November a State Department intelligence estimate said that the number of Chinese in Korea "is not sufficiently extensive to indicate a plan for major operations." The estimate tended to conform with MacArthur's understanding. Toward the end of October he had told John J. Muccio, United States ambassador to South Korea, that according to his own intelligence, some 25,000 to 30,000 Chinese troops faced the Eighth Army. MacArthur added, Muccio later disclosed, that "not more than that could have crossed the Yalu, or my intelligence would have known about it." MacArthur did not mention Chinese who might be facing the Tenth Corps to the east.

The perceptive Muccio reflected,

I think that MacArthur was closed in by the operations of two of his intimates, Generals Charles A. Willoughby and Courtney Whitney, two key men vying for MacArthur's favors. And the two of them prevented MacArthur from getting the intelligence that he *had* to have in order to make the right decisions. . . . [MacArthur] had gotten to the age where he was no longer in touch with the situation. There was a failure of intelligence more than anything else [responsible] for the mess that we got into.

Willoughby, who was in charge of intelligence in MacArthur's command, was, Muccio said, filled with "disdain for the capability of Chinese, of all classes." Another woeful circumstance, according to Muccio, was that "Willoughby was working very assiduously on the history of MacArthur in the Far East—the Pacific campaigns— which was far dearer to his heart than . . . keeping in touch with what was going on in Korea."[4]

November 24, the day after Thanksgiving, had been approved by MacArthur for the start of the main drive north by the Eighth Army. In the east, elements of the Tenth Corps had already reached the Yalu. To be on hand for the jump-off in the west, MacArthur, looking smart with a checkered muffler and corncob pipe, flew to the Eighth Army headquarters on the Chongchon. According to Truman, a new intelligence estimate had been made available to MacArthur that day, saying that the Chinese had the capacity for forcing United Nations troops to withdraw to defensive positions.[5] Whether MacArthur saw the report before the attack and why Washington did not make a last-minute decision to reconsider the plans are questions that remain unanswered.

While touring the Eighth Army front on the fateful morning of the twenty-fourth, MacArthur noticed, he said later, that the ROK troops were not in good condition. "If the Chinese were actually in heavy force," he wrote, "I decided I would withdraw our troops at once and abandon any further attempt to move north."[6] Meanwhile, he watched the launching of what he called the "massive compression envelopment of North Korea." "If successful," his exultant communiqué said, "this should for all practical purposes end the war. . . ."[7] Correspondents heard him say, "I hope we can get the boys home by Christmas."

Before returning to Tokyo, MacArthur made a daring aerial reconnaissance of the Yalu area, sometimes ordering his plane to descend to an altitude of five thousand feet. Nowhere in the snowy landscape did he see any sign of a large enemy force, which must not have surprised him in view of his conviction that his air power had substantially isolated the battlefield. He decided, therefore, not to order a withdrawal of the Eighth Army. The troops pushed on. Gone now was control over events that might have been exercised by the president, the secretary of defense, and the Joint Chiefs of Staff. No one realized how dire the predicament of the Eighth Army was, especially since MacArthur's reconnaissance flight, for which he was awarded the Distinguished Flying Cross, had not been, to say the least, an efficient one. Three hundred thousand Chinese, as was later ascertained, waited in concealment south of the Yalu for the advancing Eighth Army and Tenth Corps.

As expected, of course, MacArthur's offensive got off to an encouraging start. On the left of the battle line were the United States Twenty-fourth Division, the ROK First Division, and the Twenty-seventh Brigade. The United States Twenty-fifth and Second infantry divisions and the Turkish Brigade held the center. On the right was the ROK II Corps, consisting of three divisions. In reserve was the First Cavalry. The first two hours witnessed the leading Twenty-fourth Division advance almost four miles, although ROK units on the right flank ran into tough resistance. Still, the other divisions forged steadily ahead and by late the next day the Twenty-fourth Division was within a mile of Chongju, which was only about fifty miles from the Yalu.

On the evening of November 25 the terrible blow fell. It was the start of one of the worst disasters in American military history and one that would change in many ways the history of the next two decades. The blow—it was more an explosion—came smashing out of the mountains, ravines, and forests in a wild Chinese counteroffensive heralded by bugle calls, whistles, and weird shouts, piercing the frigid night air. Its greatest weight, initially, crashed against the ROK Eighth Division on the right, routing it. To avoid detection the Chinese soldiers had moved only at night in stages to and across the Yalu and then south in the mountains toward United Nations positions. By day, they had hidden in the terrain. When MacArthur's unsuspecting men moved near enough, the Chinese went on a rampage on a wide front. In the course of the next two days the ROK II Corps was practically destroyed, exposing the right flank of the Eighth Army battle line. To avoid being overrun, General Walker's men reeled back through the snow, and some days later Walker was killed in a jeep accident. To the west, in the Tenth Corps sector, the Fifth and Seventh marine regiments were encircled near the Changjin Reservoir. The dread prospect arose that the entire Tenth Corps, which had arrived by ship, might be trapped by the Chinese against the Sea of Japan. By November 28, the whole MacArthur offensive had collapsed.

At 6:15 A.M. in Washington that day General Bradley telephoned Truman to read him a frightening message from MacArthur. It stated that the United States did not have enough forces in the field to contain the Chinese.

"We face an entirely new war," MacArthur said.[8]

Truman was bitter. In a meeting with Harriman at nine o'clock he said that the Chinese had dared to attack because of political onslaughts in the United States against the administration's foreign policy. Later in the day he blamed the hostile Hearst newspapers; Roy Howard, head of the Scripps-Howard newspapers; the McCormick newspapers—the *Chicago Tribune* and the *Washington Times-Herald*—and Joe McCarthy and others who had been trying to discredit Acheson.

After Harriman left, Truman held his usual morning meeting with his staff, none of whom knew of Bradley's call. Truman ran through pending items without mentioning Korea. What followed was vividly described by John Hersey, who, by chance, had been admitted to the conference because he was working on a profile of the president for *The New Yorker*.

When Truman had disposed of routine matters, Hersey wrote, he appeared to brace himself. "For a few moments he shifted papers back and forth and straightened a pair of scissors and two paper cutters. . . . He suddenly drooped a little; it appeared that something he would have liked to forget was back in his mind, close behind his hugely magnified eyes." The strong lenses Truman wore made his eyes dominate his face.

"We've got a terrific situation on our hands," Truman said quietly. "General Bradley called me . . . this morning. He told me a terrible message had come from General MacArthur."

Truman summarized the message and enumerated some actions that would have to be taken.

Hersey continued,

> In outlining his concrete plans and acts, the President had hidden, as indeed he had all through the staff meeting up to this point, his feelings about this new development. . . . Now he paused for a few seconds, and suddenly all his driven-down emotions seemed to pour into his face. His mouth drew tight,

his cheeks flushed. For a moment, it seemed as if he would sob. Then, in a voice that was incredibly calm and quiet, considering what could be read in his face—a voice of absolute personal courage—he said, "This is the worst situation we have had yet. We'll just have to meet it as we've met all the rest."9

The United States and Europe were thrown into a war scare. Acheson appeared before an executive session of the Senate Foreign Relations Committee. "I think," he said, "it is impossible to overestimate the seriousness of this whole matter, not merely the immediate military situation in Korea but what this means." What it meant, he admonished, was that the danger of world war had been brought "very close." "We have got to face the possibility now," he said, "that anything can happen anywhere at any time."10

Truman called the National Security Council into session. Admiral Forrest P. Sherman, chief of naval operations, said that if Chinese bombers attacked from Manchuria, the United States would have to retaliate, or it could not remain in Korea. Truman would not commit himself to an assault on Chinese territory. He would face that problem when it arose, he said.

The next day, November 29, the joint strategic survey committee, an arm of the JCS, submitted a dread report to General Collins. It said that a situation might develop in which it could become necessary to use nuclear weapons to save American troops from being overrun by the Chinese. The report and the circumstances in which it was prepared are reminders of the kind of insidious situation in which nuclear war might begin. What would the American people have demanded if, as fortunately did not happen, the Tenth Corps had indeed become hopelessly pinned against the sea and was about to be annihilated by the Chinese? What would Truman have done? What if, in the future, a large American force were to be cut off and threatened with annihilation in, say, the Persian Gulf or in South Korea, where a sizable one is still stationed, or in Central Europe, for that matter? What would the American people demand? And what would the president, whoever he might be, do? With the senseless accumulation of nuclear weapons that is taking place, an equally great danger of nuclear war lies in miscalculation of intentions or an accidental firing of an intercontinental weapon, or weapons.

In the bedlam caused by the Chinese intervention, nothing was

more incredible than that Truman should have had a press conference scheduled for November 30; that he should have gone through
with it, and that he should have been asked whether he would use
the atomic bomb in Korea. The result was a nearly worldwide up-
roar. It is highly unlikely that Truman knew about the secret Pentagon report of the day before. It is equally unlikely that he was
trying to use the press conference to frighten the Chinese and the
Soviets. He was a man under a cruel burden, and he answered
questions without adequate care as to how his words would be interpreted.

Some preliminary questions had drawn from him the comment
that he would take whatever steps were necessary to meet the new
situation. "Will that include the atomic bomb?" asked a reporter
from the New York *Daily News.* "That includes every weapon we
have," the president said. Was there, another reporter inquired,
active consideration of using the bomb? "There has always been consideration of its use," Truman replied. "I don't want to see it used.
It is a terrible weapon. . . . ." The exchange continued in that vein
until Truman also worked himself into a position of saying that the
military commander in the field would have to decide what weapons
were used.[11] The statement left the impression that MacArthur
could elect to use the atomic bomb, although everyone in the room
knew, or should have, that the law reserves such a decision to the
president.*

Only seconds after the conference ended, the United Press bul-
letined, PRESIDENT TRUMAN SAID TODAY THAT THE UNITED STATES
HAS UNDER CONSIDERATION USE OF THE ATOMIC BOMB IN CON-
NECTION WITH THE WAR IN KOREA. A similar Associated Press story
also reported that Truman had said that a decision about using the
bomb could be made by MacArthur. Shortly afterward, the White
House issued a statement saying that in no way had the president's
words changed the strategic situation in Korea and that Truman had
not authorized the use of nuclear weapons. But the news bulletin
traveled too fast.

From every corner of the globe, especially from Asians who had
seen atomic bombs used against their own people, Washington was
besieged with protests and pleas. In London, Parliament was

---

* In the Eisenhower administration field commanders in certain contingencies—
for example, immediate threat of destruction of their forces—received authority in
advance to use limited-range nuclear weapons.

thrown into such a tempest that Prime Minister Clement R. Attlee felt compelled to send a message to Truman asking if the prime minister might come to Washington at once for talks. Truman assented. Five days of meetings began in the White House on December 4 and were significant. Truman and Attlee agreed that the war should not be widened. And it was at about that time that Truman and his advisers concluded that it would not be worth the cost to mount a new attack against North Korea. They decided instead to seek a settlement at or near the 38th parallel, a decision certain to jolt MacArthur.

Such was the military situation at the moment, however, that the possibility could not be excluded that the United States would have to evacuate all of its forces from Korea. The right flank destroyed, the Eighth Army again retreated across the Chongchon and headed for the 38th parallel and South Korea. The famous Second Division was so shattered it was, momentarily, unable to fight. In the east, units of the Tenth Corps were battling to get to the port of Hungnam to be evacuated. The American people were appalled. Though in no mood for it, Truman kept a date to go to the Army-Navy football game in Philadelphia on December 2, lest cancellation of the trip stretch tension too tight. Three days later the exhausted White House press secretary, Charles G. Ross, dropped dead at his desk of a heart attack.

In the uncertain days that followed the Chinese attack, the battered Eighth Army fought off encirclement and dug in at a point in South Korea near the place where the Twenty-fourth Division task force had first met the North Korean army in June. More than 100,000 Americans and South Koreans in the Tenth Corps succeeded in escaping to South Korea by sea. A blow dreaded by Marshall, Bradley, and their colleagues, namely, a Communist air offensive from Manchuria, was never struck. Still, it was weeks before Washington could breathe easily about maintaining a foothold in South Korea. For a brief time American officials feared they might even have to sue for terms to save the troops. Acheson was worried that such an eventuality might lead to Chinese efforts to force the United States out of Japan, the accomplishment of which would have unhinged the American position in the Far East.

While the longer Vietnam War was to inflict far greater damage on American society and take a greater toll of American lives, the

Korean War was the more dangerous of the two. In Korea, the United States air force, navy, and eight-division army-and-marine force operated close to sensitive Chinese and Soviet areas in Manchuria and Siberia. The cold war was in a critical stage. Throughout Truman's tenure, Stalin ruled the Kremlin. For a time, the cream of the United States army was threatened with encirclement by Communist troops. Eventually, the United States inflicted enormous casualties on the Chinese in Korea, but against the worrisome backdrop of the Treaty of Friendship, Alliance, and Mutual Assistance that had been signed by Stalin and Mao Zedong on February 14, 1950. Article 1 provided, "In the event of one of the High Contracting Parties being attacked by Japan or states allied with it, and thus being involved in a state of war, the other High Contracting Party will immediately render military and other assistance with all means at its disposal." In reality, was not the United States allied with Japan, although legally still in occupation of the islands? Japan was the base from which American forces were operating in Korea. Peace with the Soviets hung in the balance, too. As for nuclear weapons, it was not only the threat of Chinese entrapment of American troops that raised the ultimate danger. If China had driven the United Nations out of Korea, the Americans would have taken revenge. If China's air force had attacked American forces outside Korea, in Japan, for example, Truman would have ordered a mighty retaliation.

On December 15, he proclaimed a national emergency. "Our homes, our nation, all the things we believe in are in great danger," he said on television.[12] He immediately instituted economic controls, including a program of wage-and-price controls similar to that imposed in the Second World War. Truman also moved to attain by 1952 the goals for military manpower and procurement that had originally been set for 1954. The proclamation of an emergency had the legal force of facilitating the awarding of contracts under wartime conditions. But it was also issued for psychological and political effect, demonstrating that the president was doing something about the disaster in Korea. At New Year's, 1951, the Chinese waged a new offensive that carried them across the 38th parallel in a second invasion of South Korea. Again Seoul fell to the enemy. And by then Truman had another juggernaut with which to contend.

Soon after the Chinese attack MacArthur called upon the administration for "political decisions and strategic plans . . . adequate to meet the realities involved."[13] Having at the moment exactly one army division left in the United States, with no new army or national guard divisions due to be ready before spring, the JCS told the general to preserve and consolidate the troops he had. Truman ordered General Collins to fly to Tokyo to see MacArthur. MacArthur argued with the general that the United States should accept the Chinese challenge and turn its full power toward the new undeclared war. In a second conversation Collins said that MacArthur might not be allowed to retaliate against China with air power. That, replied MacArthur, would be surrender.

In the meantime Truman, in no chummy mood over the mess in which MacArthur's end-the-war offensive had left him, was further riled over public, self-serving statements the general was making in answer to press queries. MacArthur, for example, taunted European allies, frightened over events in Asia, as being "selfish" and "shortsighted." And that was at a time when Washington was having problems holding the British in line behind Korean policy. MacArthur also claimed that when the administration had ruled out hot pursuit over Manchuria of enemy planes that had attacked United Nations positions, he was placed at "an enormous handicap, without precedent in military history."[14]

Abruptly, on December 5 Truman ordered that speeches, press releases, or other public statements dealing with foreign or military policy were to be cleared by the proper departments in Washington. Although MacArthur was not mentioned by name, the order applied to "officials in the field," as well as those in the capital. Lest there be any doubt, the Joint Chiefs of Staff immediately sent a copy of the instructions to MacArthur. In the process, legal grounds were established under which a change in command in Korea might be ordered if further unauthorized statements were made by the commander.

2

Johnson had left a call with the White House telephone operator to be awakened at 7:45 A.M. on January 30, 1968, but at 5:37 he had already been in touch with the situation room by telephone. Intelligence from Vietnam, then in the midst of the traditional Tet celebration, was arresting. By 11:45, Rostow summarized in a memorandum for the president a score of items reported by Saigon to the situation room during the morning. A sample:

Enemy forces launched coordinated mortar, rocket and ground attacks in Danang, Wheeler/Wallowa and Chu Lai areas.

Between 2:00 and 4:00 P.M. the Marble Mountain air facility received approximately 20 rounds of mortar fire with numerous Army aircraft receiving damage.

In Qui Nhon, the enemy controls the radio station and the maintenance area. . . .

In Ban Me Thuot, fighting continues within the city. . . .

In Ninh Hoa contact continues on a sporadic basis. . . .

In Tuy Hoa heavy fighting continues. . . .

In Pleiku contact continues with an unknown size enemy force in the city. . . .[15]

Shortly after noon four journalists of the *Washington Post* arrived at the White House situation room at the invitation of Rostow to examine captured enemy documents that, in Rostow's view, provided new evidence that the United States was winning the war. While the four were scanning the documents with the assistance of a briefing officer, an aide emerged from an adjacent communications center and handed the officer a slip of paper. The officer looked at it and directed that it be taken at once to Rostow's office. "Looks like some trouble in Saigon," the officer confided to the journalists. Then another slip of paper was brought out, and it was rushed to Rostow's office. Then another. And another. It was Tuesday, and Rostow was attending Johnson's weekly strategy luncheon. At 2:33 P.M. Rostow was quietly notified at the table that Bromley Smith, head of the NSC staff, needed to talk to him at once on the telephone. Rostow went into the kitchen to take the call. Within two minutes he returned to the table and was forced to interrupt a discussion. "We are being heavily mortared in Saigon," he said. He added that the Presidential Palace and bachelor officers' quarters were under fire.[16]

Johnson had returned to the Oval Office when, at 3:15, he received a typed memorandum from Rostow: "By direct telephone, NMCC [National Military Command Center] has learned that in an attack on the U.S. Embassy in Saigon, several Viet Cong got into the compound."[17]

On the other side of the international dateline it was still dark in Saigon where, at 2:47 A.M. (January 31) two sentries at the embassy in the heart of the South Vietnamese capital had radioed, "Signal

300." In the military police that code denoted an enemy attack. A small group of NLF operatives had pulled up in a small truck at the wall around the embassy, attached an explosive charge to the wall, blown a hole in it, and crawled through. Guns blazed. The American sentries who had sent Signal 300 were killed.[18]

The incident was the climax of an astonishing offensive throughout South Vietnam by nearly seventy thousand enemy soldiers and guerrillas, timed to coincide with the celebration of Tet, ushering in the Year of the Monkey. The offensive had begun the previous day in many parts of South Vietnam in ruthless disregard of the enemy's agreement to a cease-fire during the Tet observance. The timing as well as the ubiquity, coordination, and intensity of the offensive caught the American military off guard in another of the appalling series of miscalculations in the two Asian wars. The North Koreans were not going to attack. The Chinese were not going to intervene in Korea. The North Vietnamese could be forced into negotiations by bombing. The United States, as supposedly reflected in Rostow's secret documents, was winning the Vietnam War. And now Tet!

The report of a subsequent official inquiry into the intelligence deficiency at the time of Tet was particularly interesting in light of the "lessons" in the captured documents regularly read by Johnson and quietly circulated by Rostow. The report to the president's Foreign Intelligence Advisory Board said that

> . . . most commanders and intelligence officers at all levels did not visualize the enemy as capable of accomplishing his stated goals as they appeared in propaganda and in captured documents. Prevailing estimates of attrition, infiltration, and local recruitment, reports of low morale, and a long series of defeats had degraded our image of the enemy.[19]

Brutally, often murderously, the Communist forces during Tet attacked more than one hundred cities and towns, including Hue, the old imperial capital, which they held for twenty-five bloody days. They even attacked Saigon's airport, site of General Westmoreland's headquarters. "We are now in a new ball game. . . ." he said in one of his early comments on Tet, an observation resembling MacArthur's, "We face an entirely new war" after the Chinese attack.[20]

For Americans at home a picture of disaster was conveyed by newspapers, radio, and vivid television film, all focusing on the surprises, sensations, ferocity, and universality of the Communist offensive at the expense of the enormous casualties that were inflicted on the enemy. Only recently showered with optimism by Johnson, Humphrey, Westmoreland, Bunker, and Rostow, Americans were stunned and dismayed. The greatest shock to public opinion by far was the attack on the embassy compound. Essentially, it was a rather feeble assault. The NLF did not succeed in entering the main embassy building, or chancery, although initial news stories and broadcasts in the United States indicated otherwise. (Ambassador Bunker's residence was not situated in the compound.) Nevertheless, the impact of the news was such as to call into question the effectiveness of the whole American operation in Vietnam. "What the hell is going on?" Walter Cronkite demanded when the bulletins clattered into the CBS newsroom in New York. "I thought we were winning the war."[21] The same thought had occurred to millions of Americans. Johnson's standing with the people had suffered a shattering blow.

Though Johnson had been forewarned that an unusual Communist offensive was being planned for late January, he was as shocked as everyone else by its scope and especially by the attack at the embassy. The blow came at another very difficult time for him. Early in January the marines' base at Khe Sanh, near the demilitarized zone between North and South Vietnam, had been attacked, and heavy fighting was still in progress. Though the comparison was unwarranted, concern grew that Khe Sanh might become an American Dien Bien Phu. Johnson was as deeply worried about Khe Sanh as Truman had been about the fate of the Tenth Corps. Johnson had a sand-table model of the Khe Sanh battle area constructed in the situation room and used to study it in his bathrobe at night against information coming in about the day's activities. In an act without a known precedent, he required a written statement from General Wheeler confirming that the Joint Chiefs of Staff shared Westmoreland's confidence that Khe Sanh could be held.

While the outcome hung in the balance, startling events also occurred in Korea, creating an undertone of menace of a second Korean War. In Seoul, infiltrated North Korean assassins attempted, but failed, to kill President Chung Hee Park, a successor to Rhee. And on January 23, North Korea humiliated the United States by seizing the U.S.S. *Pueblo,* an intelligence ship, off the North Korean coast and imprisoning the crew. "We are going through some dangerous times," Johnson told Democratic congressional leaders on February 6.[22] Even the self-possessed Rusk was overtaxed by the strain. When a reporter at a briefing asked him why the nature of the Tet offensive had not been foreseen, the secretary of state burst out, "Whose side are you on?"[23]

Outwardly, Johnson was cool and calculating about the Tet attacks. While the fighting was still raging, Westmoreland received a message from Wheeler saying:

> The President desires that you make a brief personal comment to the press at least once each day during the current [offensive]. The purpose of such statements should be to convey to the American public your confidence in our capability to blunt these enemy moves, and to reassure the public here that you have the situation under control.

White House press secretary George Christian reinforced the message with one of his own to Bunker and Westmoreland. It said: "We are facing, in these next few days, a critical phase in the American public's understanding and confidence toward our effort in Vietnam. . . . [T]he dire prognostications of the commentators can best be put into perspective by the shared experience and wisdom of our Ambassador. . . ."[24]

At a press conference on February 2, a weary Johnson suggested that the Tet offensive had been a failure for the enemy.

> I am no great strategist and tactician. I know that you are not. Let us assume that the best figures we can have are from our responsible military commanders. They say ten thousand died, and we lost two hundred and forty-nine, and the South Vietnamese lost five hundred. That doesn't look like a Communist victory. I can count. It looks like somebody has paid a very dear price for the temporary encouragement that some of our enemies had.[25]

At the meeting with Democratic leaders on February 6, Johnson was angry at what he termed the popular pastime of stressing mismanagement in Vietnam. He said he thought there had been very little of it, adding, according to the notes of the meeting, "Anybody can kick a barn down. It takes a good carpenter to build one." He had had his fill, he indicated, of talk about "What's wrong with our country?" and said that senators Fulbright, Gruening, and Stephen M. Young, a Democrat from Ohio, were not helping a bit. Among Young's dissents had been a public call for Rusk's resignation.

As regards Tet, Senator Robert C. Byrd, a Democrat from West Virginia, incurred Johnson's resentment by saying that American intelligence was poor; that the military were not prepared; that the administration had underestimated Viet Cong morale and overestimated the popular support of the Saigon government.

"I don't agree with any of that," Johnson retorted, saying that it was known that a Communist winter offensive was planned but not known what the timing and targets were.

"We have put our best men out there," he continued. "I believe that our military and diplomatic men in the field know more than many of our congressmen and senators back here."

The criticism being heaped on the administration was "not worth much," he said, adding: "I look at all those speeches that are in the *[Congressional] Record*. I look at all the people who are going around the country saying our policy is wrong. Where do they get us? Nowhere!"

At a later meeting on February 6 with his advisers he said that he was alarmed by the attitude of Byrd and its reflection in comments by other members of Congress and by the press.

"There seems to be," he observed, "a great effort to discredit this government and its military establishment."

"If the war goes well," Rostow said, "the American people are with us. If the war goes badly, they are against us."[26]

At the meeting with the Democratic leaders Johnson had characterized Tet as a "severe defeat" for the Communists. In some ways it was. In addition to their heavy casualties they had been forced in places to relinquish earlier gains. A number of NLF cadres had been wiped out. Hanoi failed in one of its major objectives of inspiring an uprising of the South Vietnamese people against their government. In fact, the South Vietnamese army had performed well against the NLF. American forces rallied strongly. Yet, as General Vo Nguyen Giap, principal architect of the Tet offensive, said in a postwar interview, the offensive had multiple objectives, military, political, and diplomatic. One, for example, was to drive a wedge between the Americans and the South Vietnamese by demonstrating to the latter that the United States forces were not as powerful as they appeared to be. Another was to call attention to the allegedly neocolonial relationship between the United States and South Vietnam. A third was to inflict casualties that would heighten dissent against the war in the United States. This was in line with Giap's warning to the French in the earlier Indochinese War: "You can kill ten of my men for every one I kill of yours. But even at those odds, you will lose, and I will win."[27] Richard Betts has written that "in most circumstances, guerrillas win as long as they do not lose, and government forces lose as long as they do not win."[28]

A telling retrospection on the view held by Johnson regarding the Communists' "defeat" was voiced in a conversation between an American colonel and a North Vietnamese officer after the United States departure from Vietnam in 1975. The American recalled that the Communists never had defeated United States troops in a major battle. "That is correct," the Vietnamese replied. "It is also irrelevant."[29] What Johnson, Westmoreland, Rostow, and others said about Communist losses and failures was correct. It was also irrelevant when it came to convincing the American people that the Vietnam War was worth the cost the way it was going.

Tet had come at a moment when, despite orchestrated optimism, apprehension about Vietnam was coming to a head in the United States. As never before, people were asking whether the United States was not wasting tens of thousands of lives and scores of billions of dollars on a war that was burdening the conscience of some Americans, damaging the economy, tearing society with dissent, corrupting the universities, and inviting scorn from much of the civilized world. Tet redoubled the anxiety that for months had been building over the prospect of victory as a chimera. People at least had been able to see geographical evidence of progress in Korea when United Nations forces advanced at certain times. Progress in Vietnam seemed to come down to "body counts," the accuracy of which was much suspected. In Korea, Seoul was captured and recaptured by Americans and their allies. In Vietnam, the same cities, towns, villages, valleys, plateaus, highlands, and stretches of jungle had to be contested over and over. Despite their large numbers, American troops were spread so thin for guerrilla warfare that after they had taken a place and moved on, the enemy seeped back and had to be blasted out again. As seen at home, the crowning futility was the fighting in the embassy grounds nearly three years after the arrival of American combat forces in Vietnam.

Tet, of course, only reinforced Johnson's fear for the safety of Khe Sanh. As an emergency measure he sent eleven thousand more troops to Vietnam. Through Wheeler the president gloomily inquired of Westmoreland whether he might be forced to authorize use of nuclear weapons to spare the marines. Westmoreland replied that no such decision would be required at the moment. If, however, the North Vietnamese troops should attempt a massive crossing of the demilitarized zone, he said, "I visualize that either tactical nuclear weapons or chemical agents would be active candidates for employment."[30] Somehow a rumor got about that Johnson was considering using nuclear weapons. It was exploited by Senator Eugene J. McCarthy of Minnesota, who was seeking the 1960 Democratic presidential nomination as a peace candidate. The rumor also set voices buzzing in Congress and in the press. On February 16, Johnson found it necessary to call a press conference and issue a denial similar to the one the White House had issued after Truman touched off the atomic-bomb scare in November 1950.[31]

For all his troubles in Korea, Truman, unlike Johnson, did not have any serious concerns over the effect of television coverage of the war on American audiences. At the start of the Korean War an estimated ten million black-and-white sets were in use in the United States. Color television was still undergoing experimentation. In the Truman years, evening network television news programs, such as NBC's "Camel Caravan" with John Cameron Swayze, lasted for only fifteen minutes. Material from Korea on the networks typically consisted of newsreel-type shots, often of poor quality because cameras then were at the mercy of light in which action occurred. The networks usually edited any gruesome pictures out of battle scenes. Film had to be processed and flown across the Pacific to the United States, causing delay that robbed television showings of the impact of immediacy. NBC did have a thirty-minute Sunday afternoon program called "Battle Report" with Robert K. McCormick, but the content was largely supplied by administration officials. No morning network television news show appeared until "Today" was inaugurated by NBC in 1952, Truman's last full year in office. If memory serves, he never complained about television coverage of the Korean War, or press coverage for that matter. By contrast, Johnson was merely cruising in low gear for a change when he groused that liberal columnists and "TV sissies" were costing him victory in Vietnam.

Vietnam was, as the phrase went, the first television war or the first living-room war. By the time of Tet nearly one hundred million sets were in use. The sets were dominated by color, and Vietnam dominated the news. Bloodshed in battles was commonplace on the screen, and green plastic bags containing American corpses were not infrequently as familiar a sight at the dinner table as the salt and pepper. The same film was shown on European television, stirring widespread criticism of Johnson's war policy. French President Charles de Gaulle, for example, once said, "We find it detestable that a small country should be bombed by a very big one."[32] Johnson made the daily theater harder on himself by installing three television sets in his office and three in his bedroom so that he could view all the networks, singly or simultaneously—whichever choice would make his mood worse, no doubt. Yet the extent to which television affected public opinion, at least through the middle of 1967, may have been exaggerated. The question has been raised in two studies, one by John E. Mueller, a University of Rochester political scientist, and the other by Lawrence W. Lichty, professor of communications art at the University of Maryland.

Mueller found that public support for the Vietnam War, television notwithstanding, remained at a high level further into the war than had been the case in Korea, when the effect of television was minimal. The two wars, he concluded, affected public opinion similarly. What transformed public support to opposition in each case was the level of casualties. The fact that a majority of the people supported the Vietnam War as long as they did may have been due, the study suggests, to the perverse effect of the vast television coverage of antiwar demonstrations. The behavior displayed in many of the demonstrations so angered the mass of Americans that they supported the war to spite the protesters. The Lichty study concluded that, until mid-1967, television coverage of the war was "very positive: the U.S. could win in Vietnam with a minimal effort. There were always more administrative spokesmen in TV coverage, especially documentaries, than critics." Furthermore, "The gradual decline in support for the war occurred mostly among the educated few, especially the college educated, who are most likely to read newspapers and magazines and to rely upon several sources for their news. This group was also the least likely to watch television."[33]

Certainly television coverage of the Tet offensive greatly agitated the American people, and not only because of the panorama of gore, corpses, rubble, and the discouraging signs of enemy strength. In both television and newspaper photographs the horror of the war was distilled in a tableau of doom in Saigon, staged by Colonel Nguyen Ngoc Loan, chief of the South Vietnamese national police. After the Communist invaders had killed several of his men, together with the wife and children of one of them, Loan approached to within inches of a random guerrilla suspect and without a word killed him with a shot to the head with a revolver. These pictures made an indelible impact. The one piece of welcome news for the United States was that after an incredible tonnage of bombs had been dropped on the enemy, the battle of Khe Sanh was finally won after seventy-seven days.

A television show that particularly distressed Johnson was a half-hour CBS news special on February 27 by the influential Cronkite, who had gone to Vietnam to make his own assessment of the result of Tet. He asserted,

> To say that we are closer to victory today is to believe, in the face of the evidence, the optimists who have been wrong in the past. To suggest we are on the edge of defeat is to yield to unreasonable pessimism. To say that we are mired in stalemate seems the only realistic, yet unsatisfactory, conclusion. . . . [I]t is increasingly clear to this reporter that the only rational way out, then, will be to negotiate, not as victors but as an honorable people who lived up to their pledge to defend democracy and did the best they could.[34]

By February 1968 people had become increasingly pessimistic and critical of Johnson's conduct of the war. In growing numbers they appeared to conclude that it was a mistake to have gone into Vietnam in the first place and a mistake compounded not to have won the war nevertheless or gotten out of it. As the Chinese intervention had forced Truman to seek negotiations as a way out of Korea, the Tet offensive compelled Johnson to reconsider his course in Vietnam.

VII · *The Traumas*

1

In the wake of the sweeping Chinese offensive, on December 19, 1950, the Joint Chiefs of Staff sent MacArthur a tentative new directive that jarred him. Reminding the Far Eastern commander that his primary mission was the defense of Japan, "for which only troops of the Eighth Army are available,"* the chiefs directed him to remain on the defensive as long as he could hold out while still preserving his forces. Thus he was to conduct defenses in successive positions, should the Chinese continue to force his troops back. If, however, he had to pull back as far as the Kum River and the Chinese massed for a further drive from there, MacArthur was "to commence a withdrawal to Japan."[1]

MacArthur dissented and continued to dissent and in the end, in high drama, proclaimed his dissent to Congress and the American people over the head of the president. In the process he became the central figure around whose ideals and stature right-wing criticism crystallized against Truman's policy of limiting the war.

As the toll in blood and money swelled, dissent among the people against the Korean War became strong and deep. Essentially, however, it was expressed through mediums of politics—in Congress, in forums, in the press, and, above all, in the polling places in the 1952 presidential election. Dissent against Korea had none of the theatricality and fury that shook America during the Vietnam War. Korean hostilities broke out less than five years after the end of the Second World War. The American people were sitll accustomed to war, far more so than in the 1960s. They were proud and confident of their armed forces. Patriotism flourished. To the Korean War

* The Tenth Corps had been newly absorbed by the Eighth Army.

generation Selective Service had been a fact of life. Many veterans were still relishing their 1940s experiences in uniform. The fact of America's going to war to resist aggression was no shocking novelty. But when the war grew bitter and costly and months of rising casualties passed without victory in sight, public opinion on a large scale turned against it.

In particular, two historical events made a difference in dissent as between Korea and Vietnam. One was the civil rights movement of the 1960s; the other was the baby boom of the late 1940s and 1950s. The Korean War generation knew nothing about street demonstrations, marches, vigils, underground activities, urban violence, campus protest, songs, chants, and mass organization, such as were to be born of the civil rights revolution and then merged into dissent against the Vietnam War. As for the baby boom, the campuses of the Korean War period were a small world compared with the teeming universities of the 1960s. A clairvoyant Senator Lyndon Johnson could have looked at the hordes of children trudging to kindergarten in 1950 and seen a legion of college students shouting in President Johnson's face in 1967 and 1968.

Leaders of dissent were everywhere in the 1960s. In 1951, no other critic had anything like the stature of Douglas MacArthur, but what he stood for would have horrified the Vietnam War dissenters.

The JCS directive on defensive action, which jarred MacArthur, had been approved by Truman. Yet in MacArthur's opinion, it "seemed to indicate a loss of the 'will to win.'" "President Truman's resolute determination to free and unite [Korea] had now deteriorated almost into defeatism," the general was to write in his memoirs.[2] He dispatched a vigorous reply to the JCS on December 30, 1950, making it clear that he wanted the United States "to recognize the state of war which has been forced upon us by the Chinese authorities and to take retaliatory measures within our capabilities." Specifically, he recommended four momentous measures, all unacceptable to the administration.

First, a blockade of China—an act of war. Members of the JCS believed that to be effective a naval blockade would have had to include Dairen, a de facto Soviet port, and Vladivostok, the Soviets' principal Far Eastern port. Furthermore, it was evident that other United Nations allies would not join in such a potentially provocative strategy.

Second, air and naval bombardment of China on a scale necessary to destroy its industrial capacity to wage war.

Third, use of an undisclosed number of Chiang Kai-shek's Nationalist troops on Taiwan to open a diversionary second front on the Chinese mainland. To Mao, such an adventure would have had the intolerable overtones of a resumption of the Chinese civil war. A return of Nationalist forces to the mainland had a strong appeal to right-wing Republicans, however, and a sizzling episode, involving their congressional leadership and MacArthur, was in the making as a result.

Fourth, deployment of 33,000 other Nationalist troops in Korea to help stem the Chinese advance there.[3] Chiang Kai-shek had offered such a force after the North Korean invasion in June. Truman turned down the offer because of Acheson's concern that it could lead to war with China. Moreover, a later JCS study said that introduction of the Nationalist troops would not significantly affect the outcome in Korea. The troop offer was repeated after the Chinese intervention. Joe McCarthy said that Truman should be impeached if he did not accept it.

The shock of the United Nations' retreat evoked opposition to Truman's policies but not on a decisive scale.

In part, criticism was aimed at the limitations that had been placed on MacArthur's operations. Writing in *Human Events*, the conservative William Henry Chamberlain complained that MacArthur had been forced to fight "with one hand tied behind his back."

In part, the criticism sprang from a feeling that the United States ought not to have been fighting in Korea. "We should get our troops out . . . as quickly as possible," the *Detroit Times* said.

In part, the criticism was fueled by impatience over Trumans' unwillingness to strike at China. Chamberlain, for example, proposed that all the aggressive steps be taken that MacArthur had recommended in his secret message to the JCS.

In part, too, the criticism was isolationist. Said the *Topeka State Journal*, "We should withdraw our forces from Asia and after that from Europe." One of the most prominent isolationists of the Second World War period, Joseph P. Kennedy, father of John F. Kennedy, now appealed for an end of the Korean commitment and of what he called the idle attempt "to hold the line of the Elbe and the

line of the Rhine." In a televised speech that Truman labeled isolationist, former President Herbert Hoover urged that American policy concentrate on the security of the Western Hemisphere by
holding the Atlantic and Pacific oceans along with the British Isles,
Japan, the Philippines, and Taiwan. He wanted the United States to
avoid intervention on the continents of Europe and Asia.

Hoover's speech was a problem for Truman because it came at the
moment when Truman was preparing to implement the policy he
had announced in September, namely, substantially increasing the
number of American troops in Europe. His plan called for the deployment of six American divisions, the two already in Europe on
occupation duty and four others. In fact, he had just designated
General Eisenhower to be the first NATO commander. But Hoover
had warned that it would be "inviting another Korea" to send more
troops or money to Europe before Europeans had armed themselves
to build "a sure dam against the Red flood." When the new Congress convened in January 1951, conservative Republicans introduced resolutions to put both houses on record against dispatch of
troops abroad without congressional consent. The legislation
touched off what was called at the time "the great debate," which
revivified remnants of isolationist sentiment in Congress. Among the
proponents was Senator Taft who said, "The president has no power
to agree to send American troops to fight in Europe a war between
members of the Atlantic pact and the Soviet Union." Foreign en-
tanglements, so to speak, and domination of national security policy
by the Executive Branch had been growing since Franklin Roosevelt's time. Taft and other noninterventionists were really fighting
those conditions while challenging Truman's right to send troops to
Europe.

At a press conference Truman was asked whether he required
congressional approval to send the additional four divisions. "No, I
do not," he snapped. In the midst of his other troubles with Mac-
Arthur and the Chinese he remained unyielding against the challenge of the House and Senate resolutions. With a big boost from an
appeal to Congress by Eisenhower, Truman finally prevailed on the
troop issue and returned to his scourges in the Far East.

Despite MacArthur's proposals, the president and his advisers remained totally opposed to expanding the Korean War into a war
with China under existing circumstances. Their reasons were specific. They feared that Communist air power unleashed against the

vulnerable ports and airfields in South Korea and Japan at a time when masses of Chinese troops were in battle array in South Korea would endanger the existence of the Eighth Army. They feared that war against China might activate the Sino-Soviet mutual defense treaty, bringing about a third world war at a time when the Soviets were armed with nuclear weapons. Despite the crisis in Korea, the administration still regarded Western Europe as the key to United States security and did not want American forces immersed in Asia, leaving Europe vulnerable to Soviet attack. Finally, in the opinion of the Joint Chiefs of Staff, the United States was not yet prepared for a major war.

The chiefs rejected MacArthur's recommendations. They reiterated that he should hang on in Korea, inflicting casualties on the Chinese unless and until the safety of the Eighth Army was in peril, and then set sail for Japan. MacArthur replied that his forces were not strong enough to hold in Korea and to defend Japan. He warned of falling morale among his troops. Secretary Marshall was nettled. When a general complained of the morale of his troops, Marshall remarked to Rusk, it was time to take a look at the general's morale. Finally in his message, MacArthur perturbed Truman by saying that "under the extraordinary limitations and conditions imposed upon the command in Korea its military position is untenable, but it can hold for any length of time up to its complete destruction if overriding political considerations so dictate." Another perimeter defense around Pusan was being prepared. "We were at our lowest point. . . ." Marshall said later.

Truman presided at a National Security Council meeting that produced a directive, concluding, in effect, that, after all the costs and anguish of the previous six months, the evacuation of Korea would be necessary if the Chinese kept advancing. Truman sent a considerately worded letter to MacArthur explaining why the administration was taking the course it took. Until the United States and its European allies had been adequately rearmed, Truman said, "we must act with great prudence in so far as extending the area of hostilities is concerned. Steps which might in themselves . . . lend some assistance to the campaign in Korea would not be beneficial if they thereby involved Japan or Western Europe in large-scale hostilities."

Nevertheless, Truman assured MacArthur that the Chinese would not have heard the last of it if their forces should drive the United

Nations out of Korea. "[W]e shall not," the president said, "accept the result politically or militarily until the aggression has been rectified."[4]

General Bradley later testified on Capitol Hill that expulsion from Korea was something that the United States could not have accepted "as a final solution."

"[I]f we had been driven back to Pusan beachhead, even if we had been able to hold it, or if we had been driven out, I think our people would have demanded something else be done against China," he said.[5]

Indeed at a critical point in January 1951 the views of MacArthur and the Joint Chiefs of Staff were not so divergent as they later came to seem. After receiving and rejecting MacArthur's bomb-and-blockade proposals, the chiefs themselves, without approval of higher authority, tentatively agreed upon a blockade of China, Nationalist military operations against the mainland Chinese, and American air and naval attacks on China in the event of Chinese assault against United Nations forces somewhere outside Korea, if evacuation were required. None too soon all such contingency plans became unnecessary.

Unexpectedly, in mid-January the administration was treated to an astonishing development. In the prevailing gloom, General Collins was sent back to the Far East for a reassessment. What he found in Korea did not square with MacArthur's messages. Indeed the army chief of staff had scarcely arrived when the Eighth Army began a counterattack, a reconnaissance in force that inflicted casualties on the Chinese near Osan. The Eighth Army that Collins saw was in fairly good shape, was improving rapidly, and was imbued with reasonably good morale.

When General Walker was killed, he was succeeded as Eighth Army commander by General Ridgway, former deputy chief of staff of the army for operations, who, in the Second World War, had commanded the Eighty-second Airborne Division in Sicily and Normandy and later XVIII Airborne Corps. In taking command in Korea, he did an outstanding job in revising, reorganizing, and refitting the routed ground forces. When MacArthur had talked about the necessity of evacuating to Japan as quickly as feasible, he appears to have overlooked not only the recuperative power of the Eighth Army but also the ravaging effect of winter upon the Chinese troops and the disadvantage of their long supply lines, which were at the mercy of American pilots. Now the Eighth Army was on its way north again, soon to inflict ghastly casualties on the overextended Chinese. It was to be only a matter of weeks before the Americans would recapture Seoul for the second time and would move up once again to the 38th parallel. This time, except for tactical purposes and short distances, United Nations forces would not be allowed by the president to cross the parallel with the aim of reunification of Korea. And that was a policy MacArthur still could not swallow.

On March 15, 1951, in violation of Truman's December 5 order against unauthorized statements, MacArthur publicly criticized the strategy of stopping the Eighth Army's advance at or near the parallel. Answering a question from Hugh Baillie, president of the United Press, he opposed such a halt as an act that fell short of "accomplishment of our mission in the unification of Korea." Truman tolerated that firecracker, only to have a bomb go off in his face a week later.

At the United Nations a consensus was developing behind the proposition that return of UN forces to the area of the 38th parallel created an opportune moment for seeking a settlement with China. Discussions led to a plan for President Truman, as executive agent of the United Nations, to declare a desire for peace. The Joint Chiefs of Staff and the State Department drafted a declaration to the effect that the UN command was ready to enter into arrangements with the Chinese for a cease-fire as a forerunner to negotiations that might produce a broad settlement in the Far East. While circulating the draft for approval of other United Nations members with units in Korea, the chiefs routinely notified MacArthur on March 20 that a presidential statement regarding a settlement would be issued shortly.

Late in the evening of March 23, Washington time, news came bursting in from Tokyo that MacArthur had issued an ultimatum to China. The essence of his statement, addressed to the Chinese military command, was: Confer in the field with MacArthur on armistice terms or China would be wiped out. The deed blew the United Nations initiative to bits. As the biographer William Manchester wrote of MacArthur and his conduct at that stage of the Korean War, "He simply could not bear to end his career in checkmate."[6] The statement was an egregious violation of Truman's order of December 5. In spirit it was completely out of tune with the conciliatory character of Truman's pending declaration, now sabotaged. The MacArthur statement was also usurpation of the conduct of foreign policy by a field commander. News of it caused a donnybrook at the United Nations. Who spoke for the United States, allied diplomats demanded: Truman or MacArthur? "The President, although perfectly calm," Acheson wrote later, "appeared to be in a state of mind that combined disbelief with controlled fury." On the spot, Truman dictated a message to MacArthur reminding him of the December order and stating, "The President has also directed that in the event Communist military leaders request an armistice in the field, you immediately report that fact to the JCS for instructions."[7]

Out of sight, another fuse was burning toward the powder. Joe Martin, Republican leader of the House of Representatives, had delivered a Lincoln Day speech in Brooklyn advocating that Chinese Nationalist troops open a second front on the mainland. He said, "What are we in Korea for—to win or lose? . . . If we are not in Korea to win, then this administration should be indicted for the murder of thousands of American boys."

Martin endured a good deal of Democratic criticism for it and, on March 8, wrote to MacArthur, an old friend, seeking his advice on the question, "either on a confidential basis or otherwise." On March 20, MacArthur wrote: "Your view with respect to the utilization of the Chinese forces . . . is in conflict with neither logic nor . . . tradition."[8] The letter was a case of a military commander's conveying to the political opposition his support of a policy opposed by the president. And he did not indicate that the letter was confidential.

Truman was at his desk on the afternoon of April 5 when Roger Tubby, then an assistant White House press secretary, brought him a bulletin off a news ticker. Martin, worried about the Korean situation, had read MacArthur's letter to the House. "It makes me boil," Tubby said.[9]

At first glance, Truman took the bulletin calmly. On his desk lay a copy of the new issue of *Life*. Pointing to it, Tubby said, "They want us to attack China." An editorial in the Henry Luce magazine, echoing the conservative Republican line, asserted that the United States should "take full advantage of whatever the Nationalists can do now to help us now in the struggle for Asia," even if that help might assume the form of "a limited beachhead invasion, presumably in South China."[10]

"Well," Truman said, "I think they are maneuvering the general out of a job."

"Good!" Tubby exclaimed. The common view in the White House staff was that the relief of MacArthur was long overdue.

Truman told Tubby that MacArthur had been guilty of a "doublecross," apparently referring to the torpedoing of the cease-fire offer.[11] Truman considered that a graver offense than the letter to Martin.

"This stuff makes me boil, too," Truman said. "You know, I can work up to a boil. I can take just so much. I am talking to Marshall on this."

On his calendar he jotted, "The situation with regard to the Far Eastern General has become a political one."

Later, he noted, "Rank insubordination . . ."

During a tense, secretive week in the White House Truman held a series of meetings with four advisers: Marshall, Acheson, Harriman, and Bradley. "I've come to the conclusion," the president wrote in his diary, "that our Big General in the Far East must be recalled. I don't express any opinion or make known my decision [while the advisers were deliberating]."[12] Considering the upheaval that the removal of MacArthur was certain to cause, Acheson and Marshall at first counseled a cautious approach. Harriman outspokenly favored relief of the general. As chairman of the JCS, Bradley withheld an opinion until he could sound out the chiefs. When he did so, they unanimously recommended relief on three counts. The first was that MacArthur's statements showed that he was not in sympathy with the government's policy of limiting the war to Korea. The second was that he had violated the president's order regarding clearance of statements. The third was that as a military officer MacArthur had not submitted to civilian control. At a meeting on April 9, Bradley reported the chiefs' opinions to the president. Marshall, Acheson, and Harriman declared themselves in favor of relief. Shortly after 1:00 A.M. on April 11, 1951, the news was flashed to the world from the White House press room: TRUMAN FIRES MACARTHUR.

The reason the news came at such an hour was that the original plan for personal, courteous notification to MacArthur misfired because of a communications breakdown in Pusan. Unaware of events in Washington, Secretary of the Army Pace was visiting Korea. The plan as of April 10 was for Truman to inform Pace of his decision and direct him to fly to Tokyo to notify MacArthur at his residence. Then, during the evening of the tenth, not only did communications go out in Korea, but reporters from the *Chicago Tribune* and the Mutual Broadcasting System called Bradley's office about a tip that an important resignation was expected in Tokyo. Mutual said it was setting up for a big story out of Japan. The assumption of a number of Truman's advisers was that MacArthur had learned of the president's decision and was going to beat him to the punch. If so, Tubby argued, MacArthur might denounce administration policies and say that he could no longer serve in such a situation. The resulting sensation would indeed have put Truman in a hole, and Tubby and others argued that the White House could not run the risk. Truman decided that the proposed Pace mission was hopeless in the circumstances and that the order should be sent directly to MacArthur and announced. The unintended effect was that MacArthur appeared to have been treated shabbily, magnifying the explosion that daylight would bring.

The passions that were released simultaneously in all parts of the country were rare in the United States. "The people in my section at least," a southern senator said, "are almost hysterical."[13] To millions, MacArthur was an illustrious patriot suddenly cast down by a politician in Washington, a politician who deliberately would not allow MacArthur to win a war against Communism. A Wisconsin newspaper, the *Fond du Lac Commonwealth Reporter*, attributed Truman's decision to appeasement of the "yapping yahoos of the British Socialist Government." Suspicion that MacArthur's downfall was a concession to Great Britain and other members of the United Nations added more than a touch of fury to the reaction. And in London, as if in confirmation, Parliament cheered when the news came. Truman's announcement was a catalyst for unleashing against himself the frustrations of a lengthening limited war with no prospect now of a great MacArthur victory, such as had thrilled Americans during the war in the Pacific. By a multitude of conservatives, anti-Communists, chauvinists, and fundamentalists of one sort and another, Harry Truman was hated for having done something that, ironically, history would regard as one of his most justified, necessary, and courageous acts. In the eyes of the dissenters the difference between the politician and the exalted figure in Tokyo was captured in a closing line in the five-star general's letter to Martin in which he said, "There is no substitute for victory."

Taft, Wherry, the Senate minority whip, and their colleagues led Republicans in a blaze of rhetoric at the Capitol. Joseph and Stewart Alsop were to write that the Taft-Wherry wing of the Republican party "clearly sees MacArthur as the ideal rallying point for an all-out attack on Truman and, through Truman, on American foreign policy." In a fiery speech at a meeting in Joe Martin's office, attended by representatives of the Republican National Committee, Taft suggested that Truman be impeached. Elsewhere, Joe McCarthy said, "The son of a bitch should be impeached." In a front-page editorial the *Chicago Tribune* declared: "President Truman must be impeached and convicted. . . . [H]e is unfit, morally and mentally, for his high office." When the Senate convened on April 11, William E. Jenner, a Republican from Indiana, said: "[T]his country is in the hands of a secret inner coterie which is directed by agents of the Soviet Union. . . . Our only choice is to impeach President Truman."[14] The proprietors of the *Fort Wayne News-Sentinel* took it upon themselves to telegraph every member of the Indiana congressional delegation to urge the "immediate impeachment" of Truman and Acheson. The Hearst, McCormick, and Scripps-Howard newspapers treated MacArthur's removal as if it were a national disaster. Hearst's *New York Journal-American* suggested that Truman may have acted under the influence of "some kind of mental or neural anodyne" administered by a State Department agent. Not to be outdone, McCarthy attributed Truman's condition on the night of April 1–11 to "bourbon and benedictine."[15]

The Illinois state senate adopted a resolution condemning Truman for "irresponsible and capricious action." The Los Angeles City Council adjourned "in sorrowful contemplation of the political assassination" of MacArthur. In San Gabriel, California, the president was burned in effigy. In New York, longshoremen walked off their jobs to demonstrate against him. He was denounced from pulpit to barroom. The White House was engulfed with angry telegrams. In Tokyo, MacArthur told Ridgway he had learned from physicians that, as Ridgway recalled MacArthur's words, Truman "was suffering from malignant hypertension; that this affliction was characterized by bewilderment and confusion . . . and that . . . he wouldn't live six months."[16] Several days after his action, Truman was lustily booed to his face at the season-opening baseball game in Washington. Nothing like it had happened in a baseball park since Herbert Hoover's appearance at the World Series of 1931. Harriman wrote to Eisenhower, "The Roosevelt-Truman haters are having a chance to let off their spleen."[17]

Truman stood his ground and said little. To General Eisenhower, then in Europe as commander of NATO forces, he wrote, "I was sorry to have to reach a parting of the way with the big man in Asia, but he asked for it and I had to give it to him."[18]

After a tumultuous hero's welcome in San Francisco on his return from Tokyo, MacArthur flew to Washington and addressed a televised joint session of Congress on April 19. The speech was a highly charged attempt to force a reversal of Truman's Far Eastern policy. To say that the United States could not mount as strong a defense in Asia as in Europe, MacArthur insisted, was defeatism.

"You cannot," he said, "appease or otherwise surrender to Communism in Asia without simultaneously undermining our efforts to halt its advance in Europe."

Then the peroration, which had the effect of rekindling resentment in and out of Congress over the general's removal: "'Old soldiers never die; they just fade away.'" And like the old soldier of that ballad, I now close my military career and just fade away—an old soldier who tried to do his duty as God gave him the light to see that duty. Goodby."[19]

2

The Johnson administration was born of violence in Dallas, and violence, despite Johnson's efforts at conciliation, was to be its lot. When news of the Tet attack on the embassy in Saigon arrived in Washington, the Reverend Dr. Martin Luther King, Jr., had only 65 days to live, Robert Kennedy only 127. The bright times that had seemed to stretch ahead of Johnson on the morrow of his election in 1964 turned into times of riots, fires, bombings, and death at home as well as in Vietnam. One of the bright times was when he signed the Voting Rights Act in August 1965, saying that, finally, "perhaps the last of the legal barriers tumbling." But in that same August blacks in the Watts section of Los Angeles engaged in six days of sniping, looting, and bombing that left thirty-four persons dead and more than one thousand injured.

The tumbling of legal barriers did not meet the immediate rising expectations of blacks for better jobs, better homes, better schools, a better life. On a wide front their dissatisfaction flowed into a militancy under the slogan "Black Power." In May 1965 a wave of riots, arson, and shooting rose in the South. In the North, too, the conditions of blacks precipitated racial trouble. Five days of violence in Newark in July caused the death of twenty-six persons. Then disturbances rocked Spanish Harlem. Then, one of the worst race riots in American history exploded in downtown Detroit. Homes, buildings, stores went up in flames. In four days, forty-three persons were killed in desolate streets. Governor George Romney of Michigan called out the national guard, and Johnson felt compelled to send federal troops and tanks. The murder of King in Memphis on April 4, 1968, set off rioting in 110 cities. Thirty-nine persons, mostly blacks, were killed. Twenty-five hundred were injured. Seventy-five thousand national guard and federal troops were sent into the streets of America. As black smoke from burning buildings drifted over the White House and the cherry blossoms, Washington was in a state of seige. Machine guns were mounted on the steps of the Capitol, and troops sealed off black neighborhoods. And race riots were only part of the national trauma.

Thousands of antiwar demonstrations swept from coast to coast, ranging in method from praying to dynamiting. The participants included clergymen, professors, black leaders, white civil rights activists, pacifists, housewives, entertainers, writers, artists, lawyers, doctors, drifters, draft-card burners, self-aggrandizers, dreamers, and tens of thousands of college students. Some of the students rebelliously chanted, "Hell, no, we won't go!" although perhaps a fair percentage of them grew up and voted for Ronald Reagan. Drug addiction, the sexual revolution, and a surge of defiance by youths, many of them radicalized through participation in the civil rights movement, contributed to the social convulsion that multiplied the burdens of those who were conducting the war. "One of the things that divides us," Johnson said, "is that a great number of the hawks want us to do more, but the other side is more vociferous." He squirmed under the crescendo of criticism over bombing, saying, "I am like the steering wheel of a car without any control. The Senate won't let us play down the bombing issue."[20]

Dissent assumed myriad forms. The Dow Chemical Company was harassed at every point because it manufactured napalm, the use of which was excoriated by opponents of America's war-making. Protesters disrupted trading on the New York Stock Exchange on one occasion; on another, they interrupted an Armed Forces Day parade in New York. A Rutgers University professor's statement that he would welcome an NLF victory became an issue in the gubernatorial election in New Jersey in 1966. But Governor Reagan of California, speaking in Albany, Oregon, in 1967, said the country's longing for an American victory was wearing thin. "Isn't it time," he asked, "we either win this war or tell the American people why we can't?" The folk singer Joan Baez joined others in a lawsuit to recover the percentages of their 1965 and 1966 federal taxes that had been spent for military purposes. The opening of a motion picture on the Green Berets was picketed in New York. In many demonstrations around the country, the flag of North Vietnam was unfurled as a sign of contempt for American society.

Johnson chose the occasion of a Jewish Labor Committee dinner in New York on November 9, 1967, to denounce in a speech "those who say: 'What America built is rotten. Let's tear it apart.'" All the things promised for his Great Society would come in time, he said, but would not come easily.

> It will not come at all if we ever yield to the forces of division and the forces of paralyzing dissension. And let me tell you, my friends, tonight those forces are abroad in this land at this hour. They are the enemies of constructive action. Men who want to move this nation forward must join us in resisting them.[21]

The jibes of college students were particularly painful to Johnson because of what he had done for education. He had hoped to win the good opinion of youth and believed his programs had earned it. Reedy wrote,

> Nothing bewildered him more than the seiges of the White House by half-naked hippies chanting, "Hey! Hey! LBJ! How many kids have you killed today?" He thought he had done everything for them—college loans, scholarships, subsidies— and he considered their conduct nothing but the grossest ingratitude. They were not showing the same concern for his problem that he had shown for their problems, or at least that was the way he reasoned.[22]

Considering his efforts on behalf of civil rights, Johnson could not have felt very differently about the blacks' dissent. Martin Luther

King himself had urged blacks to take part in antiwar demonstrations. He perceived that Vietnam was diminishing the Great Society, which held promise for blacks, and that the casualty lists contained the names of a disproportionately high number of black servicemen.

The physical appearance of many of the protesters grated on Johnson. "When he was a young man, as soon as you graduated from college you were very careful to comb your hair right and tie your tie right, get a pressed shirt, pressed suit, and you'd start making the rounds looking for a job. . . ." Reedy told Merle Miller. "The long hair bothered him, the careless, sloppy clothes, the blue jeans. He'd look around the White House and he'd see a lot of young people that looked exactly like his ideal of what young persons should look like. And so to him that was the real American youth."[23] In 1967, an off-Broadway play, *MacBird!*, smeared the president so viciously that *The New Yorker* rejected an advertisement for it on the grounds of taste.

Johnson was stung by radicals carrying signs that labeled him a war criminal and a killer, while exalting Ho Chi Minh. At the previously mentioned meeting with Democratic leaders on February 6, 1968, Johnson asked Senator Mansfield to make a speech condemning Ho for what Johnson called the dirty tactic of violating the Tet truce. "But nobody says anything bad about Ho," he grumbled. "They call me a murderer. But Ho has a great image." It was not unusual in those days before the boat people and the oppression of South Vietnam for some war critics, including Mary McCarthy and Susan Sontag, to portray Hanoi's leaders as saintly.

In time, Johnson could barely move about the country without demonstrators crowding near his limousine or shouting imprecations outside hotels at which he was staying. Things came to a point where he could be assured of decorous settings for speeches only on aircraft carriers or military installations. In November 1967, he undertook a 5,100-mile tour of such havens in order, he said, to salute the men "who keep me free." He quoted former President Eisenhower as having told him that the American people had forgotten what it meant to be patriotic. Returning from the tour, Johnson spent the final Saturday night at Williamsburg, Virginia, to attend a Gridiron Club dinner. On Sunday morning, he did the proper thing by going to an Episcopal service at Bruton Parish Church. The Reverend Cotesworth Pinckney Lewis made the most of the situation by preaching on the evils of the Vietnam War. "We are appalled," he said, "that apparently this is the only war in our history which has had three times as many civilian as military casualties." The president's hour of worship made front pages across the country.

Several days later at a press conference he shrugged off the incident, saying that thirty-five presidents before him had had to endure such experiences. He turned angrily, however, on dissent in the form of "storm-trooper bullying, throwing yourself down in the road, smashing windows, rowdyism, and every time a person attempts to speak to try to drown him out."[24]

"The fact that a generation of Americans could be alienated from the values of their forefathers was something beyond his ken," Reedy wrote.[25]

"I know that in some quarters today patriotism is regarded with puzzlement or disdain," Johnson said in his speech to the national convention of the American Legion in Washington in 1966. Probing for an answer, he added: "Many people feel a deep sense of rootlessness in the swirling currents of modern life. They are strangers to their neighbors and their community, and so they feel estranged from their country."[26]

One of the targets of dissent was a deplorable situation that had come about in the raising of military manpower. Middle- and upper-middle-class young men on a large scale were avoiding military service, especially in combat units, while blacks and whites at the lower end of the economic scale were carrying the burden of the horror in Vietnam.

In the First and Second World Wars the problem of fairness was greatly reduced because full mobilization was in effect. Since Johnson had rejected full mobilization in the Vietnam War, fairness became elusive. Young men could volunteer not only for a particular branch of the armed services but for a particular line of duty. Volunteers tended to come from the educated classes, and, for the most part, they chose duties that did not put them in the line of fire.

For most of the rest of its military manpower the country relied on the Selective Service system, which had become distorted before the United States entered the Vietnam War. For one thing, the need for military manpower had been very low. For another, the baby boom had produced such an extraordinarily large number of draft registrants that Selective Service, which acted under legislation passed by Congress, was practically giving away deferments and even creating new categories of deferments to dispose of the load.

Draft classifications were especially favorable to college students and professionals, and remained in existence when Johnson turned to combat in Vietnam. To retain their deferments, many college seniors flocked to graduate schools. Others had the wherewithal to pay for professional draft-deferral advice. Still others knew the ropes well enough to flee to Canada. When the casualty figures began coming in from Vietnam, the evidence of the class system in operation was abundant. Not only was Selective Service itself laboring under a conservative bureaucracy, but Congress was inert in the face of the scandal. In particular, the conservative South Carolinian, Mendel Rivers, as chairman of the House Armed Services Committee, thwarted reform, even after Johnson had appointed a commission under the respected Burke Marshall of Yale Law School that recommended some necessary changes. But then there was no ground swell of public opinion demanding a change in the painful and dangerous situation.

While Johnson was struggling to hold things together in Washington, hundreds of college buildings around the country were seized by students, and many of the buildings were damaged. Some demonstrators blocked the entrance to military bases and actually invaded certain of them. Others interrupted the movement of troop trains by standing on the tracks. A pacifist in the Catholic Workers movement immolated himself in front of United Nations headquarters; another young protester committed self-immolation in front of the Pentagon. Marchers in the streets chanted "Sieg Heil" and carried banners flaunting "Amerika," and not infrequently were clubbed or temporarily blinded by tear gas. Several hundred marchers were arrested in October 1967 in a thirty-two-hour demonstration at the Pentagon, celebrated by Norman Mailer, a participant, in *The Armies of the Night*. The event involved so many different sequences that a true account was next to impossible. To Mailer, the conflict was dominated by horrible brutality inflicted upon young women by soldiers and United States marshals. To Johnson, the occasion was one for pride in the restraint, firmness, and professional skill of the soldiers and marshals in the face of "irresponsible acts of violence and lawlessness by many of the demonstrators."[27] To the outside observer, it was fresh evidence that at the approach of a presidential election year the atmosphere in the United States was poisonous.

Occasionally, Johnson met with a body of distinguished advisers outside the administration, an establishmentarian group if ever there was one dubbed the "Wise Men." They included Acheson, McGeorge Bundy, then president of the Ford Foundation, Clark Clifford, Henry Cabot Lodge, Averell Harriman, former Secretary of the Treasury C. Douglas Dillon, General Omar Bradley, Maxwell Taylor, Justice Fortas, and Arthur H. Dean, former special ambassador to Korea during the truce negotiations. On November 2, 1967, Johnson told the "Wise Men," who still supported him on Vietnam, that he was, in the words of the minutes,

> deeply concerned about the deterioration of public support and the lack of editorial support for our policies. He pointed out that if a bomb accidentally kills two civilians in North Vietnam, it makes banner headlines. However, [the enemy] can [lob] mortar shells into the [Presidential] Palace grounds in Saigon and there are no editorial complaints against it.[28]

By the time of Tet the loss of press support for Johnson's war policies had become a hemorrhage. Ever since Eisenhower had set out to secure the independence of South Vietnam, the American press in general had stood staunchly behind the domino theory. Matters began to change after Johnson made Vietnam America's war and the credibility of the administration became suspect. *Time* and *Life*, in the forefront of Johnson's supporters from the outset, were critical of war policy by the fall of 1967. *Newsweek* turned the same corner. *The New Yorker* took to carrying long, dissenting articles, and its "Talk of the Town" page now mixed humor with tracts heavy with the idealism of the peace movement. The staple of *The New York Review of Books* became antiadministration dissertations, accompanied by David Levine's drawings caricaturing the president as a sick man. The bombing of North Vietnam had set the once supportive *New York Times* against Johnson's Vietnam policies; the paper's Op Ed Page was filled with antiwar sentiment. The *Los Angeles Times* cooled on the war in 1967. The *Washington Post* also did an about-face from what Senator Fulbright had once denounced as obsequious backing of Johnson's conduct of the war. Even the *Wall Street Journal* deserted the president after Tet.

"We think," the *Journal* said in its lead editorial on February 23, 1968, "the American people should be getting ready to accept, if they haven't already, the prospect that the whole Vietnam effort may be doomed, that it may be falling apart beneath our feet."

Except, however, for his press conference of February 1, in which he called the enemy offensive a failure, Johnson had little to say publicly about the war immediately after Tet. The White House revealed that he was preparing a major televised address, but it was not scheduled until March 31. The expectation, even among his speech writers, was that he would reaffirm his goals and appeal to the people to hold firmly to the course.

VIII · *Undone*

1

When, at the end of a stormy presidency studded with historic decisions, Truman delivered his farewell address on television, he said that his most important decision had been to intervene in Korea to wage a limited war in order to avert a world war. It was also a decision that was to inflict heavy damage on his leadership and on the Democratic party.

Narrowly defined, the United Nations' effort had been a success. In a historic exercise of collective security, the non-Communist forces had driven the invading North Koreans back across the 38th parallel. Aggression had been repulsed, the status quo restored. The Chinese offensive, too, had been contained.

Significantly also, Truman's foreign policy had withstood MacArthur's challenge, enjoying the continuing support of the bipartisan coalition that had backed Roosevelt's and Truman's aims abroad. In the showdown with MacArthur, Truman was supported by *The New York Times*, the *New York Herald Tribune*, the *Washington Post*, the *Baltimore Sun*, the *Christian Science Monitor*, the *Chicago Sun-Times*, the *St. Louis Post-Dispatch*, the *St. Louis Globe-Democrat*, the *Boston Globe*, the *Minneapolis Tribune*, and *America*, a national Catholic weekly. Notably, Truman received timely help from joint hearings by the Senate Armed Services and Foreign Relations committees. Called as an inquiry into the relief of MacArthur, they delved into the origins, conduct, and prospect of the war.

Starting with MacArthur, all of the main participants in military leadership and war policy, excluding the president, of course, were sworn as witnesses. For weeks the hearings proceeded, patiently and fairly, giving everyone his say, and, inevitably, driving home to the public a realization of what might have been involved in Mac-Arthur's proposal to wage war upon China with air and naval power. If the hearings did not arrest the decline in the president's popularity, they did shield him from protest over MacArthur's removal. For Truman would have had the utmost difficulty governing throughout his remaining twenty-one months in office had the military leadership sided in the moment of crisis with MacArthur. Instead, the esteemed Secretary of Defense George Marshall, General Bradley, chairman of the Joint Chiefs of Staff, and each of the three chiefs, respectively representing the army, navy, and air force, testified in support of Truman's action. Bradley was the most succinct in stating the case against MacArthur's plan for attacking China. "Frankly, in the opinion of the Joint Chiefs of Staff," Bradley testified, "this strategy would involve us in the wrong war, at the wrong place, at the wrong time, and with the wrong enemy."[1] He meant that the ultimate enemy was the Soviet Union.

The stand of the military robbed the raucously supported Mac-Arthur challenge of most of its force. Marshall and Bradley and possibly some, or all, of the three chiefs had not been at ease with the thought of relieving MacArthur. Privately, before the president acted, Bradley suggested to Marshall that the latter, as secretary of defense, write to MacArthur and tell him how his statements had put Truman in an impossible situation. The two drafted a letter but never sent it. "You'd never in the world have got him relieved," Truman said eight years later, "if the Chiefs of Staff had been in control of the policy of the country."[2] When Marshall, Bradley, and the chiefs were forced by Truman to render a judgment, it came down against MacArthur and eventually cooled the crisis.

No more acceptable for all that, however, was the war as it dragged on with growing casualties, higher taxes, and irritating economic controls. The earlier feat of driving the North Koreans out of South Korea no longer satisfied a public opinion now impatient with the unending checkmate near the 38th parallel. By and large, Truman was never as popular as his recent image suggests. Heavy political liabilities had accumulated around him, and the war simply raised the level of disgust with all the miseries in Washington.

Preposterous as it might seem today for anyone to have tried to depict as "soft" on communism an administration that had gone to war against Stalin's client state and had fostered the Marshall Plan, NATO, and the Truman doctrine, the Republicans to a large extent succeeded in doing just that. The demagoguery of McCarthy, the Red-baiting by Nixon, Wherry, and the China lobby, and the calamitous Hiss case had combined to convince millions of Americans that the administration harbored Communists in positions where they could influence foreign policy.

Corruption had also been exposed in the administration without implication of Truman personally. First there were rather petty cases of favoritism, featuring gifts of a mink coat and deep freezers. Then there was alleged influence-peddling by "five-percenters," schemers who charged a fee of that amount on the total of a government contract they might procure for a client. After that came revelations of alleged political influence in the obtaining of loans from the Reconstruction Finance Corporation, since abolished. Next, tax fixing in the Bureau of Internal Revenue. Finally, laxity and worse in the Department of Justice. Truman shocked a good many voters by firing first T. Lamar Caudle, assistant attorney general in charge of the tax division, and, ultimately, the attorney general himself, J. Howard McGrath, who had been Democratic national chairman at the time of Truman's dazzling victory in 1948.

The war, the Red bugaboo, and the scandals gave the Republicans an effective war cry for the 1952 campaign: "Korea, Communism, and Corruption."

The Fair Deal had been stranded by the war. Truman's State of the Union message of 1951, which in other circumstances would have been the critical year for his liberal domestic program, dealt almost exclusively with Korea, rearmament, taxes, and the perceived Soviet menace. "In the months ahead," he said, "the government must give priority to activities that are urgent, like military procurement and atomic energy and power development. It must practice rigid economy in its non-defense activities. Many of the things we would normally do must be curtailed or postponed."³ In particular, the high hopes of 1949 for civil rights legislation died, increasing the certainty that a day of reckoning was coming on that issue. Given the powerful conservative forces in Congress during Truman's second term, civil rights bills would have been up against a high wall in any case. To make matters worse, Truman had to mute his differences with southerners in order to win their support for war policy, especially after China's intervention and the political bedlam caused by his relief of MacArthur.

After all the high promise of the 1948 victory, the only major new domestic legislation Truman was able to get through Congress was the National Housing Act of 1949, a law that widened the federal government's role in housing and slum clearance. In words that were to have a hollow sound in later years it proclaimed the goal of "a decent home and a suitable living environment for every American family." The effectiveness of the legislation depended on continuous ample funding by Congress, but it was not forthcoming, in large part because of the Korean War. Military and diplomatic questions dominated Truman's second term. During the Korean War, nevertheless, he did achieve a gratifying measure of success in keeping prices steady after an initial rise.

Not until fifteen years later when inflation began in the latter part of the Vietnam War to sap their standard of living did people appreciate what Truman had done to stabilize the economy during the Korean War. In contrast to Johnson, who was to insist on heavy funding for domestic programs in wartime, Truman not only imposed wage and price controls but also got Congress to pass three tax bills in the months after the North Korean invasion. He was convinced that Roosevelt had relied too much on borrowing to finance the Second World War, thereby causing the national debt to balloon. In coaxing three tax bills out of the legislators, Truman's most effective argument was that borrowing, as he said in a special message in 1951, "would only transfer the financial problem to our children and . . . increase the danger of inflation with its grossly unfair distribution of the burden."[4] When Truman left office, the people were at least spared the pains of inflation that was to be a legacy of the Johnson administration.

By the time of the Senate hearings in the spring of 1951 it was evident to Marshall and Acheson that the Chinese must have known that they had achieved what they could in Korea without a major change in strategy, involving a heavy commitment of fresh troops. After all, the Chinese aims in Korea were limited, too; these had been achieved when United States forces were driven out of most of the North. Heavy losses of men were doubtless hard on Mao's new regime. Furthermore, his Soviet allies had concluded that it was time for a settlement, lest the war spread dangerously. Recent Chinese attacks had been repulsed repeatedly by Ridgway's forces with what Marshall called "tremendous" losses. Testifying at the hearings early in May, for example, he said:

If they renew the attack and they meet the same result that came from their attack of the last two weeks, we will have almost destroyed again, or ruined the fighting power of, some, I think it is, thirty-four new divisions. . . . If we break the morale of their armies, but more particularly, if we destroy their best-trained armies, as we have been in the process of doing . . . it seems to me you develop the best probability of reaching a satisfactory negotiatory basis with those Chinese Communist forces. . . .[5]

Seizing the opportunity presented by the military situation, Trygve Lie, secretary general of the United Nations, stated that the principal purposes of the United Nations would be fulfilled by a cease-fire along the 38th parallel, assuming that it would be followed by restoration of peace and security in the area. Diplomats went to work. On June 23, 1951, Jacob Malik, head of the Soviet delegation to the United Nations, said on radio that his government believed the war could be settled. After preliminary exchanges the North Koreans agreed to participate in a cease-fire conference.

The conference began on July 10, at Kaesong, later moving to Panmunjom. While negotiators wrangled, the fighting continued since, as Ridgway was to note, "the negotiations were just an extension of the battlefield. Whatever was eventually agreed on would necessarily reflect the military realities; and it was the bitter task of the solider to impress the enemy with our ability to resist all his efforts to move the battle line farther south."[6] The cease-fire talks were so long and sour and the concomitant fighting so heavy at times that the negotiations brought no surcease for Truman's troubles. By the end of 1951 his popularity, as reflected in the Gallup poll, had fallen to an unprecedented low point of 23 percent. Although he rarely showed it, with his remarkable resilience at the age of sixty-eight, he endured, as 1952 dawned, moments of deep dejection, even indulging in reveries, recorded in his diary, about the atomic annihilation of Moscow, Leningrad, Stalingrad, Odessa, Dairen, Port Arthur, Peking, Shanghai, Vladivostok, and Mukden. "This is the final chance," he jotted in his diary of January 27, 1952, "for the Soviet Government to decide whether it desires to survive or not."[7] After relieving his frustrations in that fashion, possibly after downing one bourbon too many, he would return briskly to his desk the next morning, ready for business.

In the spring of 1952 Truman was wounded in the crossfire between the Korean War and a national steel strike. The steel companies and the United Steelworkers of America were deadlocked over the terms of a pending labor contract. When the union decided to strike, Truman was beset by conflicting advice about the effect of a walkout. A number of civilian advisers maintained that an adequate supply of steel was on hand for military purposes, a judgment that was subsequently widely accepted. The Pentagon, on the other hand, warned him that a strike would cause a serious shortage of steel, especially of certain specialized products essential for fighting the war. Truman was determined not to risk a shortage for the battlefield.

A few courses were open to him for keeping the factories producing. A principal option was the Taft-Hartley act, with its provision for postponement of a strike for an eighty-day cooling-off period. To many, that seemed the most sensible and proper approach. But there were flaws in it. And Truman was adamant in believing that in the situation that had developed, invocation of Taft-Hartley would be unfair to the union. The year 1952 was a presidential election year, and the Taft-Hartley act was anathema to organized labor, chief ally of the Democratic party. Another possible option, over which his advisers were divided, was for the president to seize the strike-threatened steel industry and run the plants. The Selective Service law authorized seizure under certain conditions but was in many ways unsuited to the threatened steel strike because the legislation had not been intended to deal with labor disputes.

Blaming the corporations for the dispute, on April 8 Truman put the country in turmoil and precipitated a constitutional conflict by announcing on television that he would seize the steel industry. In an executive order he based his authority on "the Constitution and laws of the United States, and as President and Commander in Chief of the armed forces"—the very authority he had asserted in sending troops to Korea and Western Europe without the approval of Congress.

The government's takeover of the steel industry whipped up the hottest domestic controversy Truman had ever faced. Fourteen separate resolutions of impeachment of the president were introduced in Congress. His friend, Senator Lyndon Johnson, said that Truman's order was evidence of a trend toward dictatorship. Big Business and Republican conservatives charged that a dictatorship had already begun. Truman had pushed to new lengths the legal power of the president at a time when his political power had been eroding under the acid of "Korea, Communism, and Corruption."

The companies took the case to the United States District Court for the District of Columbia, challenging the president's inherent right to seize. The case was heard by a strict constructionist, Judge David A. Pine. In defending the government, Assistant Attorney General Holmes Baldridge delivered what he later confessed to be a bad argument. Pine ruled that seizure was "illegal and without authority of law." The union struck but returned to work at Truman's urging, as the plants were still in government hands, pending appeal to the Supreme Court.

A high personal drama, unperceived at the time, was involved in the appeal. Even as President Johnson was to use Associate Justice Abe Fortas of the Supreme Court as a regular counselor, Truman often sought the advice of Chief Justice Fred M. Vinson. When the strike was brewing, Vinson, a companion and confidant of Truman's, counseled him to seize the steel industry and advised him that he had the legal grounds on which to act. In what a *New York Times* editorial two decades later called a breach of ethics and the separation of powers, Vinson's advice was given at a time when it appeared probable that the case would eventually come before the highest court, provided the president took the chief justice's advice.[8] When that came to pass and the justices filed in on June 2 to hand down their decision, the outcome of a great issue hung on whether the chief justice had been able to carry a majority of the court with him. He had not. By a vote of six to three, the Supreme Court found Truman's act unconstitutional. The court upheld Pine's decision, thereby narrowing the powers of the president. With his critics shouting in glee, Truman turned the plants back to the companies.

This time the union went on strike and stayed on strike for fifty-three days, halting steel production in the midst of a war. "How the President got through it all with his far greater burdens and his advanced years attests to his remarkable stamina," the assistant White House press secretary Roger Tubby observed in his personal journal. "But even he was played out." Joseph H. Short, the White House press secretary, told Tubby on one occasion that he "thought the President would collapse on his way to his room." At another time when some papers were to be signed, according to Tubby, Truman deferred the task until a moment "when I'm not so shaky."

He confessed to feeling "terribly tired" and to having fallen asleep in a chair the day before.[9]

Truman did not enter his name in the Democratic presidential primary in New Hampshire in February 1952. Apparently without any instruction or urging from Washington, a Manchester lumber dealer filed petitions for him anyhow. Truman ignored the election, and he was soundly defeated by a Democrat he disliked, Senator Estes Kefauver of Tennessee (Truman referred to him as Cowfever). Though the president had ignored the New Hampshire race, the outcome was an embarrassment to him. The next day he told reporters that primaries were "just eyewash."

On March 29, 1952, Truman spoke at a Jefferson-Jackson Day dinner at the National Guard Armory in Washington. Handed to the press in advance, his text read like typical election-year oratory of the day, ranging from Teapot Dome to Hoover's handling of the Great Depression. And when he delivered it, that was the way it sounded until the very end when, without any warning whatever, he said: "I shall not be a candidate for reelection. I have served my country long and, I think, efficiently and honestly. I shall not accept renomination. I do not feel that it is my duty to spend another four years in the White House."[10]

Some guests were so astonished that they were not sure they had heard him correctly. A collective gasp filled the armory. For months politics had been dominated by speculation as to whether Truman would run again. The suddenness of his announcement raised some questions as to whether the burden of the Korean War had caused him to bow out. In fact, he had never intended to run in 1952, and his wife, Bess, was determined that he should not. On April 16, 1950, more than two months before the Korean War began, he wrote a memorandum for his file commending the two-term tradition and stating that he would not accept renomination. He informed his staff secretly during a vacation in Key West, Florida, on November 19, 1951.

With or without Truman on the ticket, the Democratic party was in a grievous condition in 1952. Roosevelt had been elected and reelected for four terms, the last of which, all but eighty-two days, had been served by Truman. Then, when Truman upset Dewey in 1948, assuring at least twenty continuous years of Democratic power, the political rhythm of the country was unduly interrupted. The monopoly of power in the executive branch had been partly to blame for wrongdoing by easygoing office holders who had grown to feel immune to punishment for shady dealings. The administration had run down. Furthermore, defeats in five consecutive presidential elections had frustrated Republicans to the point where they encouraged the likes of Joe McCarthy as a last resort to finding a way back to power. It was a nasty time. Democratic leadership had aged. The erstwhile "solid South" had come to despise liberal Democratic programs as a threat to its racial mores. The Democratic nominee, Governor Adlai E. Stevenson of Illinois, was an admirable figure, but ten of him could not have defeated the war hero and astute politician Dwight Eisenhower in a year of Republican resurgence. And always in the background loomed the Korean War.

2

As the drafting of Johnson's much-awaited post-Tet speech of March 31, 1968, progressed, he betrayed the exhaustion of recent months. Visitors who saw him for the first time in a while were shocked by his drooping look and the deep furrows in his forehead. Even those who met with him frequently noticed the ravages. "And I think he was a little tired spiritually, too, at the end," General Wheeler was to recall. "He felt very keenly—and it had its effect on him—the loss of his popularity in the country. This was something that bothered him a great deal." Wheeler observed that Johnson was distressed that he would not go down in history as a peacetime president. "[H]e found himself as a 'war president' and, incidentally, in a very difficult time because of the dissent. . . ." Wheeler said. "This, of course was particularly abrasive to him."[11]

During Westmoreland's visit to Washington in November 1967, Johnson and the general had a talk in the White House late one night. Johnson confided that he had decided not to run for reelection in 1968.

"The primary reason, as he discussed it with me," Westmoreland remembered, "was his state of health. He had had a heart attack [in 1955]. He was tired. He had been carrying a terrible burden for a very long time. Mrs. Johnson, of course, had carried a burden almost comparable."[12]

Johnson is said to have brooded on the ordeal of Woodrow Wilson after Wilson had suffered a stroke in office. Johnson reminded Westmoreland of the trial that could face any semi-invalid in the White

House. According to Westmoreland, Johnson sought, and obtained, the general's assurance that the morale and effectiveness of the troops in Vietnam would not be affected by his departure from office.

Whether Johnson had by then made an irrevocable decision to retire at the end of his term is uncertain. Since the late summer of 1967, according to White House press secretary George Christian, the president had been discussing the future and expressing hope that he would not have to run. At one point he considered making an announcement of withdrawal from the race in December 1967. Christian, Horace Busby, another White House assistant, and Governor John B. Connally, Jr., of Texas, a close friend of the president's, all helped draft an appropriate statement. December passed without an announcement. Johnson considered making the statement in his 1968 State of the Union message but did not.

"I was a strong advocate of Johnson's not running again," Christian said afterward. "I thought the country was so divided that he was not doing himself or the country any favors by running. . . . Even if he were elected, it would be increasingly difficult to govern the country, and the people were ready for a change, some change in direction. And it was too late to try to mount some sort of public-opinion offensive."[13]

Affairs were in a wretched state early in 1968. The nation was demoralized. Not only had Tet disturbed the composure of the American people about the war at a critical time, but domestic problems related to Vietnam had grown very serious, too. For years the United States had been spending more money abroad than it had earned abroad. The balance of payments deficit had diminished the gold supply. In November, Great Britain devalued the pound sterling. Panic ensued in the world gold market. Speculation spread that the dollar also might have to be devalued. Johnson summoned reporters to the LBJ Ranch on New Year's morning, 1968, and announced what he called decisive steps to reduce the balance-of-payments deficit by $3 billion in the next twelve months.

"We cannot tolerate," he said in a statement, "a deficit that could threaten the stability of the international monetary system, of which the U.S. dollar is the bulwark. We cannot tolerate a deficit that could endanger the strength of the entire free world economy and thereby threaten our unprecedented prosperity at home."[14]

The measures included restraints on direct American investment and lending abroad and voluntary postponement of nonessential travel by American citizens outside the Western Hemisphere.

Outlays for the Vietnam War were wrenching the domestic economy. Although inflation had set in after American forces were committed to combat, Johnson persisted in a policy of guns *and* butter. In 1966, he did prevail on Congress to restore automobile and telephone excise taxes temporarily. In his State of the Union message of 1967 he recommended a two-year surcharge of 6 percent on corporate and personal income taxes. In the State of the Union message of 1968 he was still asking for the surcharge and in much more urgent circumstances, warning of the danger that "failure to act on the tax bill will sweep us into an accelerating spiral of price increases . . . and a continuing erosion of the American dollars."[15]

Foreshadowing years of instability, prices had risen. Interest rates had climbed. Budget deficits swelled. Home builders had been squeezed. The cost of medical care had gone up. Whereas within months of the outbreak of the Korean War, Truman had been able to get three large tax bills through Congress and had instituted a comprehensive program of economic controls, the economy during the Vietnam War had been subject to no comparable restraints. A number of economists have attributed the onset of the inflation of the 1960s and 1970s to Johnson's inability to get adequate tax bills passed. Wage-and-price controls he eschewed altogether.

Under pressure of inflation Congress had been reducing appropriations for Great Society programs. John Gardner, one of the most prominent members of the cabinet, resigned as secretary of health, education, and welfare partly because he did not receive the funds needed to realize his objectives. As Johnson had feared from the beginning, many conservatives seized upon the war as an excuse to vote against liberal measures. In his speech at the Jewish Labor Committee dinner in November 1967 he had attacked "the old coalition of standpatters and nay-sayers."

> They never wanted to do anything. But this year they say they can't do it because of Vietnam. That is just pure bunk. This crowd was against progress before Vietnam. They are against progress tonight, and they will be against progress tomorrow. And they will be against it when the war is over and when it is nothing but a dim memory.[16]

Vietnam had brought the Democratic party to the brink of a split.

With Allard K. Lowenstein, a kinetic New York liberal, as the catalyst, an antiwar faction bent on denying Johnson the nomination had been coalescing since early 1967. The dissidents' greatest need, of course, was a potent candidate. To Lowenstein, the logical man was the junior senator from New York, Bobby Kennedy. Kennedy brooded about running but would not agree to it. Then a voice from Minnesota said, "There comes a time when an honorable man simply has to raise the flag." Eugene McCarthy, poet, scholar, and one of the leading senate doves, entered the Democratic primary in New Hampshire, with a horde of students trudging through the snow at his heels. Still, speculation persisted that Kennedy would yet seek the nomination. Johnson had long suspected that he would, according to George Christian.

On January 30, 1968, Kennedy met with a group of reporters at what is called the Godfrey Sperling breakfast, a modern Washington press institution named for Godfrey Sperling of the *Christian Science Monitor*, its founder and moderator. At the table in the President's Room at the National Press Club, Kennedy said that he could conceive of no circumstances in which he would be a candidate. "My running," he said, "would automatically elect a Republican by splitting the Democratic party, and Democratic candidates would be beaten all over the country."

As Kennedy was about to leave, a reporter came in with bulletins from a news ticker about enemy attacks all over South Vietnam. The Tet offensive had just begun. At least one reporter present had a feeling that when Kennedy read the bulletins, he could have bitten his tongue for having declared that he would not be a candidate. A few minutes later, before climbing into his limousine outside the building, Kennedy told the reporter that Johnson felt he had to keep the war going as proof of his manhood.[17] What an irony it was: Kennedy's denouncing Johnson in 1968 for not stopping the war lest he lose his manhood, and Johnson's telling Doris Kearns in 1969 that when he became president, he feared to abandon South Vietnam lest Kennedy accuse him of losing his manhood.

McCarthy's campaign in New Hampshire had been considered a farce at first, but Tet gave it a boost. Like Truman in 1952, Johnson did not enter the primary. Local Democrats, in an action reminiscent of the Truman experience, had organized a write-in vote on the president's behalf. The election was on March 12. Johnson was the speaker at a dinner of the Veterans of Foreign Wars in Washington that evening before the body of the returns had begun arriving from up north. "I had an early report from New Hampshire this morning on these unbiased television networks," he told the guests. "They had counted twenty-five votes there—the first twenty-five. And the vote for LBJ was zero. I said to Mrs. Johnson, 'What do you think about that?' She answered, 'I think the day is bound to get better, Lyndon.'"[18] It was one of the infrequent occasions on which Lady Bird Johnson was mistaken.

By the time her husband had returned to the White House his jest was no longer funny. McCarthy won a resounding psychological victory. The president had received only 49 percent of the Democratic votes to McCarthy's 42 percent. But through a peculiarity of the selection system, McCarthy won twenty of twenty-four delegates to the Democratic convention. Furthermore, it was apparent from public opinion polls that he would defeat Johnson in the forthcoming Wisconsin primary. Yet McCarthy was in for about as hard a blow as Johnson. On behalf of Kennedy, Richard Goodwin, a longtime associate of the Kennedys who had been helping McCarthy, told him in New Hampshire on the night of the voting that Kennedy was considering running after all. He announced his candidacy on March 16 and set out on a blazing campaign tour. Of all the unlikely tricks of history, Bobby Kennedy had seized in the Vietnam War the very role of leader of the dissidents Douglas MacArthur had played in the Korean War—the fiery Kennedy representing the Democratic Left in contrast to the icy MacArthur speaking for the Republican Right.

The convergence of Tet and the Democratic split put Johnson in an intolerable situation. At luncheon with his highest advisers on March 22 he said he felt that a dramatic shift had occurred in public opinion about the war. According to the minutes, he added, "[A] lot of people are really ready to surrender without knowing that they are following a [Communist?] party line."[19]

Sometimes in those months Johnson, who was not a regular communicant in any church, became so consumed with anxiety that late at night he would order his limousine and a Secret Service detail and drive to St. Dominic's Roman Catholic Church in a poor section of southwest Washington for private prayers with a few priests and Christian brothers. The church, where the president's daughter Luci had received instructions when converting to Catholicism before marriage, was run by the Dominican order.* Johnson discovered it while attending mass there with her. Beginning in 1966, he returned for consolation from time to time, including a night when he had ordered the bombing of fuel dumps near Hanoi and Haiphong. Priests and brothers arranged a special prayer service for him in the chapel connected with the church on such occasions. It was a service typical of one that may be observed in Catholic or Episcopal churches, consisting of readings from the scriptures and psalms and sometimes the singing of hymns. Only Johnson, the Secret Service, and a couple of the clergy would be present during the late-night visits. "The president seemed to be very sincere," the Reverend Norman Haddad, a frequent participant, recalled recently. "It was no kind of show."

In the context of war policy and the presidential campaign, a climactic event had occurred at the end of February when Wheeler returned from a trip to Saigon, bringing a new request for reinforcements from Westmoreland. Ostensibly speaking on Westmoreland's behalf, Wheeler presented to Johnson on February 28 the case for about 206,000 more men. *The New York Times* broke the story, and it created a hullabaloo. To meet such a request Johnson would have been compelled, in an inflation-ridden election year, to call up reserves. An estimated $10 billion would have to have been added to the budget in 1969 and $15 billion in 1970.

In fact, Westmoreland had not taken it upon himself to ask for 206,000 more men to handle the military situation created by Tet. The plot was more complex than that. The nub of it was the worry of the Joint Chiefs of Staff about the inadequacy of the total military establishment in a dangerous period. Judging that Tet had created an atmosphere in which Johnson might feel forced at last to mobilize reserves, Wheeler put Westmoreland up to requesting a large number of troops in the expectation that the chiefs could retain a sizable portion of them for assignment outside Vietnam. Wheeler's presentation depressed Johnson and drove him into a profound review that was to bring a turning point in Vietnam policy. It came at a time when the Pentagon had passed into new hands. McNamara

* Luci once referred to Brother Fabian Butler as her "little monk." The president also spoke of "the little monks," but the Dominicans at the church are not monks. Monks generally confine their lives to monasteries.

had just departed for the World Bank. As his successor as secretary of defense, Johnson had chosen Clark Clifford.

Clifford was and is a shrewd, handsome, personable denizen of the inner sanctums of Washington, through whose walls he could still hear the wash of political currents on the outside. Very likely, Johnson wanted a hard-liner at McNamara's old desk. What he got was a skeptic. By and large, Clifford had favored Johnson's war policy for the first couple of years. In June 1967 Johnson had sent him and Maxwell Taylor on a mission to the Asian and Pacific nations allied with the United States in Vietnam to appeal to them to expand the size of their military contributions. To Clifford's dismay, as he wrote later, "our plea fell on deaf ears." "I returned home," he wrote, "puzzled, troubled, and concerned. Was it possible that our assessment of the danger to the stability of Southeast Asia and the Western Pacific was exaggerated? Was it possible that those nations which were neighbors of Vietnam had a clearer perception of the tides of world events in 1967 than we? Was it possible that we were continuing to be guided by judgments that might once have had validity but were now obsolete?"[20] From private conversations with Clifford in the summer of 1967, friends concluded that he thought the United States should get out of Vietnam.

He was present on February 28, 1968, when Wheeler asked for 206,000 additional men. Johnson was unwilling to make a commitment on the spot. Instead he selected a high-level committee headed by Clifford to take an intensive fresh look at Vietnam and to hand him on March 4 recommendations based on "the lesser of evils." In questioning military leaders in the committee sessions regarding future prospects in the war, Clifford became more convinced than ever that American policy had reached a dead end. The recommendations he submitted were essentially middle-of-the-road in character, containing something that would appeal to the various constituencies, including the military—for example, early approval of a reserve call-up of 245,000 men, which, of course, never came. The eye-catcher was the recommendation on immediate reinforcements for Westmoreland. The Clifford committee recommended not 206,000 men but 23,000. Thenceforth, the new secretary of defense used his diplomatic skills to curb military escalation in Vietnam and encourage negotiation. William Bundy credits the influence of Clifford's actions and recommendations, in particular, with turning Johnson around on the bombing policy, as does Harry McPherson.

At the March 4 meeting at which the recommendations were submitted and on at least two other occasions during that period, Rusk, the one who was a reigning culprit in the eyes of intellectual doves, urged Johnson to halt the bombing of North Vietnam north of the 20th parallel. Such a decision would have put about 90 percent of North Vietnamese territory off limits to American bombers. Influenced by a study done by a group of British intellectuals, including the economist Barbara Ward, the secretary of state was willing to test the reaction of Hanoi at that stage to a new initiative for peace. He made the point that since the monsoon season was at hand, cessation of bombing would not greatly affect the general military situation for the time being. Rusk also pressed the case for turning over a larger share of the fighting to the Saigon government's forces, or what was to become known in the Nixon administration as "Vietnamization" of the war.

Almost everywhere Johnson looked now, even among the previously supportive "Wise Men," representing the viewpoint of business, industry, and the legal profession, he could detect a loss of hope for the American commitment and a desire for disengagement from Vietnam. To a politician of Johnson's sensibilities, the degree of trauma in the country, the defections in Congress, and the chaos in the Democratic party surely signaled the end not only of escalation but also of his own political career. As Christian had sensed, it was too late for the president to undertake an offensive. A Johnson campaign for reelection would have put the country in shock.

The opening line of Johnson's address to the people on Sunday evening, March 31, was arresting. Speaking from the Oval Office over all the networks, he did not say that he wanted to talk about the war. "Tonight," he began, "I want to speak to you of peace in Vietnam and Southeast Asia."[21]

Going on to say that he was prepared "to move immediately toward peace through negotiations," he announced a halt in air and naval attacks on the almost 90 percent of North Vietnamese territory lying north of the demilitarized zone. Even the remaining limited bombing would be stopped, he said, if Hanoi would end its offensive operations. Then he called for formal peace talks and appealed to Ho Chi Minh to cooperate. Johnson promised to help strengthen South Vietnamese forces for their own defense. As for American forces, the request for 206,000 more men had gone out the window. Johnson noted that the previous authorized force level for the Americans was

525,000. He recalled sending another 11,000 for the Tet emergency. In the next five weeks, he disclosed, he would send only another 13,500 support troops, obtained in part by a call-up of certain reserve units. Again he urged Congress to pass a wartime surcharge on income taxes. This time, Congress was to respond favorably, but too late to reverse the swell of inflation.

As in the case of Truman's speech in the National Guard Armory almost exactly sixteen years earlier, a text of Johnson's speech had been distributed to reporters in advance; they immediately spotted an absence of comment about the political campaign or Johnson's own plans. His words unfolded simply as a statement concerning a decision to concentrate on a settlement rather than on continued prosecution of the war in the familiar pattern. Then at the end, exactly like Truman, he veered without pause or warning in a new direction that left the television audience as nonplussed as the audience in the armory in 1952.

Seeking peace, Johnson said, he would not allow the presidency to become entangled in election-year politics. He did not believe that he should devote "an hour or a day of my time to any personal partisan causes or to any duties other than the awesome duties of this office. . . . Accordingly, I shall not seek, and I will not accept, the nomination of my party for another term as your president."

3

Neither Truman nor Johnson was able to end the war in which he had committed American troops to combat. Both presidents were compelled to leave Washington with a deep sense of unfulfillment after final months of cruel disappointments. In 1953, President Eisenhower assumed responsibility for the Korean truce talks. In 1969, President Nixon and Henry Kissinger took over the Vietnam peace talks, which had opened in Paris not long after Johnson's March 31 speech. The talks sputtered on for another five years, during which more Americans were to be killed in Vietnam than had died there before, and still worse antiwar upheavals were to shake the United States.

Worn by the steel strike, resentful over Adlai Stevenson's tactic of distancing himself from the outgoing Democratic administration, angry at Eisenhower's campaigning, Truman was also frustrated by the intractability of the North Korean negotiations at Panmunjom.

In July 1952, as the national conventions were stirring up the issues at home, the Korean truce talks drearily passed the one-year mark. An impasse had developed on the matter of repatriation of prisoners of war. After the Second World War Soviet citizens who had defected to the German army had good reason to dread repatriation. Upon Stalin's demands, however, the United States and Great Britain sent them home, much to Truman's later regret. In Korea, a somewhat similar situation arose. The North had captured thousands of South Koreans as well as Chinese loyal to the Nationalists. The North Koreans pressed the captives into military service, during which many of the captives surrendered to United Nations forces. In the truce talks the North Korean government demanded they be returned with the rest of the prisoners. American negotiators suspected that the captives would be severely punished or killed and suggested instead that the South Koreans in question be released to the Rhee government and the Chinese Nationalists sent to Taiwan. A secondary consideration was involved. If the prisoners held by United Nations forces were returned to death or slavery, American psychological warfare would be impaired in the future. In other wars prisoners would not defect to the United States if they knew they might later be sent home to be tortured to death.

Washington espoused a doctrine of voluntary repatriation based upon the moral principle that only prisoners who volunteered to return would be placed in the hands of the Kim Il-sung regime. A strategic as well as a humanitarian aspect was at stake. If prisoners had a choice of returning or not, then in a future war Communist troops, whether of the Soviet Union or another nation, who were taken prisoner, might well decide not to return home. Such a procedure indeed could pave the way in war for wholesale defection by Communist soldiers who preferred a free society. Communist negotiators at Panmunjom could see that possibility as well as anyone else and continued to demand repatriation by force, if necessary. Truman would not budge. "We will not buy an armistice," he said, "by turning over human beings for slaughter or slavery."[22] Presaging American strategy in the Vietnam War, the United States heavily bombed cities of North Korea to compel the Communist negotiators to settle, but the truce talks ground to an indefinite halt on October 8, 1952. That was right in the middle of the presidential election campaign in the United States. Heavy fighting was resumed, helping the Republican cause. Eisenhower sank the Democrats in a speech in Detroit on October 24.

On national television he characterized Korea as "the burial ground for twenty thousand American dead" and heaped blame on the Truman administration for it. He promised, if elected, to give priority "to the job of ending the Korean War until that job is honorably done." Then: "That job requires a personal trip to Korea. I shall make that trip. Only in that way could I learn how best to serve the American people in the cause of peace. I shall go to Korea."[23]

Truman was furious. After the Republicans had won a huge victory and the president-elect had visited Korea, he publicly accused Eisenhower of "a piece of demagoguery." Acting on his good instincts, he did arrange for Eisenhower's son, John S. D. Eisenhower, an infantry officer serving in Korea, to be brought home for his father's inauguration without his father's knowledge. But for Truman's pains Eisenhower was angry at him and let him know it on the ride from the White House to the Capitol on Inauguration Day. Eisenhower thought a soldier's place in war was with his division.*

Johnson's final months in office were even more turbulent than Truman's. On the evening of the fourth day after his withdrawal speech, Johnson was preparing to fly to Honolulu for another conference on Vietnam. An aide handed him a note, "Mr. President: Martin Luther King has been shot." Johnson canceled his flight and went on television. "I ask every citizen," he said, "to reject the blind violence that has struck Dr. King, who lived by nonviolence. . . ." The fires were already burning. Almost exactly two months later, Johnson was asleep on June 5 when his telephone rang at 3:31 A.M. Rostow was calling. He had just been notified by the Situation Room that Robert Kennedy had been shot in Los Angeles in the flush of his celebration of his victory in the California Democratic primary. In agitation, Johnson telephoned Attorney General Ramsey Clark, J. Edgar Hoover, director of the Federal Bureau of Investigation, and James J. Rowley, head of the United States Secret Service, and later appointed a distinguished committee to study the causes of violence. Robert Kennedy's death left Johnson in fresh

---

* Later, Eisenhower sent Truman an apologetic note, thanking him for what he had done.

alarm over the state of public order in the United States.

Johnson did not attend the Democratic National Convention in Chicago in August, but his name darkened, it must be said, a convention that was perhaps the most riotous political event in modern American history, a stew of passion and violence in the convention hall and streets alike. With Kennedy out of the picture, Vice-President Humphrey, favorite of the party regulars, was practically certain of the nomination, barring some last-minute conflict between him and Johnson.

A primary issue before the delegates was what the Democratic platform should say on Vietnam. Operating through powerful party regulars, Johnson was determined that his policy not be repudiated. The antiwar faction despised his handling of the war and believed that the Democrats would lose in November unless its nominee broke with the president on Vietnam—an excruciating problem if the nominee were to be Johnson's vice-president, who had loquaciously supported Johnson's policies. On the eve of the convention, Soviet troops marched into Czechoslovakia, keeping hardline anti-communism fashionable in the United States and strengthening Johnson's forces at the convention when it came to the foreign policy plank. The antiwar faction demanded that the plank call for a halt in all bombing of North Vietnam, not just the bombing above the demilitarized zone. Johnson balked, claiming that if the bombers were grounded altogether, North Vietnamese troops would flood through the zone, imperiling American forces in the South. Reflecting his own policy, he demanded a plank that advocated a complete bombing halt only when Hanoi's response would justify it. That statement and other phrases in the administration draft made the plank appear to the antiwar faction as an outright endorsement of Johnson's policy in Vietnam.

Humphrey would not risk Johnson's seizing the nomination from him if Humphrey were to side with the antiwar faction. Lamely, he said that he had not come to Chicago to repudiate the president. The convention adopted the plank that Johnson demanded, and Humphrey lost an opportunity to run as his own man in the matter of peace in Vietnam. Instead he set out on an erratic campaign with the enmity of many voters friendly to the antiwar movement who might otherwise have been his supporters. On occasion during the fall, notably in a speech in Salt Lake City, he suggested that if he were president, he would approach a Vietnam settlement differently from Johnson. Johnson was furious, according to his special counsel, Harry McPherson. As McPherson later put it, Johnson "rubbed Humphrey's nose in it" every time Humphrey tried to break free on Vietnam policy.[24] To this day some doubts persist as to whether Johnson wanted Humphrey to win or whether he secretly preferred Nixon, who was well established as a hard-liner on the war.

Late in the fall, Hanoi offered to make certain concessions in the peace talks if all bombing were stopped unconditionally. On October 31, practically on the eve of the election, Johnson completely halted three and a half years of bombing, ultimately to be resumed by President Nixon. Humphrey's supporters were enraged that Johnson had not acted quicker as a way of rescuing the Democratic cause. On the other hand, of course, Johnson, about to step into the dock of history, did not want to act before he was sure a bombing halt was for the best, lest it appear that he had played politics with an issue of peace or war. Working out an understanding about the bombing halt with Hanoi and Saigon while under the pressure of the presidential campaign threw Johnson into some all-night frenzies. "A terribly dismal day for the president—he's worked so hard he's snakebitten," a participant remarked to colleagues after one session. After another, the participant expressed concern that Johnson was "just plain paranoid now." The next line in the still-private note reads, "It's an awfully good thing Administration is coming to a close."

Winner by an inch, Nixon called on Johnson on November 11 as part of the transition between administrations. In reference to Vietnam during the campaign Nixon had said that it was time for new leadership not tied to the policies of the past. He had vaguely but effectively intimated that he had a plan for ending the war. According to the White House notes of his conversation with the president, Nixon said that in general, he "found no significant differences between his views on Vietnam and those of the present administration."[25]

When, with the war in Korea still being fought, Eisenhower was inaugurated on January 20, 1953, it brought to an end nearly twenty years of Democratic rule, which had begun when Hoover left office on March 4, 1933.

Harry and Bess Truman took a train back to Independence, and he carried their bags to the attic. At a rousing send-off at Union

Station in Washington he had predicted that he would live to be one hundred years old. Bess made it to ninety-seven, but when he died on December 26, 1972, he was eighty-eight. Still, he had lived long enough to have seen the public image of a man whose leadership in the White House had been shredded, finally, by a costly, inconclusive war in Asia take an extraordinary turnabout. When polled on two occasions, a majority of historians have listed him among the near-great presidents. Popular culture has celebrated him in song and skit. His courage, outspokenness, honesty, simplicity, and other old-fashioned virtues have won the affection of a later generation. The irony was that the misfortunes of a man he had detested, Richard Nixon, were largely responsible for the steep rise in Truman's reputation by filling the American people with a yearning for someone just like Truman. After Watergate, stonewalling, Vietnam, and the credibility gap, the memory of Truman emerged as a sign that the country had had a better past after all.

While Eisenhower was applying himself to the Korean War, Stalin died of a stroke on March 5, 1953. A marked drop in tension followed. Heavy losses in Korea were wearing on the Chinese. Eisenhower pushed matters toward a truce by threatening through intermediaries to use nuclear weapons. The fighting in Korea ended on July 26, 1953.

Nixon's inauguration on January 20, 1960, while the war in Vietnam was still being fought, again brought an end to Democratic rule that had begun eight years earlier when Eisenhower left office on January 20, 1961.

After a rollicking luncheon at the Cliffords', Lyndon and Lady Bird Johnson went to Andrews Air Force Base, outside Washington, for their last ride on Air Force One, which flew them to Texas and retirement at the LBJ Ranch. It was a warm, moonlit night along the Pedernales River when they arrived. The bitterness of the Korean War had not followed Truman home. The Vietnam War, destined to last until April 30, 1975, was different. Its hatreds dogged Johnson to the end. He did not share Truman's good fortune in living long enough to see his public image restored from the ravages of Vietnam. In contrast to Truman, who survived the presidency by almost twenty years, Johnson lived only four years more. He died on January 22, 1973, at the age of sixty-five.

Not even the harshest critics gainsay his accomplishments in domestic reform, especially in civil rights. In the case of Vietnam, the opposite has been true. Maybe he has received even more blame for it than he deserves. War and the manner in which it is fought are usually a form of national expression. The Vietnam War was the product of many hands at work and many minds in assent. Would Johnson not have been acclaimed by his contemporaries and posterity if he had won a swift, clear-cut victory in Vietnam? Could not the same be said of Truman in Korea? Grenada was an outing next to those wars, and behold what a hero it made of Reagan. Above all, when it comes to the good opinion of posterity, stands the question of character. Truman has been rescued from the grime of the presidency because his character has come to have an enduring appeal to the American people. Johnson may always be accepted as a giant, but his character was not one that a later generation, at this point, looks up to.

In Korea and Vietnam a total of 111,185 Americans died or were killed—53,246 in Korea, 57,939 in Vietnam. There is no way to rationalize the outcome of those two wars that justifies such a sacrifice. To be sure, neither Truman nor Johnson planned, or even dreamed of, such results, but that does not alter the conclusion.

Surely, the United States occupation of southern Korea in connection with the ending of the war in the Pacific was a raw mistake. As in the case of a number of great problems—the atomic bomb, primarily—Korea instantly and unexpectedly fell into Truman's inexperienced hands the afternoon Roosevelt died. As with most of those other great problems, the question of Korean policy was thrust at Truman in a status that was still tentative yet set upon a course that a vice-president taking over the White House was likely to follow. In the global chaos of mid-1945 a bequeathed policy of Korean trusteeship and American participation in the interim administration of Korea was not one that was likely to have been chosen for serious reappraisal early in a new administration. The new secretary of state, James F. Byrnes, already immersed in the developing cold war in Europe, was quite ready to carry on the Roosevelt administration policy of supposedly temporary American intervention in southern Korea. Truman fully supported Byrnes. A policy shaped in one administration was applied in another.

Almost immediately, Americans became entangled in a hostile rivalry with the Soviets in an outer corner of the Aisan mainland far removed from any requirements of American security. Why should the United States have emerged from the Second World War as special protector of the people who lived in southern Korea? Once that role was assumed as a result of the occupation and the resulting Soviet-American rivalry, Americans were saddled with an obligation never envisioned in the war aims of 1941–42.

Strategically, it was not critical that southern Korea be kept out of the Soviet orbit. As the preeminent sea, air, and nuclear power, the United States at that time could have entered into, if necessary, a permanent and mutually satisfactory arrangement for the defense of Japan and the other islands of the American defense perimeter in the Far East. The United States would obviously go to their defense today. Had the United States in 1945 stayed clear of Korea, which few Americans knew or cared about then anyhow, Korea would not have become involved in the cold war. It was because Korea was a combustible cold war issue in June 1950 that the pressures on Truman for military intervention were all but irresistible.

More than thirty years later, the Korean War still has not been settled. Forty thousand American military personnel are stationed in South Korea now. In November 1983, President Reagan himself was at the demilitarized zone between the still hostile North and South, straining through binoculars for sight of any Communist troops, who might suddenly march against Seoul again. He was on the ramparts of one of the most sensitive borders in the world. As matters stand, a new and more terrible war in Korea is always a possibility.

One of the worst aspects of the Korean War was the subtle ways in which it influenced the American commitment in the Vietnam War. It was not just that Truman felt compelled to send arms and money to Bao Dai and thus involve the United States in the civil war in Indochina. Because of Chinese military intervention, Korea so magnified American fears of Communist Chinese aggression throughout Asia that the Eisenhower, Kennedy, and Johnson administrations moved into Vietnam in one way or another to build a dike. And the model they had before them was Korea. If the United States had succeeded by force of arms in erecting a barrier to preserve an independent South Korea, then why could it not do likewise in Vietnam with money, military assistance, advisers, helicopters, and, finally, American bombers and a half-million American troops?

The Korean model was misleading from the start. South Korea had an effective government, controlling not only the city but the countryside. The Saigon government did not control the agricultural areas of South Vietnam, a remnant of the recent French Indochinese empire. Beginning with Eisenhower and continuing through the Kennedy and Johnson administrations, American plans were based upon, and American resources poured into, an ineffective government. The United States went to the defense of a nation that was not really a nation in the sense understood by Americans. Finally, the North Koreans ultimately accepted a truce. The North Vietnamese, completely lacking in what Americans considered reasonableness, did not. Instead they kept forcing Americans to spend ever more blood and money until the effort became too extravagant even for the United States.

Washington did not achieve a great deal toward its aims of deterring future wars by confronting aggression in Korea and "aggression" that was really civil war in Vietnam. The last thirty years have witnessed incessant warfare in one part of the world or another. If it has been the secret intention of the Soviet Union at any time since the Second World War to provoke a military showdown with the West, the Kremlin undoubtedly has been deterred by the nuclear weapons of the United States, not by the American stands in Korea and Vietnam. Upholding the United Nations in Korea did not arrest the decline of that organization.

In Vietnam in particular, American policymakers held that failure to oppose Communist aggression would revive isolationism. But the Vietnam War produced a new wave of isolationism, as reflected, for example, in the nomination of George McGovern for president by the Democrats in 1972. The very thought of another Korea or Vietnam still chills American enthusiasm for overseas military adventures, beyond a pushover like Grenada. In Congress and, in fact, in the military, the "Vietnam syndrome" cools talk of intervention in Central America or the Middle East. Indeed, the Vietnam experience pulverized the internationalist bipartisan establishment that had shaped American foreign policy since about 1940. The escalation ordered in Vietnam by Johnson and later Nixon was a primary cause, and Truman's intervention in Korea without a congressional declaration a secondary one, in the passage of the War Powers Act of 1973, curbing the president's authority for long-term commitment of American forces abroad without a declaration of war by Congress. Although it was technically invoked by Congress after President

Reagan dispatched marines to Lebanon in 1983, the constitutionality of the act has yet to be tested.

The American misadventure in Vietnam was a hopeless case of myopia, of focusing on one troubled area without looking at the broader interests of the United States. Americans became captives of a state of mind symbolized by the domino theory and overheated by dogmas of the cold war. Anticommunism led Truman and Johnson too far afield. Their objectives outran their power. The Second World War created an illusion that American power could prevail in large areas of the globe. To have pushed farther in the Korean and Vietnam wars might, as the two presidents saw it, have provoked another world war. On the other hand, waging limited wars with no final, satisfying victory in sight finally deprived Truman and Johnson of public support.

Limited war creates difficulties for a democratic system with its tolerance of dissent, especially when, as in Vietnam, many people come to regard it as an unjust war. Intolerance of limited war presents a serious problem in the long run, because unlimited war is now out of the question if civilization is to survive. As is apparent around the globe today, war is a condition of human life. If the United States becomes involved in future hostilities of significant size, the American people will have to learn once again to cope with limited war.

The moral of Korea and Vietnam, which would be just as true of Central America in 1984, for example, is that use of military power to resolve problems of political, ideological, and economic origins, though perhaps not always futile, is treacherous indeed. That which may look relatively easy for a great power to accomplish may lead instead to unimaginable complications, particularly in a setting of difficult terrain and guerrilla traditions. Thus the first steps that Truman and Johnson took in the belief that they were measured and cautious ones proved to be dangerous and irreversible because events unforseen by the two presidents took control.

Above all, nothing is more misleading, more evanescent than the enthusiastic popular support a president may receive when he initially embarks on a limited war for such purposes as putting down indigenous communism or providing credibility for diplomatic obligations in other areas or exerting proper American leadership or defending American interests that turn out not to be vital ones. As

Harry Truman and Lyndon Johnson learned to their distress, casualties, taxes, inconveniences, and military humiliations rob people of their faith in a war rather quickly if a truly vital national interest or the nation's honor is not at stake. After a couple of years of involvement in Korea and in Vietnam, many, perhaps most, Americans could not remember for what it was they were supposed to be fighting, a familiar phenomenon that could as well occur, if the occasion were presented, in Central America. The fates of Truman and Johnson are a good place for any president to begin when pondering whether, in a world grown very dangerous, there is not a better way to deal with a problem than military intervention.

Central America, of course, has a different history from that of Korea and Vietnam. Central America is a neighbor of the United States; it lies within the United States' traditional sphere of influence. While there is wide agreement that Fidel Castro and Soviet officials have actively encouraged revolution in Central America, impartial experts do not believe they have supplied most of the weapons to revolutionaries. In a recent book Walter LaFeber, one of this country's foremost diplomatic historians, argues that it is not international communism but nationalism that provides most of the fuel for revolution in Nicaragua and El Salvador.[26] Indeed, LaFeber's controversial thesis is that the long history of United States military and economic intervention has produced revolutionary societies in Central America.

In any case, the pitfalls of Korea and Vietnam are reminders that we should not lose sight of. Those two wars demonstrated how hard it is for a president, once committed, to pull back in time to avert disaster. Wars not only take on lives of their own, as the saying goes, but they also develop constituencies—powerful ones. George Ball's futile warning to Lyndon Johnson not to risk a large military commitment in Vietnam is as pertinent now as it was then. "Once on the tiger's back," Ball said, "we cannot be sure of picking the place to dismount."[27]

Notes

The following abbreviations are used in the notes:

FRUS   *Foreign Relations of the United States, Diplomatic Papers*, cited by year and volume. U.S. Government Printing Office, Washington, D.C.

HSTL   Harry S Truman Library, Independence, Missouri

LBJL   Lyndon Baines Johnson Library, Austin, Texas

OHT   Oral History Transcript. Both of the libraries have compiled extensive interviews relating to the respective presidencies.

PPP   *Public Papers of the Presidents of the United States: Harry S Truman* and *Public Papers of the Presidents of the United States: Lyndon B. Johnson,* cited year by year. U.S. Government Printing Office.

PSF   President's Secretary's File. Harry S Truman Library

ROK   Republic of Korea

NSC   National Security Council

JCS   Joint Chiefs of Staff

The notes also contain citations from Roger W. Tubby's journal. A former State Department press officer, Tubby transferred to the White House in 1950 as an assistant press secretary and in 1952 became the White House press secretary. His journal is deposited at the Yale Library but is closed. He gave the author of this book complete access to the parts of it pertaining to the Truman administration.

I. *The Triumphs*

1. *The New Republic,* November 15, 1948, p. 1.
2. Clark M. Clifford Papers. State of the Union, 1949. Drafts. Box 23. HSTL.

3. *PPP*. Truman. 1949, p. 1 ff.
4. Charles E. Wilson to President Truman, December 1, 1948. Truman to Wilson, December 18, 1948. PSF: General File "W" Folder.
5. *PPP*. Truman. 1948, p. 121 ff.
6. *The New Republic*. November 14, 1964, p. 3.
7. Merle Miller, *Lyndon: An Oral Biography* (New York, 1980), p. 496.
8. *PPP*. Johnson. 1963–64, vol. 1, pp. 704, 705.
9. *PPP*. Johnson. 1963–64, vol. 2, p. 1604.
10. Ibid., p. 1607.
11. Ibid., pp. 1656, 1657.
12. Ibid., p. 1658.
13. Ibid., p. 1653.
14. John J. Muccio to George C. Marshall, November 9, 1948. *FRUS*, vol. 6, p. 1323.
15. *PPP*. Johnson. 1963-64, vol. 2, p. 1611 ff.
16. *New York Times*, November 28, 1964, p. 1.
17. *The Pentagon Papers*, (*New York Times* edition) (New York, 1971), pp. 326, 170–73.
18. *United States-Vietnam Relations 1945. Study Prepared by the Department of Defense* (U.S. Government Printing Office, 1971), Book 4, IV. C. 2, p. 54.

II. *The Traps*

1. The physician present related this episode to a young colleague, who years later privately passed it on to the author.
2. The author was present on the occasion.
3. Ed. Robert H. Ferrell, *Dear Bess: The Letters from Harry to Bess Truman, 1910–1959* (New York, 1983). See, for example, pp. 62, 60, 78, 96, and 254.
4. The late Paul Porter recalled Truman's words in an interview with the author in 1972.
5. Diary of Eben A. Ayers (assistant White House press secretary), entry of September 14, 1945. HSTL.
6. Related by William P. Rogers in a speech at the John F. Kennedy Library in Boston, April 26, 1983.
7. Bryce N. Harlow, OHT, LBJL.
8. *Dear Bess*, op. cit., p. 525.
9. Ibid., p. 39.
10. Ronnie Dugger, *The Politician: The Life and Times of Lyndon Johnson. The Drive for Power—from the Frontier to Master of the Senate* (New York, 1982), p. 86.
11. *PPP*. Truman. 1948, p. 339.

12. R-G 332 (U. S. Theaters of War, World War II, USAFIK), "XXIV Corps Journal." Box 22. 1945–December 1948. Washington National Records Center, Suitland, Md.

13. *FRUS*. 1944, vol. 5, pp. 1224–28.

14. *FRUS*. 1945, vol. 6, pp. 1039.

15. *FRUS*. 1946, vol. 8, pp. 713, 714.

16. *FRUS*. 1950, vol. 7, pp. 11–14.

17. *PPP*. Truman. 1949, p. 279.

18. *FRUS*. 1949, vol. 7, pt. 2, pp. 760–78.

19. *Khrushchev Remembers*, with an introduction, commentary and notes by Edward Crankshaw (Boston, 1970), pp. 367, 368.

20. *PPP*. Truman. 1950, p. 453.

21. Harry S Truman, *Years of Trial and Hope* (Garden City, N.Y., 1956), p. 332.

22. *FRUS*. 1946, vol. 8, pp. 77, 78.

23. Warren I. Cohen, *Dean Rusk* (Totowa, N.J.), p. 288.

24. *The Pentagon Papers* (*New York Times* edition), p. 27 ff.

25. *FRUS*. 1949, vol. 7, pt. 1, pp. 105–10.

26. *The Pentagon Papers* (*New York Times* edition), p. 10.

27. Notes on the President's Meeting with Undersecretary of State James Webb, March 26, 1950. Webb Folder. Box 6, Personal Files. HSTL.

28. *PPP*. Truman. 1951, p. 7.

29. Ibid., p. 1140.

30. Notes on the President's Meeting with Undersecretary of State James Webb, op. cit.

31. *United States-Vietnam Relations*, cited chap. 1, n. 18, Book 9. V. B. 3., p. 5.

32. *The Pentagon Papers* (*New York Times* edition), p. 10.

33. Ibid., p. 7.

34. Dwight D. Eisenhower, *The White House Years. Mandate for a Change* (Garden City, N.Y., 1963), p. 347.

35. Leslie H. Gelb, with Richard K. Betts, *The Irony of Vietnam: The System Worked* (Washington, D.C., 1979), p. 68.

36. *The Pentagon Papers* (*New York Times* edition), p. 1.

37. Larry Berman, *Planning a Tragedy: The Americanization of the War in Vietnam* (New York, 1982), p. 13.

38. Ibid., pp. 15, 16.

39. Theodore C. Sorensen, *Kennedy* (New York, 1965), p. 640.

40. Ibid., p. 651.

41. Norman Podhoretz, *Why We Were in Vietnam* (New York, 1982), pp. 19, 20.

42. *The Irony of Vietnam*, op cit., p. 70.

43. *The Pentagon Papers* (*New York Times* edition), pp. 90, 91.

44. Sorensen's *Kennedy*, op cit., p. 703.
45. *The Pentagon Papers* (*New York Times* edition), p. 80.
46. Arthur M. Schlesinger, Jr., *A Thousand Days: John F. Kennedy in the White House* (Boston, 1965), p. 341.
47. *Washington Post*, March 30, 1984, p. D 3.
48. Herbert S. Parmet, *JFK: The Presidency of John F. Kennedy* (New York, 1983), p. 330.

III. *The Pressures*

1. *PPP*. Truman, 1952–53, p. 1197 ff.
2. Journal of Joseph E. Davies, entry of April 3, 1945. Joseph E. Davies Papers, Library of Congress, Washington, D.C.
3. W. Averell Harriman and Elie Abel, *Special Envoy to Churchill and Stalin 1945–1946* (New York, 1975), p. 550.
4. Interview with John R. Steelman (the assistant to President Truman), August 24, 1974. Also Steelman. OHT. HSTL.
5. *PPP*. Truman. 1947, pp. 178, 179.
6. *NSC-7*. Modern Military Branch, National Archives, Washington, D.C.
7. *FRUS. 1948*, vol. 2, pp. 930, 931.
8. *United States Relations with China, with Special Reference to the Period 1944–1959* (a State Department white paper), pp. 107–09.
9. President Truman's Conversation with George M. Elsey, July 16, 1950. Korea—June 16, 1950 Folder. Box 71. George M. Elsey Papers. HSTL.
10. *Congressional Record*, vol. 95, pt. 2, p. 1950 ff.
11. *Committee on International Relations. Selected Executive Session Hearings of the Committee, 1945–1950, vol. 7. United States Policy in the Far East, pt. 1. Historical Series. U.S. House of Representatives.* Government Printing Office, pp. 179–81.
12. *Congressional Record*, vol. 96, pt. 1, p. 889.
13. *United States Relations with China*, op. cit., p. xvi.
14. Margaret Truman (with Margaret Cousins), *Souvenir: Margaret Truman's Own Story* (New York, 1956), p. 275.
15. Lyndon Baines Johnson, *The Vantage Point: Perspectives of the Presidency 1963–1969* (London, 1971), p. 45.
16. Tom Wicker, *JFK and LBJ: The Influence of Personality upon Politics* (New York, 1968), p. 205.
17. George Reedy, *Lyndon B. Johnson: A Memoir* (New York, 1982), p. 147.
18. *The Irony of Vietnam*, cited chap. II, n. 35., p. 91.
19. Doris Kearns, *Lyndon Johnson and the American Dream* (New York, 1976), p. 253.

20. John P. Roche. OHT. LBJL.
21. *The Politician,* cited chap. II, n. 10, p. 150.
22. Telephone conversation with Chester V. Clifton, August 25, 1983.
23. *PPP.* Johnson. 1963–64, vol. 1, p. 8 ff.
24. *Lyndon B. Johnson: A Memoir,* op. cit., p. 146.
25. Zbigniew Brzezinski. OHT. LBJL.
26. *PPP.* Johnson. 1963–64, vol. 1, p. 8.
27. *Lyndon B. Johnson: A Memoir,* op. cit., pp. 148, 149.
28. Eric F. Goldman, *The Tragedy of Lyndon Johnson* (New York, 1968), p. 381.
29. Harry C. McPherson. OHT. LBJL.
30. Ernest R. May, "Commentary," a paper delivered at the conference "Some Lessons and Non-Lessons of Vietnam. Ten Years After the Paris Peace Accords." Woodrow Wilson International Center for Scholars, Washington, D.C., 1983.
31. *The Politician,* op. cit., p. 220.
32. *The Vantage Point,* op. cit., p. 47.
33. *The Politician,* op. cit., p. 306.
34. *The Pentagon Papers* (*New York Times* edition), p. 127 ff.
35. Richard M. Helms. OHT. LBJL.
36. *The Pentagon Papers* (*New York Times* edition), p. 128. *The Irony of Vietnam,* op. cit., p. 92.
37. *The Pentagon Papers* (*New York Times* edition), p. 190.
38. Ibid., p. 274 ff.

IV. *The Commitments*

1. Interview, March 14, 1979, with James E. Webb, who was present on the occasion.
2. *Military Situation in the Far East. Hearings Before the Committee on Armed Services and the Committee on Foreign Relations. United States Senate. Eighty-second Congress. To Conduct an Inquiry into the Military Situation in the Far East and the Facts Surrounding the Relief of General MacArthur. . . ,* p. 948.
3. *FRUS.* 1950, vol. 7, p. 140.
4. Except where otherwise indicated, the ensuing account of the meeting at Blair House on June 25, 1950, is based on *FRUS.* 1950, vol. 7, pp. 157–65.
5. *The History of the Joint Chiefs of Staff. The Chiefs of Staff and National Policy, vol. 3. The Korean War, pt. 1. Historical Division. Joint Secretariat. Joint Chiefs of Staff,* pp. 100, 101.
6. Matthew B. Ridgway, *Soldier: The Memoirs of Matthew B. Ridgway* (New York, 1956), p. 192.

7. John D. Hickerson. OHT. HSTL.

8. Account of the meeting of June 26, 1950, is based on *FRUS*. 1950, vol. 7, pp. 178–83.

9. Thomas Terry Connally, as told to Alfred Steinberg, *My Name is Tom Connally* (New York, 1954), p. 346.

10. *Years of Trial and Hope,* cited chap. II, n. 21, pp. 338, 339.

11. *The Vantage Point* (cited chap. 3, n. 15), p. 573.

12. *FRUS*. 1950, vol. 7, pp. 248–50.

13. Ibid., pp. 250–53.

14. *Years of Trial and Hope,* op. cit., p. 343.

15. *PPP*. Truman. 1950, p. 529.

16. Roy E. Appleman, *United States Army in the Korean War. South to the Naktong, North to the Yalu (June–November 1950).* Office of the Chief of Military History. Department of the Army. 1961. U.S. Government Printing Office, p. 61.

17. *PPP*. Truman. 1950, pp. 502–06.

18. Korea—Congressional Leaders. 11:00 A.M. 6/30/50 Folder. Elsey Papers. Box 71. HSTL.

19. *FRUS*. 1950, vol. 7, p. 336.

20. *The Vantage Point,* op. cit., p. 112.

21. William Bundy. OHT. LBJL.

22. Stanley Karnow, *Vietnam: A History* (New York, 1983), p. 369.

23. Ibid.

24. *PPP*. Johnson. 1963–64, p. 927.

25. *The Vantage Point,* op. cit., p. 115.

26. *Lyndon B. Johnson: A Memoir,* cited chap. III, n. 17, p. 150.

27. Interview with Frank Church, September 7, 1983.

28. *The Irony of Vietnam,* cited chap. II, n. 35, p. 103.

29. Earle G. Wheeler. OHT. LBJL.

30. *PPP*. Johnson. 1963–64, vol. 2, p. 1126.

31. Ibid., p. 1164.

32. Ibid., p. 1391.

33. Hugh Sidey. OHT. LBJL.

34. *Planning a Tragedy,* cited chap. II, n. 37, pp. 34, 35.

35. *PPP*. Johnson. 1965, vol. 1, p. 4.

36. Ibid., p. 21.

37. Ibid., p. 33.

38. Ibid., p. 73.

39. *Planning a Tragedy,* op. cit., pp. 37, 39.

40. William Bundy. OHT. LBJL.

41. *The Vantage Point,* op. cit., p. 124.

42. Ibid., p. 125.

43. Ibid., p. 126.

44. Ibid., pp. 126, 127.
45. William Bundy. OHT. LBJL.
46. *Planning a Tragedy.*, op. cit., p. 53.
47. George W. Ball, *The Past Has Another Pattern: Memoirs* (New York, 1982), p. 381.
48. Philip L. Geyelin, *Lyndon B. Johnson and the World* (New York, 1966), p. 222.
49. *PPP*. Johnson. 1965, vol. 1, p. 278.
50. Quoted in *Planning a Tragedy*, op. cit., p. 54.
51. *The Irony of Vietnam*, op. cit., p. 121.
52. Ibid., p. 122.
53. *Planning a Tragedy*, op. cit., pp. 91, 92.
54. Ibid., pp. 56, 57.
55. *The Irony of Vietnam*, op. cit., pp. 372–74.
56. *The Past Has Another Pattern*, op. cit., pp. 393, 394.
57. *The Irony of Vietnam*, op. cit., p. 371.
58. *Planning a Tragedy*, op. cit., pp. 84, 85.
59. Ibid., pp. 187, 189.
60. *Lyndon B. Johnson and the World*, op. cit., p. 221.
61. William Bundy. OHT. LBJL.
62. Ibid.
63. *Lyndon B. Johnson: A Memoir*, op. cit., p. 148.
64. *The Vantage Point*, op. cit., p. 146.
65. *Planning a Tragedy*, op. cit., pp. 103, 104.
66. Ibid., pp. 89, 90, and 93, 94.
67. Ibid., p. 107.
68. Herbert Y. Schandler, *The Unmaking of a President: Lyndon Johnson and Vietnam* (Princeton, 1977), p. 3.
69. William Bundy. OHT. LBJL.
70. *PPP*. Johnson. 1965, vol. 2, p. 795.

V. *The Caldrons*

1. *United States Army in the Korean War*, cited chap. IV, n. 16, pp. 107, 108.
2. *Time*, November 27, 1950.
3. *New York Times*, August 13, 1950, p. 3.
4. *FRUS*. 1950, vol. 1, p. 234 ff.
5. *PPP*. Truman. 1950, p. 527 ff.
6. Interview with W. Averell Harriman, June 26, 1974.
7. *New York Herald Tribune*, September 27, 1950, p. 8.
8. *Congressional Record*, vol. 96, pt. 11, p. 15412.
9. *FRUS*. 1950, vol. 7, pp. 712–21.

10. *The History of the Joint Chiefs of Staff,* cited chap. 4, n. 5, p. 230.
11. *FRUS.* 1950, vol. 7, pp. 759–62.
12. Ibid., p. 826. Also *United States Army in the Korean War.,* op. cit., p. 608.
13. *The History of the Joint Chiefs of Staff,* op. cit., p. 243.
14. *FRUS.* 1950, vol. 7, 839.
15. *The History of the Joint Chiefs of Staff,* op. cit, p. 262.
16. John J. Muccio. OHT. HSTL.
17. Letter, Truman to Nellie Noland, October 13, 1950. Ed. Robert H. Ferrell, *Off the Record: The Private Papers of Harry S Truman* (New York, 1980), pp. 195, 196.
18. Interview with Henry J. Nicholson of the Secret Service, October 6, 1978.
19. *PPP.* Truman. 1950, p. 674.
20. James F. Schnabel, *United States Army in the Korean War. Policy and Direction: The First Year.* Office of the Chief of Military History. United States Army, Washington, p. 197.
21. *The Vantage Point,* cited chap. 3, n. 15, p. 153.
22. Earle G. Wheeler. OHT. LBJL.
23. Ibid.
24. *The Wilson Quarterly.* Summer 1983, p. 116.
25. Wheeler. OHT. LBJL.
26. BDM Corporation, *The Strategic Lessons Learned in Vietnam* (McLean, Va.), vol. 3, section 2, p. 21.
27. Cyrus R. Vance. OHT. LBJL.
28. Harry C. McPherson. OHT. LBJL.
29. *PPP.* Johnson. 1965, vol. 1, p. 394 ff.
30. George E. Christian. OHT. LBJL.
31. Wheeler. OHT. LBJL.
32. Barry Zorthian. OHT, pt. 4, p. 10. LBJL.
33. William Bundy. OHT. LBJL.
34. Ibid.
35. Ibid.
36. *The Unmaking of a President,* cited chap. 4, n. 68, p. 38.
37. David Kraslow and Stuart H. Loory, *The Secret Search for Peace in Vietnam* (New York, 1968), p. 137.
38. William Bundy. OHT. LBJL.
39. Zbigniew Brzezinski. OHT. LBJL.
40. McPherson. OHT. LBJL.
41. Ibid.
42. Memo for the President from Jim Jones. Tuesday Luncheon. September 12, 1967. Meeting Notes File. LBJL.
43. Wheeler. OHT. LBJL.

44. *Vietnam: A History,* cited chap. 4, n. 22, p. 415.
45. *The Unmaking of a President,* op. cit., p. 309.
46. *Lyndon B. Johnson: A Memoir,* cited chap. III, n. 17, p. 147.
47. Sam Houston Johnson, *My Brother Lyndon* (New York), 1969, p. 210.
48. Interview with Frank Church, September 7, 1983.
49. Liz Carpenter, "Why I Believe LBJ Was a Winner," *Parade* magazine, June 5, 1983, p. 6.
50. Zorthian, OHT, pt. 2, pp. 17, 18, 19. LBJ.
51. Lewis J. Paper, *John F. Kennedy: The Promise and the Performance* (New York, 1975), p. 113.
52. Telephone conversation, September 1983, with Bromley Smith, former head of the National Security Council staff.
53. *The Pentagon Papers* (*New York Times* edition), pp. 489, 490.
54. John P. Roche. OHT. LBJL.
55. *The Pentagon Papers* (*New York Times* edition), p. 472.
56. *PPP.* Johnson. 1965, vol. 1, p. 3 ff.
57. Michael Maclear, *The Ten Thousand Day War: Vietnam: 1945–1975* (New York, 1981), p. 233.
58. *PPP.* Johnson. 1965, vol. 1, p. 394 ff.
59. Frances FitzGerald, *Fire in the Lake: The Vietnamese and the Americans in Vietnam* (New York, 1972), p. 311.
60. Interview with Bill D. Moyers on "Vietnam: A Television History," pt. 4. Public Broadcasting System, 1983.
61. *The Pentagon Papers* (*New York Times* edition), pp. 474, 475.
62. Arthur M. Schlesinger, Jr., *Robert Kennedy and His Times* (New York, 1981), p. 799.
63. Chalmers M. Roberts, *First Rough Draft* (New York, 1973), p. 250.
64. *Robert Kennedy and His Times,* op. cit., pp. 825–27.
65. *The Pentagon Papers* (*New York Times* edition), pp. 483–85; 502–09.
66. *United States–Vietnam Relations 1945-1967,* cited chap. 1, n. 18, Book 5, IV. C. 6, pp. 81–89.
67. Ibid, pp. 93–95.
68. *The Pentagon Papers* (*New York Times* edition), pp. 527–29.
69. Ibid., p. 531.
70. *United States–Vietnam Relations,* op. cit., Book 6, IV C. 7(b), pp. 43–54.
71. *The Pentagon Papers* (*New York Times* edition), p. 577 ff.
72. Ibid., p. 283.
73. *Lyndon Johnson and the American Dream,* cited chap. III, n. 19, p. 320.
74. *New York Times,* December 30, 1966.
75. *The Vantage Point,* op. cit., p. 368.
76. *United States–Vietnam Relations,* op. cit., p. 91.

77. Townsend Hoopes, *The Limits of Intervention* (New York, 1969), p. 89.
78. *PPP*. Johnson. 1967, vol. 2, p. 816 ff.
79. *Robert Kennedy and His Times*, op. cit., pp. 883, 884.
80. *United States–Vietnam Relations*, op. cit., Book 6, IV. C. 7(b), p. 101.
81. *The Vantage Point*, op. cit., pp. 372–78, 600, 601.
82. Telephone conversation with Robert S. McNamara, September 27, 1983.
83. *First Rough Draft*, op. cit., p. 264.
84. *PPP*. Johnson. 1967, vol. 2, p. 1048.
85. Peter Braestrup, *Big Story: How the American Press and Television Reported and Interpreted the Crisis of Tet 1968 in Vietnam and Washington*. Abridged edition (New Haven, 1977), p. 51.
86. Ibid., pp. 51, 52.

VI. *The Disasters*

1. *The History of the Joint Chiefs of Staff*, cited chap. IV, n. 5, pp. 301, 302.
2. Memorandum for the President, November 10, 1950. PSF. Subject File: NSC Meetings. Memos for the President. Meeting Discussions (1950) Folder. Box 220.
3. *FRUS*. 1950, vol. 7, pp. 1013, 1014.
4. John J. Muccio. OHT. HSTL.
5. *Years of Trial and Hope*, cited chap. II, n. 21, p. 381.
6. Douglas MacArthur, *Reminiscences* (New York, 1964), p. 372.
7. *Military Situation in the Far East*, cited chap. IV, n. 2, pp. 3491, 3492.
8. *FRUS*. 1950, vol. 7, pp. 1237, 1238.
9. John Hersey, "Profiles," *The New Yorker*, April 14, 1951.
10. *Reviews of the World Situation: 1949–1950. Hearings Held in Executive Session Before the Committee on Foreign Relations. United States Senate, First and Second Sessions . . . Historical Series:* U.S. Government Printing Office), pp. 370, 372, 374.
11. *PPP*. Truman. 1950, p. 724 ff.
12. Ibid., p. 741 ff.
13. *FRUS*. 1950, vol. 7, pp. 1320–22.
14. *Military Situation in the Far East*, op. cit., pp. 3532–34.
15. Memos for the President. National Security File. NSC History. March 31 Speech. Box 47, vol. 2, nos. 6, 7, 8, 9, 10. LBJL.
16. President's Daily Diary, January 30, 1962. LBJL.
17. Memos for the President. National Security File. NSC History. March 31 speech. Box 47, vol. 2, nos. 6, 7, 8, 9, 10. LBJL.

18. Don Oberdorfer, *Tet! The Story of a Battle and Its Historic Aftermath* (New York, 1971), chap. 1.
19. *The Unmaking of a President*, cited chap. IV, n. 68, p. 76.
20. Ibid., p. 107.
21. *Tet!*, op. cit., p. 158.
22. Notes on the President's Meeting with the Democratic Congressional Leadership, February 6, 1968. The President's Appointment File, February 5, 1968. LBJL.
23. *First Rough Draft*, p. 261.
24. *The Unmaking of a President*, op. cit., p. 83.
25. *PPP*. Johnson. 1968, vol. 1, p. 161.
26. Notes for the President's Meeting with Senior Foreign Policy Advisers, February 6, 1968. President's Appointment File, February 5, 1968.
27. *Vietnam. A History*, cited chap. 4, n. 22., pp. 535, 536.
28. *The Wilson Quarterly*. Summer 1983, p. 99.
29. Ibid.
30. *The Unmaking of a President*, cited chap. IV, n. 68, pp. 89, 90.
31. *PPP*. Johnson. 1968, vol. 1, p. 234.
32. Arthur M. Schlesinger, Jr., *The Bitter Heritage: Vietnam and American Democracy* (Greenwich, Conn., 1966), p. 68.
33. Summaries of the studies were presented at the conference "Some Lessons and Non-Lessons of Vietnam. Ten Years After the Paris Peace Accords." Woodrow Wilson International Center for Scholars, Washington, D.C., 1983.
34. *Tet!*, op. cit., pp. 251, 252.

VII. *The Traumas*

1. *The History of the Joint Chiefs of Staff*, cited chap. IV, n. 5, pp. 397–99.
2. *Reminiscences*, cited chap. VI, n. 6., p. 378.
3. *Years of Trial and Hope*, cited chap. II, n. 21, pp. 435, 436.
4. *The History of the Joint Chiefs of Staff*, op. cit., pp. 399–401.
5. *Military Situation in the Far East*, cited chap. IV, n.2, pp. 2625, 2626. The Bradley testimony is in the "Declassified Hearing Transcripts." These were released years after the issuance of the first classified hearings in 1951 and are on microfilm in the National Archives.
6. William Manchester, *American Caesar: Douglas MacArthur 1880–1964* (Boston, 1978), p. 617.
7. Dean Acheson, *Present at the Creation: My Years in the State Department* (New York, 1969), p. 519.
8. Joseph W. Martin, Jr., as told to Robert J. Donovan, *My First Fifty Years in Politics* (New York, 1960), pp. 103–205.

9. Roger Tubby's journal, entry of April 5, 1951.
10. *Life*, April 9, 1951, p. 36.
11. Roger Tubby's journal, entry of March 21, 1951.
12. Truman, handwritten diary entry, April 5, 1951. PSF: Diaries. Diary 1951 Folder. Box 278.
13. *New York Times*, April 12, 1951, p. 11.
14. *Congressional Record*, vol. 97, pt. 3, pp. 3618, 3619.
15. *American Caesar*, op. cit., pp. 650, 651.
16. M. B. Ridgway, memorandum for diary 12 April 1951 (paraphrase of MacArthur), box 20 Ridgway ms. Also Ridgway oral history, 81 American Military Institute, Carlisle, Pa. Quoted by Barton J. Bernstein in *International Historical Review*, April 1981, p. 268.
17. W. Averell Harriman to Dwight D. Eisenhower, April 26, 1951. Harriman's Private Papers, Washington, D.C.
18. Truman to Eisenhower, April 13, 1951. PSF: General, NAT Folder No. 1. Box 132.
19. *Military Situation in the Far East*, op. cit., p. 3533 ff.
20. For the President from Jim Jones. Meeting With Foreign Policy Advisers, November 2, 1967. Meeting Notes File. Box 2. LBJL.
21. *PPP*. Johnson. 1967, vol. 2, p. 1007 ff.
22. *Lyndon B. Johnson: A Memoir*, cited chap. III, n. 17, p. 145.
23. *Lyndon: An Oral Biography*, cited chap. I, n. 7, p. 595.
24. *PPP*. Johnson. 1967, vol. 2, p. 1045 ff.
25. *Lyndon B. Johnson: A Memoir*, op. cit., p. 9.
26. *PPP*. Johnson. 1966, vol. 2, p. 935.
27. *PPP*. Johnson. 1967, vol. 2, p. 936.
28. For the President from Jim Jones. Meeting with Foreign Policy Advisers, November 2, 1967. Meeting File Notes. Box 2. LBJL.

VIII. *Undone*

1. *Military Situation in the Far East*, cited chap. IV, n. 2., p. 732.
2. Harry S Truman, *Truman Speaks* (New York, 1960), p. 24.
3. *PPP*. Truman. 1951, p. 12.
4. Ibid., p. 135.
5. *Military Situation in the Far East*, op. cit., pp. 352, 365.
6. Matthew B. Ridgway, *The Korean War* (Garden City, N.Y., 1967), p. 88.
7. PSF; Longhand Notes File. Longhand Personal Memos, 1952. Folder no. 1. Box 333.
8. *New York Times*, August 28, 1982.
9. Roger Tubby's Journal, entry of April 13, 1952.
10. *PPP*. Truman. 1952–53, p. 225.

11. Earl G. Wheeler. OHT. LBJL.
12. William C. Westmoreland. OHT. LBJL.
13. George E. Christian. OHT. LBJL.
14. *PPP*. Johnson. 1968–69, vol. 1, p. 1 ff.
15. Ibid., p. 31.
16. *PPP*. Johnson. 1967, vol. 2, p. 1009.
17. The author was the reporter.
18. *PPP*. Johnson. 1968–69, vol. 1, p. 381.
19. March 22, 1968. Meeting Notes File. Box 2. LBJL.
20. *Foreign Affairs,* July 1969, pp. 606, 607.
21. *PPP*. 1968–69, vol. 1, p. 469 ff.
22. *PPP*. 1952–53, p. 321.
23. *New York Herald Tribune,* October 25, 1952, p. 8.
24. Harry C. McPherson. OHT. LBJL.
25. Notes on the President's Meeting with the President-elect, Richard Nixon, November 11, 1968. Meeting Notes File. Box 3. LBJL.
26. Walter LaFeber, *Inevitable Revolution. The United States in Central America* (New York, 1983), pp. 275, 276.
27. *The Past Has Another Pattern,* cited chap. 4, n. 47, p. 382.

Index

Chinese intervention in Korea and,
128–129, 146, 164
civil rights program of, 2–3, 10, 164
Cold War and, 31–33
Congressional approval for Korean action avoided by, 53–54, 57
corruption in administration of, 164
crossing 38th parallel approved by,
83–87
domestic failures of, 3, 5, 164–165
economic controls instituted by, 132,
165
Eisenhower's relations with, 12, 146,
154, 178, 180
in election of 1948, 1, 2, 164, 169
European defense policy of, 78, 146
exhaustion of, 166, 168–169
Fair Deal of, 1, 5, 164
foreign policies established by, 9, 14
inflation controlled by, 165
invasion of North Korea approved by,
83–87
JCS and, 81, 83, 91, 144
Johnson and, 42, 51, 167
Korean War buildup under, 51, 52,
75
limited intervention policy of, 23–24,
187
MacArthur relieved by, 151–154,
162–163, 164
MacArthur's disagreements with,
147–148, 149–151
MacArthur's relations with, 88–89,
90, 133, 146
Marshall Plan approved by, 34
national emergency proclaimed by,
132
North Korean War preparations and,
19–20
nuclear weapons programs approved
by, 14, 77
present-day image of, 182–183, 184
renomination refused by (1952), 169
on repatriation issue, 179
Republican criticism of, 37–38, 76,
98, 163–164
reserves called up by, 70

as senator, 13
settlement at 38th parallel sought by,
131, 149
State of the Union message of (1949),
1–3
steel industry seized by, 167–168,
178
unauthorized statements banned by,
133, 149–150, 151
universal military training (UMT)
proposed by, 75
unpopularity of, 145, 152–154,
163–166
Vietnam policy of, 6, 20–23, 28
war with China opposed by, 146–147
Truman, Margaret, 20, 38
Truman Doctrine (1947), 17, 23, 34, 35,
43, 163
Tubby, Roger W., 47, 150–151, 152,
168
Turkey:
in Korean War, 79, 127
Soviet designs on, 16
Truman Doctrine and, 23, 33–34, 43
Twenty-fifth Infantry Division, U.S.:
in Korea, 74, 127
in Vietnam, 113
XXIV Corps, U.S., 15, 16
Twenty-fourth Infantry Division, U.S.,
73–74, 88, 127, 131

Ugly American, The (Lederer and Burdick), 26
United Kingdom, *see* Great Britain
United Nations, 6, 87, 162, 186
Korean War force of, 79–81
Korean War truce sought by, 80–81,
149, 166
League of Nations compared to, 49
peacekeeping role of, 36–37
South Korea established under auspices of, 6, 17–18, 36
see also Security Council, U.N.
United Press, 130
United Steelworkers of America, 1952
strike of, 167–168